R J Memett

U of A

Methuen's Old English Library

General Editors:
  ARTHUR BROWN and ALAN BLISS

AN OLD ENGLISH GRAMMAR

Methuen's Old English Library

Poetry

THE DREAM OF THE ROOD
Edited by Bruce Dickens and Alan S. C. Ross.

THE BATTLE OF MALDON
Edited by E. V. Gordon.

THREE NORTHUMBRIAN POEMS
Edited by A. H. Smith.

JUDITH
Edited by B. J. Timmer.

DEOR
Edited by Kemp Malone.

JULIANA
Edited by Rosemary Woolf.

CYNEWULF'S ELENE
Edited by P. O. E. Gradon.

THE SEA FARER
Edited by I. L. Gordon.

THE WANDERER
Edited by T. P. Dunning and Alan Bliss

Prose

THE PARKER CHRONICLE: 832-900
Edited by A. H. Smith.

AELFRIC'S COLLOQUY
Edited by G. N. Garmonsway.

SERMO LUPI AD ANGLOS
Edited by Dorothy Whitelock.

Studies

EARLY MIDDLE ENGLISH LITERATURE
By R. M. Wilson.

AN
OLD ENGLISH
GRAMMAR

by

RANDOLPH QUIRK

*(Professor of the English Language in the
University of London, University College.)*

and

C. L. WRENN

Methuen & Co Ltd

11 NEW FETTER LANE LONDON E.C.4

First published September 1st, 1955
Second edition 1957
Reprinted five times
Reprinted 1969

2·7

S.B.N. 416 77240 4

PRINTED IN GREAT BRITAIN

BY R. & R. CLARK, LTD., EDINBURGH

AND BOUND BY HUNTER & FOULIS EDINBURGH

CONTENTS

PREFACE

THIS *Grammar* is designed especially for the literary student of English, who has long been neglected in favour of his philologically inclined colleague and who is felt to be in need of a single compact grammar which will put the emphasis where he needs it most and serve as a companion to all his undergraduate studies in Old English. It has also been felt that Old English studies stood in need of a grammar which was primarily concerned with that form of Old English in which most of the literary remains of importance have come down to us—the Classical Old English of about A.D. 1000 rather than with 'early West Saxon' or the other Old English dialects, however interesting these may be to the philological enquirer.

With the aim, then, of presenting a grammar of literary Old English to literary students, we have forsaken the historical in favour of a descriptive approach wherever this seemed expedient and practicable, and we have tried to avoid assuming a knowledge of—or indeed interest in—Germanic philology as such. The treatment of inflexions, syntax, word-formation, and phonology represents an attempt to describe realistically the forms that occur most prominently in the important literary manuscripts, systematised in a manner that seems most significant for the Classical Old English which they generally present, though this has meant to some considerable extent the replacing of categories, classifications, and even technical terms that were evolved for and suited to the structure of the 'Germanic dialects' as a whole. On the other hand, we have resisted changes of this kind wherever the traditional framework seemed readily comprehensible to non-specialists and unlikely to mislead the student who has not had a philological training. Moreover, the *Introduction* aims not only at providing a minimum background of knowledge, but also at indicating the kinds of evidence on which the grammatical description is based.

Among the features to which we attach importance are the

relatively detailed and practical treatment of *Syntax* and the attempt to make naturally intelligible the actual processes of the sound-changes described in the *Phonology*. We have sought throughout to help the student who has deeper linguistic and mediæval interests to advance his studies by means of the notes set in small type, where more advanced matters could be touched upon and works of scholarship cited for further reading. In the treatment of *Inflexions*, these notes have often been used also to deal with the variant and exceptional forms, and by this means we have been able to keep the paradigms free from confusing by-forms. Particular care, too, has been taken with the typography throughout, with the aim of achieving clarity and ease of reference.

Our thanks are due to a long line of distinguished predecessors whose grammars of Old English we have been more eager to consult and copy than to replace; the many references in our notes by no means constitute an adequate expression of our debt. More specifically and personally, we should like to thank those colleagues and friends who have helped us with advice and criticism at various stages of our work: Mr G. N. Garmonsway, Professor Daniel Jones, Professor Helge Kökeritz, Professor Sherman M. Kuhn, Dr W. R. Lee, Professor Francis P. Magoun Jr., and Professor F. Norman. In particular, we are deeply grateful to Professor Norman Davis for his learning, patience, and labour in making detailed criticisms and improvements. Finally, we have special pleasure in acknowledging a most sympathetic and helpful general editor in Professor A. H. Smith.

R. Q.
University College, Durham
C. L. W.
Pembroke College, Oxford

We are greatly indebted to many colleagues and friends, in private discussion or through reviews, for a good number of the corrections and improvements incorporated in this edition.

R. Q.

October 1957

C. L. W.

ABBREVIATIONS

a(cc).: accusative
adj.: adjective
adv.: adverb
Angl.: Anglian (see § 4)
AS: Anglo-Saxon
A.V.: Authorised Version
C: complement
Cl: Class
comp.: comparative
cons.: consonant
d(at).: dative
ed.: edition (by)
EETS: *Early English Text Society*, London
f(em).: feminine
Fr.: French
g(en).: genitive
Germ.: German
Gmc: Germanic (see §§ 3, 178)
Go.: Gothic (see § 178)
IE: Indo-European
imperat.: imperative
impers.: impersonal (see § 120*e*)
ind(ic).: indicative
infin.: infinitive
i(nstr).: instrumental
Ital.: Italian
J. Engl. and Germ. Phil.: *Journal of English and Germanic Philology*, Urbana
Kt: Kentish (see § 4)
l(WS, OE): late (West Saxon, Old English)
Lat.: Latin
lit.: literally
m(asc).: masculine
ME: Middle English
Mod.(E.): modern (English)
Mod. Lang. Rev.: *Modern Language Review*, Cambridge
MS(S): manuscript(s)

n(eut).: neuter
n(om).: nominative
Nb: Northumbrian
N.E.D.: *New* (or *Oxford*) *English Dictionary*, ed. J. Murray and others, Oxford 1888-1933
O: object
OE: Old English
OHG: Old High German
OIr: Old Irish
ON: Old Norse
p(ers).: person
P.B.B.: *Beiträge zur Geschichte der deutschen Sprache und Literatur* Halle
pl.: plural
PMLA: *Publications of the Modern Language Association of America*, Baltimore
pple: participle
pres.: present
pret.: preterite
Pr.OE: Primitive Old English (see § 178)
pron.: pronoun
reflex.: reflexive
resp.: respectively
RP: Received Pronunciation (the educated speech of Southern England)
S: subject
sc.: understand (Lat. *scilicet*)
sg.: singular
subj.: subjunctive
superl.: superlative
s.v(v).: under the word(s)
Trans. Phil. Soc.: *Transactions of the Philological Society*, London
V, vb(s): verb(s)
WS: West Saxon (see §§ 4f)

SYMBOLS

´ `   indicate heavy and secondary stress resp. (see § 12)

- ᵕ   indicate length and shortness resp. in vowels (see § 10)

[ ]   enclose *phonetic symbols*, on which see § 176

:   after phonetic symbols denotes length; between forms denotes a correspondence

~   expresses a relationship, alternation, or correspondence

- -   denote that the forms they precede, follow, or surround are partial; thus *gifan, -ie-*

/   between forms indicates alternation or equivalence; thus *ð/þ*

( )   enclose alternative forms or parts of forms; thus *sind(on)*

>   means 'changed to' or 'becomes'

<   means 'changed from' or 'derived from'

*   denotes a reconstruction (see § 178)

I

INTRODUCTION

General

1. *Old English* is the name given to the language or group of closely related dialects of the Germanic inhabitants of Britain from the first conquests in the middle of the fifth century till the close of the eleventh. The period of 'Old English' thus extends from the earliest permanent settlements of the Anglo-Saxons till the time when the effects of the Scandinavian invasions and of the Norman Conquest began to be felt on the language, and the changes in scribal habits threw into relief the linguistic changes that had been going on during the last century or so of the West Saxon tradition. But since the earliest surviving written monuments scarcely go back beyond the end of the seventh century, when the vernacular begins to appear in charters and in the one extant poem of Cædmon, the language to be studied in fact covers approximately the four centuries from A.D. 700 to 1100. Our knowledge of OE is inevitably limited in general to literary and learned usage, though some occasional glimpses of the spoken language may be had from such texts as Ælfric's *Colloquy* and from relics of an oral poetic tradition preserved in the formulaic style of *Beowulf*.

For a reliable succinct account of all the literary monuments of the period, see *A Literary History of England* (edited by Albert C. Baugh, New York 1948), Book I, Part I: 'The Old English Period' by Kemp Malone.

2. The Term 'Old English'

In the eighteenth and nineteenth centuries the term *Anglo-Saxon*, adapted in the early seventeenth century from Lat. *Anglo-Saxonicus*, was the commonest name for the language; but, although still sometimes used by scholars, it has gradually been replaced in the last hundred years by the more scientific term *Old English*. For the peoples, as distinct from their language, the Lat. *Anglo-Saxones* was the noun often used from the ninth century to distinguish the 'English Saxons' from the 'Old Saxons' or inhabitants of the Saxon homeland who had not migrated: and hence *Anglo-Saxon* is still properly used as the name of the pre-Norman Germanic inhabitants of Britain. Camden, the antiquarian scholar who first applied the Lat. *Anglo-Saxonicus* to the language, rendered it however into English as 'English Saxon'—a term which the Elizabethans had already used. The Anglo-Saxons themselves, though they did occasionally render as *Angul-Seaxan* the Lat. *Anglo-Saxones* in charters from the late ninth century, regularly called their language, including all its dialects, *Englisc*, though this term originally had meant Anglian (§ 4). While *Old English* preserves the idea of historic continuity in our language, it is also true that modern literary English descends more directly from an East Midland (Anglian) dialect than from the southern and south-western language of Anglo-Saxon Wessex in which nearly all the OE texts have survived—from the language of King Offa the Mercian rather than from that of King Alfred the Great. For literary monuments, therefore, the notion of a *direct* continuity from Old to Modern English is to some extent misleading.

Bede distinguished the *Angli Saxones* or Germanic conquerors of Britain from the *Antiqui Saxones*, the 'Old Saxons', and from this distinction the term 'Anglo-Saxon' ultimately arises. The term *Saxon* was applied to the conquered people of England by Latin-writing chroniclers of the twelfth and thirteenth centuries, and hence the use of 'Saxon' from the fourteenth century onwards to describe both the people and their language. Indeed, the first OE dictionaries and grammars, written in Latin in the sixteenth and seventeenth centuries, generally employ the term *Saxonicus*, which became 'Saxon' in the next century for such purposes and is still sometimes found. The popular, wider, non-technical use of *Anglo-Saxon* to cover the English-speaking world dates from early Victorian times. See N.E.D., s.vv. *Anglo-Saxon* and *Saxon*, and cf also Kemp Malone in *Review of English Studies* v (1929), pp. 173-85. In the S.W. Midland prose life of St Margaret, of about 1200, occurs the expression *ald Englis* for 'Old English' (*Seinte Marherete*, ed. F. Mack, EETS, p. 52, l. 32).

3. Position and Relationship

Old English is a member of the western branch of the Germanic family of languages and therefore belongs ultimately to the Indo-European stock. It shares the fundamental characteristics of IE with most other European languages, though these remoter basic qualities have been much obscured by distance in time and space. More clearly, it shares special Germanic features which distinguish it, together with the languages of Germany, Scandinavia and the Netherlands, from other branches of IE. Such special Germanic features include the following:

(*a*) the First Consonant Shift, by which Gmc consonants underwent characteristic changes in pronunciation, such as the voiced plosives *b*, *d*, *g*, *gw* becoming the voiceless plosives *p*, *t*, *k*, *kw* (see § 179);

(*b*) the fixing of the stress of words generally as near to the beginning as possible, or on the root-syllable (see §§ 12 ff);

(*c*) the strong tendency, resulting from (*b*) but varying in intensity among different Gmc languages, to weaken and lose inflexional endings;

(*d*) the development of derived or secondary verbs (consonantal or 'weak' verbs), formed from other words and distinguished by preterites and past participles formed by means of a dental suffix;

(*e*) the syntactical distinction between the two types of adjective inflexion—the indefinite and definite declensions (see §§ 50-4, 116);

(*f*) certain strata of vocabulary peculiar to the Gmc languages;

(*g*) the two-tense system. Verbs in the Gmc languages show by inflexion only two tenses, present and past; in OE, time-relations other than simple present and simple past had for the most part to be inferred from the context, just as in Mod.E. we allow a present tense form to indicate future time after *when*: 'When I come home I shall tell you my news'; even the complex Mod.E. expressions of time-relation like

'I would have had' use only a two-tense distinction in the component verbs.

Within the Gmc group of languages, OE has further special characteristics which it shares with the group generally termed *West Germanic*, which comprises the languages of the Netherlands, Germany, and eastern Switzerland. Within this West Germanic group, OE has still closer affinities with Frisian (though the earliest Frisian texts go back only to the thirteenth century) and Old Saxon (the language of the continental Saxons).

For an effective presentation of the facts of the Gmc languages, see Antoine Meillet, *Caractères généraux des langues germaniques* (Paris 3rd ed. 1927), and Edward Prokosch, *Comparative Germanic Grammar* (Philadelphia 1939); cf also H. M. Chadwick, *Origin of the English Nation* (Cambridge 1907). For a recent discussion, see Ernst Schwarz, *Goten, Nordgermanen, Angelsachsen* (Berne 1951). The best small handbook is still H. Hirt, *Handbuch des Urgermanischen* (Heidelberg 1931-4).

4. Dialects

It is possible that OE was already to some extent divided into three main dialects when the first settlements were made from the Continent. These would roughly correspond to the three racial or tribal divisions of the Gmc invaders described by Bede, and are therefore known as *West Saxon* or the Saxon dialect of the kingdom of Wessex (other Saxon dialects existed but did not attain to writing), *Kentish*, and *Anglian*, derived respectively from Saxons, Jutes and Angles. The Jutish or Kentish dialect covered a wide area in the S.E. of England, including for a time S. Hampshire and Wight; West Saxon expanded all over the S. and S.W. with the growing importance of Wessex; the Anglian dialects covered the Midlands and N.E. of England and parts of S. Scotland, and through geographical and political factors became divided into *Northumbrian* and *Mercian*. It is therefore customary to regard OE as comprising four principal dialects: *West Saxon, Kentish* or South Eastern, *Mercian* or W. Midland, and *Northumbrian*. Of the language of the E. Midlands almost nothing is known in the OE period, though ME evidence makes it seem that it must have had marked features distinguishing it from Mercian. Indeed, the only OE dialect of which we can gain an extensive and continuous knowledge is West Saxon. Moreover, WS was the only dialect to become literary in prose, and in the later OE period it was Wessex that provided the dialect which became the cultural language of the whole of England, though somewhat influenced and modified by neighbouring dialects. It was in this literary or classical *koiné*, basically WS, that nearly all the earlier poetry was copied, and so preserved, at the time of the Benedictine Renaissance at the close of the tenth century and early in the eleventh century. It is therefore this WS, in which almost all writings of any real literary merit are to be read, that has always been taken as the basis for the study of OE and for the making of grammars and dictionaries.

On the origin of the OE dialects, see K. Brunner (ref. as in § 24), § 2 and Anm. 1.

For an important re-examination of some of the questions relating to classical OE and especially to the language of OE poetry, see K. Sisam, *Studies in the History of Old English Literature* (Oxford 1953).

5. Standard Language

The Elizabethans, Lawrence Nowell, Joscelyn, and others, who revived the study of 'Saxon' in the sixteenth century, took classical OE of the later period as their basis, and this practice was followed in dictionaries and grammars till the middle of the nineteenth century. Subsequently, from the pioneering work of Henry Sweet onwards, the language of King Alfred, generally under the name *Early West Saxon*, has become the regular medium for all grammatical text-books, and OE of the later period has often for teaching purposes been 'normalised' in spelling on this 'Early West Saxon' basis. Yet King Alfred's prose, though outstandingly important, survives only in one complete MS that is actually contemporary (MS Bodley Hatton 20 of his translation of St Gregory's *Cura Pastoralis*), and it is only in the common literary OE of a century later that prose becomes of really high literary value. It was into this same form of OE that nearly all earlier poetry was copied. While accepting, therefore, the traditional practice of taking WS as the norm of OE grammatical investigation, this book will, as far as is practicable and desirable, take the literary language of Ælfric (himself a grammarian) as its foundation, since almost all texts likely to be read by the literary student of OE are extant only in this classical OE *koiné*.

Of Sweet's writings, the most important for the question of WS in its Alfredian form as a basis for study are the following: the introductory apparatus to his ed. of *King Alfred's West Saxon Version of Gregory's Pastoral Care* (EETS, London 1871-2); 'Dialects and Prehistoric Forms of English', *Trans. Phil. Soc.* 1875-6; *History of English Sounds* (Oxford 1888). For a discussion of the whole problem of normalisation of OE, see C. L. Wrenn, 'Standard Old English', *Trans. Phil. Soc.* 1933, pp. 65 ff. Since this grammar is intended primarily for the literary rather than the philological student, the non-WS dialects will be noticed only incidentally.

6. Periods

The history of OE is usually divided into the two main periods, *Early OE* (from about A.D. 700 to 900) and *Late OE* (from about A.D. 900 to 1100). But in fact the only considerable work of 'Early OE' upon which any thorough grammatical study can be based is that of King Alfred, which came at the very end of this 'Early OE' period, and only in the case of his *Cura Pastoralis* translation (since the MSS of all his other works are later) does his work survive in the forms of a scribe who wrote in one of his scriptoria. Moreover the extant MSS of the Alfredian WS already shew marks of a transition to Late OE, just as, similarly, the OE of the eleventh century begins to shew marks of the transition to Middle English.

We take, then, classical OE as the literary standard language of England from about 900 to 1100, particularly as written at its best by Ælfric and his contemporaries, and with this form of OE as its normative basis, this grammar will, as far as possible, draw its illustrative material from the texts which the student will in fact normally read, such as *Beowulf* and the selections in the *Anglo-Saxon Readers* of Sweet and of Wyatt.

Before Alfred's reign there are only one or two charters in WS, while for the non-WS dialects there are scattered remains in Northumbrian, Mercian, and Kentish. For an account of these, see K. Luick, *Historische Grammatik der englischen Sprache* (Leipzig 1921) §§ 21-7. F. Mossé, in his *Manuel de l'Anglais du Moyen Âge: Vieil-Anglais* (Paris 1944), suggests dividing OE into four periods: (*a*) pre-Alfredian, (*b*) Alfredian, (*c*) period of Ælfric and Wulfstan, (*d*) period of transition which he would end at 1150. Literary OE MSS continued to be copied till late in the twelfth century.

Orthography and Pronunciation

7. The Alphabet

The Germanic invaders brought to Britain a rough method of writing magical formulae and epigraphs called *runes*. This runic writing consisted at first of some 24 symbols to be scratched upon or coloured into stone or hard wood or metal—signs which generally by means of straight lines could very roughly represent common sounds. These runes, at first the secret of a priestly class (the OE word *rūn* means 'secret'), were employed in England to some extent after the conversion to Christianity for religious inscriptions such as that on the Ruthwell Cross, and also at times more widely; but they were unsuitable for any sort of continuous writing and remained only as tokens of antiquarian interest in the late OE period. The OE alphabet used throughout the MSS is the Irish form of the Latin letters, with some slight additions and modifications. It was first employed to express the vernacular in writing in the early Christian centres in Northumbria, whence it spread, aided by the Roman missionary influences from Canterbury, throughout the country.

The late OE runic letters, with their meanings explained in order with a commentary, are to be found conveniently in Bruce Dickins, *Runic and Heroic Poems of the Old Teutonic Peoples* (Cambridge 1915), in the *Runic Poem*. See further, C. L. Wrenn, 'Late Old English Rune-Names', *Medium Ævum* i (1932), H. Arntz, *Handbuch der Runenkunde* (Halle, 2nd ed., 1944), and R. Dérolez, *Runica Manuscripta* (Bruges 1954).

8. This Irish-Latin alphabet (as adopted in England, commonly known as *Insular Script*) had characteristic forms for *f, g, r,* and *s,* among other less individual features, and it may still be seen to some extent in the present-day forms of Irish letters. These Celtic-Roman letters were employed to represent as phonetically as possible the sounds of OE, with the same values as they had when used to represent Latin in the

contemporary pronunciation; it is largely from our knowledge of this Latin pronunciation and from the transliteration of Latin words into OE that we are able to infer the pronunciation of OE, together with further assistance from the development of OE forms in later English and from their cognates in the other Gmc languages.

At first the Latin letter *u* was used for the OE sound [w] and the biliteral *th* for the voiced [ð] and voiceless [θ] sounds heard in Mod.E. in the words *this* and *thin* respectively. But in the later eighth century the letter *d* was also often used for these latter sounds, since in Irish usage *d* sometimes was the sign of a voiced fricative. But, with the firm establishment of the Christian church and culture, two runic symbols came to replace *th*, *d*, and *u* in these functions, since runes were perhaps no longer felt to be a heathen peril: [ð] and [θ] came to be represented by þ, and [w] by ƿ. A third new symbol was added to the Irish-Latin alphabet by drawing a fine line through the upper part of the Insular *d* so as to form ð, and by the ninth century ð and þ were being used indifferently for the two sounds [ð] and [θ]. To distinguish the characteristic OE fronting and raising of the Gmc ă to a sound approximately like that of the *a* in Mod.E. (RP) *hat*, [a] or [æ], the Latin biliteral *ae*, æ was used for both the long and the short sounds.

It is convenient to have names for these symbols which find no place in Mod.E. spelling: þ and ƿ are known by their runic mnemonic names 'thorn' and 'wynn' respectively; ð is called *eth* (*eð* is the Icelandic name for this letter as adopted from OE) and æ is called 'ash', the OE word *æsc* 'ash' being the name of the corresponding runic letter.

Phonetic terms and symbols are more fully explained in § 176.

9. All printed books in OE used the MS forms of most letters (the 'Anglo-Saxon' or 'Saxon' characters) till the middle of the nineteenth century, when the current practice of printing in roman type came in. All OE books agree however in retaining the symbols þ, ð, and æ; a few also retain the runic ƿ, but *w* is now normal practice so as to avoid confusion with þ and þ. As has been said, among the more remarkable features of the

Insular script was a special form of *g*, written ʒ; this symbol is retained by some grammarians, including Professor Brunner in German and Miss Wardale in English, but an increasing majority prefer to use the ordinary roman symbol *g*, for there seems little reason to retain the OE ʒ while ignoring the fact that the OE script had special forms of *f*, *r*, and *s* also. In this grammar, *þ*, *ð*, and *æ* will be used, but all other letters will be given their modern roman form.

10. Fairly often, but without any discernible regularity or method, OE scribes used a mark over vowels resembling an acute accent, a form taken from Latin practice. This accent seems sometimes to have been an indication of stress (but not of length), and sometimes to have been used to avoid ambiguity when two different words were written with the same letters (such as *gōd* 'good' and *god* 'God'). It will normally be ignored in this grammar, but vowel-length will be regularly indicated by a macron (¯), leaving short vowels unmarked.

Some carefully written MSS, such as the best of Ælfric, shew a regular distinction (which is graphic rather than phonetic) of *þ* initially as against *ð* medially and finally: *þis* as compared with *ōðer* and *mōnað*. Sometimes vowel-length is indicated by doubling, as in *good* for *gōd*. The first OE printed book was made by one John Day in 1567; it is Ælfric's homily on the Easter Mass (*De Sacrificio in Die Pasce*) and the title is of some interest: *The Testimonie of Antiquitie shewing the Auncient fayth / in the Church of England touching the sacrament of the / body and bloude of the Lord here publickly preached and also received in the saxons tyme aboue 600 yeares agoe.* For a full account of OE scribal practice, see W. Keller, *Angelsächsische Palaeographie* (Berlin 1906).

11. Vowel-Length

As we have just seen, vowel-length is not regularly indicated in OE, nor does the metre serve as a systematic basis for ascertaining it. The Latin so-called *apex* over vowels to shew length, from which the OE accents on vowels were adapted, did not regularly refer only to quantity even in Irish, and where its occurrence in OE seems to indicate a long vowel this is probably only because such vowels were often heavily stressed. It was, in fact, probably as a means of indicating stress and intonation that the accents were used in so far as such use was deliberate. The doubling of vowels which is fairly often to be

AN OLD ENGLISH GRAMMAR

met with in early MSS is a much more reliable sign of length. In general, however, the length of OE vowels is to be determined from etymology, cognate forms in other languages, later development, and (to a very limited extent) from metre. But while the length of a vowel as suggested by etymology is generally taken in grammars as the norm, it must be remembered that in later OE quantity was often changed by the shortenings and lengthenings explained in § 199.

12. Stress

The stress or intensity of utterance of OE was much the same as in Mod.E. It is probable that there were four clearly observed grades: heavy (1), secondary (2), light (3), weak (4); thus a word like *gelustfullīce* 'joyfully' would have a stress pattern 4-1-2-3-4. In practice, however, we need distinguish only three approximate types: *heavy* stress (which may be indicated by an acute accent), *secondary* or medium stress (which may be indicated by a grave accent), and weak stress (which is generally left unmarked).

OE words normally had the heavy stress on the initial syllable—generally the root—but there were the following exceptions:

(a) In compounds of noun plus noun, or noun plus adjective, the root syllable of the second element carried a secondary stress: cf *mánnes* 'man's' beside *máncỳnnes* 'mankind's', where the second element *cynnes* exists as a separate word.

(b) Prefixes are as a rule unstressed, unless they dominate the meaning, and the noun and verb prefix *ge-* is always unstressed.

(c) While the prefix of noun and verb compounds is normally unstressed, the emphatic prefix *bī-* (as contrasted with its weak form *be-*) has heavy stress: cf *besittan* 'to besiege' beside *bíleofa* 'food' (lit. 'by-living').

(d) While prefixes to verbs are generally unstressed, adverbial or prepositional prefixes which dominate the meaning (such as *in, ūt, æfter*) are heavily stressed: cf *oftēon* 'to deprive' beside *ingangan* 'to go in'.

(*e*) Verbs formed from nouns whose first element was a prefix carrying heavy stress, generally retain this stress on the prefix: thus *ándswarian* 'to answer', from the noun *ándswaru*.

As OE metre depends primarily on patterns of stress and on alliteration which must fall on heavily stressed syllables, a study of an exactly metred poem such as *Beowulf* will serve to confirm the rules of OE stress; the 'five types' of OE half-line are but selective, regularised and rhetorically emphatic patterns from speech. On the fundamentals of OE metre, see E. Sievers, *Altgermanische Metrik* (Halle 1893) and the very full recent study by J. C. Pope, *The Rhythm of Beowulf* (New Haven 1949).

13. One consequence of the fixing of the intensity or weight of utterance at or near the beginning of words was the weakening of final, unstressed, inflexional syllables (see §§ 3, 198). In late OE therefore the unstressed short vowels *a*, *e*, *o*, and *u* of final syllables began from about the tenth century to be weakened to a common sound called *schwa* [ə], pronounced like the final syllable of *china* or *thorough*. Since in addition final *m* tended to be pronounced as [n] in late OE, the inflexional endings *-um*, *-an*, *-on* all came to be sounded [ən], and the forms written *mannum*, *mannon*, *mannan* might all be pronounced alike [man(ː)ən]; less careful scribes might then well use one of the latter spellings to represent the form traditionally spelt *mannum*, or even (though less frequently) use *-um* to render forms historically ending in *-an* or *-on*. But on the whole the scribes tended to preserve the traditional orthography, which thus came to lag a good deal behind actual pronunciation.

Since virtually all OE texts that students will read show the distinctive inflexional endings *-an*, *-um*, *-on*, *-en*, *-að* etc. preserved in spelling, students will find it easier to learn these forms if they always give them a distinctive pronunciation, despite the fact that such pronunciation would have been archaic (to say the least) in Ælfric's time.

PRONUNCIATION

14. During the four centuries covered by its surviving records, OE must have changed considerably in pronunciation, and at varying times and speeds in its different dialects. For practical purposes, however, as with the learning of Latin, one must select one period and type of pronunciation to adopt as

a norm or standard. In what follows, the pronunciation described will for the most part be that which may be assumed to have been employed by Ælfric in the period of classical OE about the year 1000. At this time, speakers of the various dialects who were also copyists of older MSS of varying linguistic origins, transposed them into their common cultural language, in all centres generally, and wrote in that widely diffused type of late West Saxon, with elements from neighbouring dialects and a well-developed tradition, which may fairly be termed 'Classical OE'. Moreover, Ælfric himself was a careful user of this common language, and from his own Latin Grammar in OE we may learn a great deal (by studying it, so to speak, in reverse) of what was his own OE usage. We can infer that, just as there was a common written form of OE, so too there was, at least for formal purposes, a corresponding common spoken form, and it is this that we shall attempt to describe, rather than the colloquial usage which must by this time have been in varying stages of transition.

15. Vowels

OE had seven long and seven short vowels, spelt as follows: *a, æ, e, i, o, u, y*. The following illustrations show the approximate pronunciation to be attributed to the vowel symbols. OE *hām* 'farmstead' differed in its vowel [ɑ:] from *hamm* 'pasture' [ɑ] rather as Fr. *lâche* differs from *pâté* (though often before a nasal, the short *a* was pronounced like the *o* in Mod.E. *hot*). OE *æ* when short had the sound of *a* in Mod.E. (RP) *hat*, [a] or [æ], and roughly the vowel sound of Mod.E. *mare* when long, [æ:]; thus OE *mæt* and *mǣton* (pret. sg. and pl. of *metan* 'to measure') differed as regards the *æ* as Mod.E. *bat* differs from Fr. *bête*. OE *e* was similar to that in Mod.E. *egg* when short and like that in Germ. *See* when long, [ɛ] as against [e:]; for example, *eft* 'again' beside *ēst* 'favour'. The short and long *i* in *biddan* 'to pray' and *bīdan* 'to await' respectively differed as in Mod.E. *bid* [ɪ] and *machine* [i:]. Short and long *o* as in *god* 'a god' and *gōd* 'good' had respectively the vowel sounds in Mod.E. *not* [ɔ] and Fr. *beau* [o:]. Mod.E. *bush* and Fr. *fou* shew the qualities of short and long OE *u*, as in *ful* 'full' [u] and *fūl* 'foul' [uː]. The values of OE *y*, as in *lyft* 'air' and *ȳð* 'wave', may be heard in Fr. *reçu* [y] and *lune* [yː].

Another symbol, *oe*, will occasionally be found, especially in Anglian texts, representing the front-round long and short vowels like those heard in Germ. *schön* and *Göttingen* respectively; these vowels were unrounded in early WS and spelt *e* (see § 208). The symbol *æ*, while this was the usual form, was sometimes written *ae* in early MSS and also—following a Latin practice—*ę*. OE short *a* before *m* or *n* often appears as *o* (see § 186*a*), so that for example *man(n)* 'man' is often spelt *mon(n)*. This suggests that there was some fluctuation in pronunciation, and that nasals had a rounding effect on short *a*. On phonetic symbols, see § 176.

16. The values given to the vowels, like those given to the consonant-symbols of OE, probably corresponded originally to those of the letters used to write Latin as it was pronounced by the missionaries of the seventh century. It is convenient to divide the vowels, according to the part of the mouth in which they are produced, into *front* vowels (*æ, e, i, y*) and back vowels (*a, o, u*). Because the consonant *g* was vocalised after front vowels in late OE, a frequent spelling for *i* in that period is *-ig-*; for example, *bigleofa* for *bīleofa* 'food'. Similarly, because a short *i* could be sounded consonantally as [j], we often find a *g* alternating with such an *i*; for example, *herges* beside *heries* (gen. sg. of *here* 'raiding force'), *hergan* beside *herian* 'to praise'. Again, because the sounds originally written *ie* in early WS had become [ɪ], [iː] in some words, [y], [yː] in others by King Alfred's time, MSS of the period often shew *i* for *ie* and vice versa; thus *hieder* for *hider* 'hither', *hīran* or *hȳran* for *hīeran* 'to hear'. Later the results of older *ie* were mainly pronounced [y], [yː] in areas of classical OE, so that Ælfrician texts regularly shew *-y-* for early WS *-ie-*, as in *gelȳfan* for earlier *gelīefan* 'to believe' (see further, § 193).

17. Diphthongs

Diphthongs may be described as 'rising' or 'falling'; that is to say, they may be stressed more heavily on the first or on the second of the constituent vowel-sounds. OE diphthongs were generally falling; thus *féallan* 'to fall', *scēap* 'sheep', *lēoht* 'light'.

13

Diphthongs which arose from the development of a glide-vowel between palatal *c* or *g* and one of the front vowels (a special feature of WS) were probably at first rising, but the late OE and early ME evidence shews that they afterwards conformed to the general pattern of falling diphthongs. For example, non-WS *gefan* 'to give' appears in early WS as *giefan* by the development of the glide-vowel represented by *-i-*; this must at first have been pronounced with rising stress *giéfan*, but late OE *gifan* and ME *yiue* would suggest that the diphthong came to be pronounced with falling stress *gíefan* (but see §§ 193, 204). In a small number of words like *geōmor* 'sad', *geār-dagas* 'days of yore', which go back to a Gmc consonantal [j] followed by a long vowel, the *ge-* is to be taken as representing [j], a spelling devised because *g* before a back vowel would be a plosive symbol. As we are here dealing therefore with a sequence of consonant plus simple vowel rather than with a diphthong, the macron is placed only over the vowel symbol: *geōmor* [joː], *geār-* [jɑːr]. Similarly in *sceolde* 'should', *sceaða* 'foe', *geond* (*giond*) 'through', *sēcean* 'to seek', *sengean* 'to singe', and some others, we probably have simple vowels preceded by diacritics indicating the palatal quality of the consonants; cf the *i* in Ital. *mangiare* 'to eat', and the *e* in Fr. *mangeant*. Hence we should pronounce *sceolde* as [ʃɔldə], *sceaða* as [ʃaðə], *geond* as [jɔnd], *sēcean* as [seːtʃan], *sengean* as [sɛndʒan].

18. Classical OE had four diphthongs: *ea*, *eā*, *eo*, *eō*. It is to be remembered that, although in each of these, two vowel sounds were heard, they were pronounced as a single glide, with one crest of sonority, so that they formed one syllable and not two. The short diphthongs *ea*, *eo* may be assigned the pronunciation [ɛə], [eə] respectively; in the long diphthongs, the same sounds were heard, but the whole glide (and not simply the first element of it) was given greater length. Thus *weard* 'became' would be pronounced [wɛərθ], *sceāp* 'sheep' [ʃeːəp], *heorte* 'heart' [heərtə], *beōr* 'beer' [beːər].

On the other diphthongs that existed at other times and in other dialects than Classical OE of c. 1000, early WS *íe̯*, early WS and non-WS *ío̯*, see §§ 193, 205. The existence of the short diphthongs has recently been denied, and it has been suggested that (for example) *ea* represented [æ] together with a sign variously interpreted as indicating an allophonic variant of the vowel or the velar character of the following consonant. See especially M. Daunt, 'Old English Sound-Changes Reconsidered in Relation to Scribal Tradition and Practice', *Trans. Phil. Soc.* 1939, pp. 108-37, R. P. Stockwell and C. W. Barritt, *Some Old English Graphemic-Phonemic Correspondences—æ, ea and a* (Washington, D.C., 1951). For a criticism of such views and a re-examination of OE diphthongs, see S. M. Kuhn and R. Quirk, 'Some Recent Interpretations of

the Old English Digraph Spellings', *Language* xxix (1953), pp. 143-56;
cf also M. L. Samuels, 'The Study of Old English Phonology', *Trans.
Phil. Soc.* 1952, especially pp. 15-28. See further, § 202.

19. Consonants

The following consonant symbols had much the same value
as they have in Mod.E. orthography: *b, d, l, m, n, p, t,
w*, and *x* (= [ks]). *F, s, þ/ð* were voiceless fricatives initially
and finally, but were voiced between vowels (cf Mod.E. *sits*
beside *raisin*): thus *sittan* 'to sit' with [s], *genesan* 'to be saved'
with [z]; *þencean* 'to think' with [θ], *ōþer (ōðer)* 'other' with [ð];
fīf 'five' [fi:f], *ofer* 'over' [ɔvər]. *H* initially was much as in
Mod.E., but medially or finally it became a palatal or velar
fricative according to the front or back quality of the proximate
vowel and was pronounced like the *ch* in Germ. *ich* [ç] (palatal)
or *ach* [x] (velar). It may be most convenient for the non-
specialist student to pronounce both these varieties of *h* medially or finally like the *ch* in Scots *loch* or in Welsh generally;
for example, OE *hēah* 'high' as [hɛəx]. *K* is rarely used but is
sometimes found in place of *c* as the symbol for a plosive consonant (as in Mod.E.) before a front vowel: thus *kyning* 'king',
for the more usual *cyning*. OE *r* initially may well have been
strongly trilled as in Mod.Scots, but the same symbol was used
for the fricative ('burred') sound in some positions, notably
before consonants and finally (*heard* 'hard', *scūr* 'shower')—
the *r*-sound of much American speech and heard also in south-
western dialects of England. *Z* was very rare, and may have
sounded as [ts] or [dz] according to position; for example,
bæ(d)zere 'baptist'. See further, § 176.

20. One of the chief defects of the OE alphabet from a
phonetic point of view was that the symbols *c* and *g* each had
to serve for a variety of sounds. *C* was the symbol both of the
plosive consonant [k] and the affricate [tʃ], the initial sounds
in Mod.E. *keep* and *cheap* respectively, according to the back
or front quality of the proximate vowel in early OE (see § 22,
note); thus *candel* 'candle', *cōl* 'cool', *cumbol* 'banner', *cniht*
'boy' had initial [k], but *cēap* 'goods' was pronounced [tʃɛəp],
cild 'child' [tʃɪld], and *cyrice* 'church' [tʃyritʃə]. By the time

c   15

of Classical OE, the biliteral *sc* had come to represent the single consonant sound [ʃ] heard initially in Mod.E. *ship* and in the OE form *scip*; in poetry, words beginning with *sc-* could alliterate only with other words beginning with *sc-*. OE *g* (which was written with the Irish-Latin form ȝ till this began to be replaced by the Carolingian form *g* from the Continent in the twelfth century) was used as follows: initially before consonants and back vowels it represented the plosive consonant [g] as in Mod.E. *good*, for example *gāt* 'goat', *gnornian* 'to mourn', *guma* 'man'; in all positions, when the proximate vowel had front quality, it was sounded [j] (the initial sound in Mod.E. *yes*), for example *gif* 'if' [jɪf], *þegen* 'thane' [θɛjən]; after or between back vowels, it had the value of the velar fricative [ɣ] (the Germ. '*ach*-laut' voiced), sometimes heard in German *sagen*, for example *āgan* 'to own' [ɑːɣan], *fuglere* 'fowler' [fuɣlɛrə]. The biliteral *cg* was the symbol of the voiced affricate [dʒ] heard initially and finally in Mod.E. *judge*, for example *secgan* 'to say' [sɛdʒan].

The only one of these sounds which is difficult for present-day English-speakers is the [ɣ] value of *g*, and in view of the subsequent development of the words concerned, students are advised for ordinary reading purposes to pronounce this *g* as [w]; thus *dragan* 'to draw' [drɑwan], Chaucer [drɑwə(n)], *boga* 'bow' [bɔwa], Chaucer [bɔwə]. In the earlier period, OE had many long or lengthened consonants represented in writing by doubling, resembling the long consonants of Ital. in such words as *fanciullo*, *fratello*, *gatto* or the single consonant sounds heard in a few Mod.E. compounds like *lamp-post*. By the period of Classical OE, however, long consonants had been shortened in many cases, and probably universally in final position.

21. Normally, no letters are to be left unsounded in reading OE, hence the *w* of *wrītan* 'to write', the *c* of *cnāwan* 'to know', the *g* of *gnornian* 'to mourn' must be clearly heard before the following consonant. Similarly the biliteral *hw* as in *hwæt* 'what' is to be pronounced as the voiceless sound heard in Mod.Scots *what*, as distinct from the voiced labio-velar [w] (as in Mod.E. *wing*) of OE *wæt* 'wet'; so too *hl* as in *hlūd* 'loud' is to be pronounced as a voiceless *l*-sound (like that heard in Welsh *Llan-*) and *hr* as in *hring* 'ring' is to be pronounced as a voiceless *r*-sound, as distinct from the normal voiced *l* and *r*

of OE and Mod.E. alike. The OE group *ng* (for which runic writing had a separate symbol, called '*ing*') is generally the symbol of two sounds, the velar nasal [ŋ] (the final sound in Mod.E. *sing*) followed by the voiced plosive [g], resulting in the sequence heard in Mod.E. *finger* (as opposed to *singer*); *n* before *c* similarly gives [ŋ] followed by the plosive [k]; for example, OE *singan* 'to sing' [sɪŋgan], *drincan* 'to drink' [drɪŋkan].

22. There are inevitably exceptions to the above general rules of pronunciation, nor was the orthography of scribes regularly self-consistent. It is a good rule on the whole to look for guidance in doubtful cases to the practice of Mod.E. (aided if possible by ME) wherever the OE word has survived. Thus, for example, the fact that the *c* in *ælc* is an affricate and not a plosive may be suggested by the affricate in the Mod.E. form *each*. Foreign influence, however, especially Norse, may occasionally upset the correspondence, as for instance where the Norse plosive *g* has replaced the OE initial fricative in *give* and *get* (contrast Chaucer's form *yive*).

Where OE front vowels in the stem of a word are due to the *i*-mutation (see § 208) of an originally back vowel, a preceding *c* or *g* tended to remain a plosive consonant, as in *cynn* 'race' [kyn] from Gmc **kunj-*, or *cēne* 'bold' [keːnə] from Gmc **kōnj-*. Here too Mod.E. *kin* and *keen* serve as a guide and reminder.

23. In conclusion, here are the first eleven lines of *Beowulf* in a 'broad' phonetic transcription to represent the pronunciation of Ælfric's time, which was the period when the extant MS of this far older poem was copied. The text followed is that of C. L. Wrenn (London 1953):

> hwæt weː gɑːrdɛna in jɑːrdɑwum
> θēədkyniŋga θrym jəfruːnon,
> huː θɑː æðəliŋgas ɛlːən frɛmədɔn.
> ɔft ʃyld ʃeːviŋg ʃaðəna θrēətum
> mɔnəjum mæːjðum meədusɛtla ɔftēəx;
> ɛjsɔdə eərlə syθ(ː)an æːrɛst weərθ
> fēəʃaft fundən; heː θæs froːvrə jəbɑːd;
> weəks undər wɔlknum, weərθmyndum θɑːx,

17

ɔθːæt him æːjhwyltʃ θɑːra ymbsitːɛndra
ɔvər hrɔnrɑːdə hyːran ʃɔldə,
gɔmban jyldan. θæt wæs goːd kyniŋg!

We have hesitated, for reasons stated in the note to § 13, to make all inflexional endings as indeterminate as they must have been in the speech of c. 1000. Nor have we indicated the OE changes in vowel-length (see § 199), as for instance in *funden*, *gyldan*, since students will find them similarly not indicated in their texts, glossaries, and the dictionaries.

II

INFLEXIONS

General Note

24. Students who are working without a tutor and who have not previously made a start on the study of OE with the help of a primer are advised to learn by heart the paradigms and lists which are printed in **bold-face** type in the following paragraphs. They are further advised that their first steps in reading should be preceded or accompanied by a thorough study of *selected* noun, adjective, pronoun, and verb paradigms before concentrating in turn on the difficulties and exceptions presented by each of these parts of speech. Thus after learning *cyning* (§ 26), *scip* (§ 31), and *talu* (§ 36), they should proceed to the indefinite declension of adjectives (*trum*, § 50), and follow this with the personal pronouns (§ 63), *se, þæt, sēo* (§ 65), the verb *fremman* (§ 70) and 'to be' (§ 87).

Primers which are to be thoroughly recommended are Norman Davis, *Sweet's Anglo-Saxon Primer* (Oxford 1953) and P. S. Ardern, *First Readings in Old English* (Wellington, N.Z. and London 1951); more advanced linguistic students will find more detailed treatment than is possible here in J. Wright, *Old English Grammar* (Oxford 1925), R. Girvan, *Angelsaksisch Handboek* (Haarlem 1931), and K. Brunner, *Altenglische Grammatik nach . . . Sievers* (Halle, 2nd ed., 1951).

Nouns

25. OE nouns fall into three groups, *masculine, neuter* and *feminine*, according as they require one or other form of the demonstratives *se, þæt, sēo*, and enforce corresponding agreement on the other demonstratives, on adjectives, and on pronouns. It must be remembered that these three genders concern grammatical agreement and do not reflect any logical contrast between (animate) masculine and feminine and (inanimate) neuter; thus OE *bōc* 'book' is feminine, *wīfmann*

19

'woman' is masculine, and *mægden* 'girl' is neuter; but see further, § 124.

Forty-five per cent of all the nouns that the student will learn from his reading will be *masculine*; nearly four-fifths of these will have gen. sg. in *-es* and nom. acc. pl. in *-as*; about one fifth will have both gen. sg. and nom. acc. pl. in *-an*; and there will be a few very common nouns of irregular pattern.

Some thirty per cent of the nouns he meets will be *feminine*; five-sixths of these will have gen. sg. in *-e* and nom. acc. pl. in *-a* or *-e*; less than one sixth will have both gen. sg. and nom. acc. pl. in *-an*; again, he will find a small balance of irregulars.

Finally, twenty-five per cent of the nouns will be *neuter*, almost all having gen. sg. in *-es* and nom. acc. pl. in *-u* or without ending.

Regardless of gender, nouns have gen. pl. in *-(r)a* and dat. pl. in *-um*, except that nouns which have gen. sg. and nom. acc. pl. in *-an* have gen. pl. in *-(e)na*, while nouns with nom. sg. ending in a long vowel or diphthong have dat. pl. in *-m*.

For the purposes of learning OE grammar, we may conveniently classify the noun declensions in five groups:

    A—General Masculine Declension
    B—General Neuter Declension
    C—General Feminine Declension
    D—The *-an* Declension
    E—Irregular Declensions

A—GENERAL MASCULINE DECLENSION

26. The typical paradigm is as follows:

	sg.	*pl.*
nom.	**se cyning** 'the king'	**þā cyningas**
acc.	**þone cyning**	**þā cyningas**
gen.	**þæs cyninges**	**þāra cyninga**
dat.instr.	**þǣm, þȳ cyninge**	**þǣm cyningum**

In the sg., *þǣm* is dat., *þȳ* instr.; see § 65.

On this pattern are declined the majority of masculine nouns; for example, *stān* 'stone', *āð* 'oath', *bāt* 'boat', *hlāf* 'loaf', *hengest* 'horse', *æðeling* 'prince'.

Simplification of final double consonants (see § 196) some-times produces discrepancies between inflected and uninflected forms: for example, *weal(l)* 'wall', g.sg. *wealles*.

Bearu 'grove' and a few nouns with n.a.sg. forms ending in a diphthong have *-w-* before inflexional endings: *bearwes, pēo(w)* 'servant'—*pēowes, hlēo(w)* 'protection'—*hlēowes, pēa(w)* 'cus-tom'—*pēawes*.

Fæder 'father' has an uninflected d.sg. and sometimes an uninflected g.sg. *fæder* (compare § 47, *brōðor*, etc.).

On other cases of uninflected d.sg., for example *hām*, see § 115.

27. Stems in *-lh, -rh*, such as *wealh* 'foreigner', *mearh* 'horse', lose *-h-* before endings (see § 189). Monosyllables with *-æ̆-* in n.sg. have *-a-* in the pl. (see § 192). Thus:

	sg.	pl.	sg.	pl.
n.a.	wealh	wealas	dæg	dagas
g.	weales	weala	dæges	daga
d.i.	weale	wealum	dæge	dagum

The few stems ending in a vowel plus *h*, notably *eoh* 'horse', *sc(e)ōh* 'shoe', *hōh* 'heel', undergo loss of *h* with contraction in inflected cases, with lengthening of an originally short stem-vowel (see § 189); they have g.pl. in *-na* by analogy with nouns of the *-an* type (see §§ 40, 41 below); thus sg. *sc(e)ōh, sc(e)ōs, sc(e)ō*, pl. *sc(e)ōs, sc(e)ōna, sc(e)ō(u)m*, or, very late, *sc(e)ōn*.

28. With dissyllables like *heofon* 'heaven', having a short first syllable and ending in a single consonant, the second vowel is often weakened to [ə] and spelt *-e-* in inflected cases; for exam-ple, *heofenas*.

Where the first syllable is long and the second short in dis-syllabic nouns, the second vowel is syncopated (see § 195) in inflected cases; for example, *dryhten* 'lord' (g.sg. *dryhtnes*), *engel* 'angel', *dēofol* 'devil'; syncope occurs also with a few nouns which have short first syllable (thus, *fugol* 'bird', *nicor* 'monster'), though these appear also without syncope.

A long syllable is one which has a long vowel or which ends in a long consonant or in a consonant cluster. In addition to syncopated masc. forms like those of other nouns in this class, *winter* 'winter' has a d.i.sg. *wintra* (see § 43) and n.a.pl. forms on neuter patterns: *winter, wintru*.

29. (*a*) Many nouns of two or more syllables and ending in *-e* are declined as follows:

	sg.	*pl.*
n.a.	bæcere 'baker'	bæceras
g.	bæceres	bæcera
d.i.	bæcere	bæcerum

Here belong other agent nouns in *-ere* (see §§ 164, 172), and dissyllables such as *ende* 'end', *hyrde* 'shepherd', *hwǽte* 'wheat'. As well as having inflexions on the above pattern, *here* 'raiding force' sometimes has a medial [j], variously spelt, in oblique cases: g.sg. *heries*, *her(i)ges*, d.sg. *herie*, *her(i)ge*, n.a.pl. *herias*, *her(i)g(e)as*, etc. (see § 194).

(*b*) Also found with inflexions like *bæcere* are *bite* 'bite', *byre* 'son', *cyme* 'arrival', *cwide* 'saying', *gripe* 'grasp', *hyge* 'mind', *mere* 'lake', *slege* 'blow', *wlite* 'beauty'; a few, notably *hyse* 'young man', *mete* 'food', appear throughout the pl. with double consonant: *hyssas*, *mettum* (see § 194).

30. Historically, the nouns in § 29*b* do not belong to the same declension as that which gave rise to the endings of most General Masculine nouns, and many are recorded with alternative n.a.pl. forms, especially in early texts. This alternative paradigm is often found with *stede* 'place':

	sg.	*pl.*
n.a.	stede	stede
g.	stedes	steda
d.i.	stede	stedum

Wine 'friend' has, in addition, variant forms of the g.pl.: *wina*, *wini(ge)a*. A few nouns had the *-e* plural regularly: *ylde* 'men', *ylfe* 'elves', *lēode* 'people', and, above all, racial and tribal names such as *Dene* 'Danes' (g.pl. as *wine*), *Engle* 'Englishmen', *Myrce* 'Mercians' and *Seaxe* 'Saxons' (g.pl. *Myrcna*, *Seaxna*).

B—GENERAL NEUTER DECLENSION

31. Neuter nouns in general differ from masculines only in the n.a.pl., which may be in *-u* (especially short-stemmed

22

monosyllables) or have no ending (especially long-stemmed monosyllables; see § 188):

	sg.		pl.
n.a.	þæt scip	'the ship'	þā scipu
g.	þæs scipes		þāra scipa
d.i.	þǣm, þȳ scipe		þǣm scipum

The n.a.pl. ending is sometimes -*o*.

	sg.		pl.
n.a.	þæt land	'the land'	þā land
g.	þæs landes		þāra landa
d.i.	þǣm, þȳ lande		þǣm landum

32. Like *scip* are *bod* 'command', *brim* 'sea', *lim* 'limb', *gewrit* 'writing', etc. Where the stem vowel is *ĭ* in n.a.sg., it sometimes appears as *io*, *eo* in the pl.: *liomu* 'limbs' (see § 214). Where the n.a.sg. stem vowel is *ǣ*, we find -*a*- in the pl.: *fær* 'journey', *færes*, *fære*; *faru*, *fara*, *farum* (see § 192); so too *fæt* 'vessel', *swæþ* 'track', etc.; *geat* 'gate' has -*ea*- in the sg., -*a*- in the pl. (see § 204).

33. Like *land* are *bān* 'bone', *bearn* 'child', *folc* 'people', *scēap* 'sheep', *sweord* 'sword', etc. The paradigms of two common nouns in -*h*, *feorh* 'life', *feoh* 'property', are as follows:

	sg.	pl.	sg.
n.a.	feorh	feorh	feoh
g.	feores	feora	fēos
d.i.	feore	feorum	fēo

For the forms, see § 189.

Simplification of final double consonants (see § 196) produces some discrepancies as between n.a.sg. and pl. on the one hand and g.d.i.sg. and pl. on the other: thus, *bed*(*d*) 'bed' beside *beddes*, *beddum*; so too, *cyn*(*n*) 'race', *flet*(*t*) 'floor', *gied*(*d*) 'song', *wed*(*d*) 'pledge', and a few others. Similarly, derivative neuter nouns in -*en*(*n*), -*et*(*t*) double the *n* or *t* before endings; thus *wēsten*(*n*) 'desert' (n.a.pl. *wēstennu*), *fæsten* 'stronghold', *rȳmet* 'space'.

Where the medial consonant cluster in inflected forms ends in *w* (as in *bealwes* 'of evil'), the n.a.sg. and pl. ends in -*u* (*bealu*); so too, *searu* 'device', *smeoru* 'fat', *teoru* 'tar'. In *cnēo*(*w*)

23

'knee(s)', *strēa(w)* 'straw(s)', and *trēo(w)* 'tree(s)', all n.a.sg. and pl., the g.d.i.sg. and pl. may have short or long vowels: *cnĕŏwes, strĕāwa, trĕŏwum*.

34. There are many neuter nouns with n.a.sg. in *-e* which are declined as follows:

	sg.		pl.
n.a.	wīte	'punishment'	wītu
g.	wītes		wīta
d.i.	wīte		wītum

Thus, *ǣrende* 'errand', *fiðere* 'wing', *rīce* 'kingdom', *spere* 'spear', *yrfe* 'inheritance', and others.

Some nouns of this type, if they are original *ja*-stems, have alternative forms in the pl. with a palatal vowel before the endings; this phenomenon is found especially with *rīce*: n.a.pl. *rīc(i)u*, g.pl. *rīc(e)a*, d.i.pl. *rīc(i)um*; see § 194.

35. Dissyllabic nouns other than the types already mentioned display considerable variation in two respects: (*a*) the n.a.pl. (in *-u* or without ending), and (*b*) the syncope or retention of the second vowel before inflexions.

(*a*) In general, dissyllables with *short* first syllable decline like *land*, with uninflected n.a.pl.; thus *werod* 'troop', *reced* 'house', and others, but late forms with *-u* are not uncommon; *wæter* 'water' has frequent *-u* plurals (both *wæteru* and *wætru*), and *-u* forms are usual with *yfel* 'evil'. The position is similar with a number of nouns which appear sometimes spelt as dissyllables with *long* first syllable and sometimes without the second vowel in uninflected cases: thus *tāc(e)n* 'sign', *tung(o)l* 'star', *wund(u)r* 'wonder', *wǣp(e)n* 'weapon' have usually the same forms in n.a.sg. and n.a.pl., but they may also have *-u* plurals (*tācnu, tunglu, wundru, wǣpnu*). On the other hand, the majority of dissyllables with long first syllable have *-u* plurals throughout OE (*hēafod* 'head'—*hēafodu*, *nȳten* 'animal' —*nȳtenu*, *pūsend* 'thousand'—*pūsendu*), though uninflected plurals like *hēafod, pūsend* also occur.

(*b*) As regards syncope of the second vowel, this is unusual where the first syllable is short (*recedes, werodes*, etc.), though syncopated forms of *wæter* (*wætres, wætru*) are common enough.

Nouns like *tāc(e)n*, *wǣp(e)n*, on the other hand, which often lack a second vowel in n.a.sg. and pl., are very rarely without syncope in inflected cases: *tācnes*, *wǣpne*, etc. For the rest, nouns with long first syllable and with a single consonant after the second vowel normally show syncope in g.d.i.sg. and pl. (*hēafdes*), though this is usually resisted before *-u* and one finds n.a.pl. forms for the most part with the second vowel preserved (*hēafodu*).

C—GENERAL FEMININE DECLENSION

36. Many feminine nouns (especially those with short stems) have n.sg. in *-u* while many others (especially those with long stems) have n.sg. ending in a consonant; apart from this, there is no difference throughout the paradigm:

	sg.	pl.
n.	sēo talu 'the tale'	þā tala
a.	þā tale	þā tala
g.	þǣre tale	þāra tala
d.i.	þǣre tale	þǣm talum
n.	sēo ġlōf 'the glove'	þā ġlōfa
a.	þā ġlōfe	þā ġlōfa
g.	þǣre ġlōfe	þāra ġlōfa
d.i.	þǣre ġlōfe	þǣm ġlōfum

It must be noted (*a*) that the n.a.pl. of both types sometimes ends in *-e*, and (*b*) that the g.pl. ending, especially of the short-stemmed nouns, is often *-(e)na*.

37. Like *talu* are *andswaru* 'answer', *c(e)aru* 'grief', *cwalu* 'killing', *sacu* 'strife', and others; long-stemmed nouns with n.sg. in *-u* include *cȳððu* 'native land', *fǣhðu* 'feud', *gesǣlðu* 'prosperity', and *strengðu* 'strength', though all of these have both alternative sg. forms without ending and alternative a.g.d.i.sg. forms in *-u*.

38. Like *ġlōf* are *bōt* 'advantage', *brycg* 'bridge', *eaxl* 'shoulder', *ecg* 'edge', *hwīl* 'space of time', *rōd* 'cross', *sorg* 'sorrow', and many others. Several nouns which may or may not have

a final double consonant in n.sg. always have the double consonant in the rest of the paradigm: thus *ben(n)* 'wound', *hel(l)* 'Hell', *sib(b)* 'kinship', *wyn(n)* 'joy', etc., and derivatives in *-en(n)* and *-nes(s)* such as *byrgen(n)* 'tomb', *gōdnes(s)* 'goodness'.

Derivatives in *-ung* (see §§ 164, 170) such as *leornung* 'learning' have alternative forms in *-a* for a.g.d.i.sg.

Dissyllables with short first syllable, such as *firen* 'violence', *duguð* 'valour', *ides* 'woman', are declined like *glōf* without syncope of the second vowel (e.g. *firenum*); dissyllables with long first syllable, such as *frōfor* 'comfort', *sāwol* 'soul', have syncope before endings but are otherwise like *glōf*: *frōfre, sāwla*.

Inflexional endings in a number of nouns are preceded by *-w-* although in the n.sg. it may appear vocalised as *-u* or (after a long syllable) be entirely absent; thus, *beadu* 'battle', *sceadu* 'shadow' (a.sg. *beadwe, sceadwe*), *mǣd* 'meadow' (a.sg. *mǣdwe*); the paradigm is otherwise like *glōf*, and indeed oblique cases of *mǣd* sometimes lack the *-w-* (§ 187).

Clēa 'claw' is usually declined *clawe* etc.; *þrawu* 'misery' has an alternative form *þrēa* throughout the sg. and n.a.g.pl., with a d.i.pl. *þrēam*; *brū* 'eyebrow' has the following pl. forms: n.a. *brū(w)a*, g. *brūna*, d.i. *brū(w)um*; *ēa* 'river' is usually unchanged throughout the sg. and n.a.g.pl., with a d.i.pl. *ēam*, but several variants occur, notably a g.sg. *ēas*.

39. While most feminine nouns have their usual n.a.pl. in *-a*, less usually in *-e*, a number of common ones have their n.a.pl. in *-e*, less usually in *-a*; these also usually differ from the majority of feminine nouns in having identical, uninflected n.a.sg., though here again analogy sometimes causes them to adopt the commoner feminine a.sg. in *-e*. The distinctive paradigm is as follows:

	sg.	pl.
n.a.	dǣd 'deed'	dǣde
g.	dǣde	dǣda
d.i.	dǣde	dǣdum

So too, *bēn* 'prayer', *cwēn* 'woman', *fyrd* 'levy', *miht* 'power', *nȳd* 'necessity', *tīd* 'time', *wēn* 'expectation', *wyrd* 'fate', and several others.

With *ǣ* 'law' (earlier *ǣw*), we find uninflected forms throughout the sg. and n.a.pl., *ǣ*, as well as g.d.i.sg. *ǣwe*, n.a.pl. *ǣw*; *sǣ* 'sea' is sometimes masc. (g.sg. *sǣs*, d.i. *sǣ*, n.a.pl. *sǣs*, g.pl. *sǣwa*, d.i.pl. *sǣm*, *sǣwum*) and sometimes fem. (g.d.i.sg. *sǣ* or *sǣwe*, n.a.pl. *sǣ*).

D—THE *-AN* DECLENSION

40. Many masculines (with n.sg. in *-a*) and feminines (with n.sg. in *-e*) belong here, and also two neuters (with n.a.sg. in *-e*); thus *guma* 'man', *byrne* 'coat of mail', *ēage* 'eye' respectively:

	masc.	*fem.*	*neut.*
sg.n.	se guma	sēo byrne	þæt ēage
a.	þone guman	þā byrnan	þæt ēage
g.	þæs guman	þǣre byrnan	þæs ēagan
d.i.	þǣm, þȳ guman	þǣre byrnan	þǣm, þȳ ēagan
pl.n.a.	þā guman	þā byrnan	þā ēagan
g.	þāra gumena	þāra byrnena	þāra ēagena
d.i.	þǣm gumum	þǣm byrnum	þǣm ēagum

Like *guma* are *bana* 'killer', *boda* 'messenger' (and other agent nouns in *-a*; see § 161c), *nama* 'name', and many others.

Like *byrne* are *cyrice* 'church', *eorðe* 'earth', *heorte* 'heart', *hlǣfdige* 'lady', *tunge* 'tongue', and many others.

Like *ēage* is *ēare* 'ear'.

A few nouns in this class have g.pl. in *-na*, notably *wilna* (*willa* 'desire'); *tungna*, *ēagna* are alternative g.pl. forms; *oxa* 'ox' has g.pl. *oxna*, d.pl. *ox(n)um*, n.a.pl. *oxan*, *exen*.

41. A small number of masculines and feminines have n.sg. ending in a long vowel or diphthong; masculines are *gefā* 'foe', *gefēa* 'joy', *frēa* 'lord', *Swēon* (pl.) 'Swedes', *twēo* 'doubt', *wēa* 'woe'; feminines are *bēo* 'bee', *flā* 'arrow', *tā* 'toe'. These are inflected by adding *-na* to the n.sg. form for g.pl., *-m* for d.i.pl., and *-n* for the other cases.

In addition, the d.i.pl. is sometimes re-formed with *-um* (*Swēoum*), sometimes preceded by the *n* of other cases (*tānum*); *lēo* 'lion' sometimes has the *-n-* of the Latin oblique cases (*lēōnan*, *lēōnum*) and has a d.i.sg. form *lēōne*.

E—IRREGULAR DECLENSIONS

42. The nouns to be considered here are more 'irregular' than those in the preceding paragraphs only from the point of view of learning OE; in other words, these nouns have various inflexional patterns substantially different from the four main types already dealt with. If, on the other hand, we had a more strictly philological aim and were viewing the development of Indo-European nouns as a whole, we might say that the nouns in the present group were more 'regular' than many of those previously listed, since by reason of their frequency of occurrence they have retained to a much greater extent the identity and individuality of old declensional patterns, whereas many nouns in the foregoing sections have lost their former inflexions and taken on other endings.

We may sub-divide the irregular nouns into four groups, classified by the plural forms: (*a*) *-a* plurals, (*b*) *-ru* plurals, (*c*) uninflected plurals, (*d*) mutation plurals.

43. (*a*) *-a* plurals

Here belong the masculines *sunu* 'son', *wudu* 'wood', and the feminines *duru* 'door', *nosu* 'nose', *hond* 'hand':

	sg.		*pl.*	
n.a.	sunu	hond	suna	honda
g.	suna	honda	suna	honda
d.i.	suna	honda	sunum	hondum

The form *sunu* is sometimes carried through the sg. and n.a.pl. Other nouns having some forms like *sunu* and *hond*, while belonging in the main to the General Masculine or Feminine Declensions, are as follows: masc. *meodu* 'mead', *sidu* 'custom', *eard* 'native land', *feld* 'field', *ford* 'ford', *sumor* 'summer', *weald* 'forest', *winter* 'winter', and some others; fem. *flōr* (also with masc. forms of the General type) 'floor', *cweorn* 'mill'.

It will be seen that *sunu* and *hond* differ only in the n.a.sg.; on the loss or retention of *-u*, see § 188.

44. (*b*) *-ru* plurals

Here belong the following neuter nouns: *ǣg* 'egg', *brēadru* (pl. only) 'bread crumbs', *cealf* 'calf', *cild* 'child', *lomb* 'lamb':

	sg.	*pl.*
n.a.	ǣg	ǣgru
g.	ǣges	ǣgra
d.i.	ǣge	ǣgrum

Cild, cealf, and *lomb* appear also with General Neuter inflexions (like *land*, § 31), and the first two are recorded more rarely with General Masculine inflexions.

45. (c) uninflected plurals

We have here three sub-groups, the one comprising nouns in *-end*, the second a few nouns which have *-ð-* before inflexions, the third comprising some nouns of relationship.

In the first sub-group belong a considerable number of masculine agent nouns which end in *-end* (see § 171):

	sg.	*pl.*
n.a.	rīdend 'rider'	rīdend
g.	rīdendes	rīdendra
d.i.	rīdende	rīdendum

Nouns of this kind are found also with n.a.pl. in *-e* and *-as*, and sometimes with *-r-* throughout the pl.

46. In the second sub-group we have the masculines *hæle(ð)* 'hero', *mōnað* 'month'; a feminine, *mæg(e)ð* 'maiden'; and a neuter, *ealu* 'ale'; *hæle(ð)* is declined thus:

	sg.	*pl.*
n.a.	hæle(ð)	hæleð
g.	hæleðes	hæleða
d.i.	hæleðe	hæleðum

Mōnað has medial *-e-* or syncope in g.d.i.sg. and pl.: *mōn(e)ðes, mōn(e)ðe,* etc.; both *mōnað* and *hæle(ð)* also have n.a.pl. forms in *-as*. The fem. *mæg(e)ð* may or may not have syncope of the *-e-* throughout; it is uninflected in the sg. and in n.a.pl., but g.d.i.sg. may be *mæg(e)ðe*. The defective neut. *ealu* appears as *ealoð* in g.d.i.sg. and the only pl. form recorded is the gen. *ealeða*.

47. In the third sub-group are the masc. *brōðor* 'brother', and the fem. *mōdor* 'mother', *dohtor* 'daughter':

	sg.	pl.
n.a.	brōðor	brōðor
g.	brōðor	brōðra
d.i.	brēðer	brōðrum

Like these is *sweostor* 'sister' except that this is unchanged in d.i.sg.

Brōðor, dohtor, mōdor have alternative n.a.pl. forms *brōð(e)ru, dohtru, -ra, mōdra, -ru*, and the latter two are found also with mutation in g.sg. (*dehter, mēder*). On *fæder* 'father', which is declined mainly on the General Masc. pattern, see § 26. On the mutated form in *dohtor*, see § 207.

48. (*d*) **mutated plurals**

The masc. paradigm is as follows:

	sg.	pl.
n.a.	fōt 'foot'	fēt
g.	fōtes	fōta
d.	fēt	fōtum

The instr. sg. in this group is sometimes recorded in -*e* without mutation (e.g. *fōte*).

Like *fōt* is *tōð* 'tooth'; here belong also *fēond* 'foe', *frēond* 'friend' (n.a.pl. -*īe*-, -*ȳ*-), which have alternative n.a.pl. forms *f(r)ēond(as)*, *mann* 'man' and *wīfmann* 'woman' (n.a.pl. -*e*-).

The neut. *scrūd* 'garment' has forms like *land* (§ 31) but with an alternative d.sg. *scrȳd*. On *i*-mutation, see §§ 208 ff.

49. The fem. paradigm is as follows:

	sg.	pl.
n.a.	gōs 'goose'	gēs
g.	gōse	gōsa
d.i.	gēs	gōsum

Like *gōs* are *bōc* 'book', *brōc* 'breeches'; here belong also *āc* 'oak' (n.a.pl. *ǣc*), *burg* 'fortress' (n.a.pl. *byr(i)g*), *lūs* 'louse' and *mūs* 'mouse' (n.a.pl. -*ȳ*-), and a few others. Some of these are recorded with an alternative g.sg. form with mutation and without ending: e.g. *bēc, byrig*. A minor variation is repre-

sented by *hnutu* 'nut' which has g.sg. *hnute*, d.i.sg. n.a.pl. *hnyte*.
Cū 'cow' has g.sg. *cū, cūe, cȳ, cūs*, n.a.pl. *cȳ(e)*, g.pl. *cū(n)a,
cȳna; furh* 'furrow' loses the *h* before inflexions.

Adjectives

50. There are two types of inflexion, the indefinite and the
definite, for almost every adjective; on the distinction in usage
between the two, see § 116. The exceptions are *eall* 'all',
fēa(we) 'few', *genōg* 'enough', *manig* 'many', and *ōðer* 'other',
which are always indefinite; and *ilca* 'same', ordinal numerals
(except *ōðer*), comparatives, and for the most part superlatives,
which take the definite inflexion.

A. The Indefinite Declension

Although the indefinite inflexions are not exactly the same
for all adjectives, there being some points of difference over
the n.sg.fem. and n.a.pl.neut. and over the syncope or non-
syncope of medial vowels, the following paradigm may be
regarded as typical:

	masc.	*neut.*	*fem.*
sg. n.	trum 'firm'	trum	trumu
a.	trumne	trum	trume
g.	trumes	trumes	trumre
d.	trumum	trumum	trumre
i.	trume	trume	trumre
pl. n.a.	trume	trumu	truma
g.	trumra	trumra	trumra
d.i.	trumum	trumum	trumum

The *-u* of n.sg.fem. and n.a.pl.neut. is sometimes replaced by *-o*.
In late texts the n.a.pl. is often in *-e* for all genders, and we
occasionally find a weakened ending (spelt, for example, *-an*)
replacing *-um* in the d.sg.masc.neut. and d.i.pl. all genders.

51. Short-stemmed monosyllabic adjectives are declined on
the above model (e.g. *gram* 'fierce', *til* 'good'), as also compound
adjectives in *-lic* and *-sum* (e.g. *lāðlic* 'hateful', *luſsum* 'ami-

D   31

able'). Adjectives like *glæd* 'happy', *hwæt* 'bold', where the stem vowel is *ǽ*, have *-a-* before an inflexional vowel; thus a.sg.fem. *glade* beside a.sg.masc. *glædne*.

Adjectives which have *-e* in the n.sg.masc. and n.a.sg.neut. differ from *trum* in these respects only; for example, *æðele* 'noble', *dēore* 'dear', *grēne* 'green', *mǽre* 'famous', *rīce* 'powerful', *swēte* 'sweet', and many others.

Adjectives which have *-u* in the n.sg.masc. and n.a.sg.neut. differ also from *trum* in having *-w-* before *-e* and *-a*, and *-o-* before consonants; thus *gearu* 'ready' n.sg. all genders, *gearwes* g.sg.masc. and neut., *gearone* a.sg.masc., etc.; *-w-* sometimes also appears before *-um*. The neuter form *fēa* 'few' (pl. only) is often an invariable n.a. form, though separate forms *fēawe*, *-a* are also common; g.pl. is *fēa(we)ra*, d.i.pl. *fēa(w)um*, *fēam*.

Cucu (*cwicu*) 'living' is not like *gearu*, but remains almost the only trace of a lost paradigm; it is recorded with *-u* for a.sg.fem. and neut. and for n.sg. and pl. all genders, and there is an a.sg.masc. *cucone*; but the distinctive inflexions of *cucu* are rare, a more frequent form being *cwic*, inflected like *trum*. Also declined like *gearu* are *fealu* 'dark', *geolu* 'yellow', *nearu* 'narrow', and a few others.

52. Long-stemmed monosyllables differ from *trum* in being uninflected in n.sg.fem. and n.a.pl.neut. where *trum* has *-u* (see § 188); thus *blind* 'blind', *dēad* 'dead', *eald* 'old', *lāð* 'hostile', *sōð* 'true', *wīs* 'wise', and many other common adjectives. So too compound adjectives in *-isc*, *-lēas*, *-weard*, and other long-syllabled elements (see §§ 165, 171 f). Present and past participles belong here also, except that the former have *-e* in n.sg.masc. and n.a.sg.neut.

The uninflected forms of certain adjectives sometimes end in a single, sometimes in a double consonant: e.g. *eal(l)* 'all', *grim(m)* 'grim'; they usually have the single consonant before endings beginning with a consonant (*grimne*, *ealre*), the double consonant before endings beginning with a vowel (*grimme*, *eallum*).

Adjectives whose uninflected stem ends in *-h* lose the *h* in inflected forms (see § 189); thus *þweorh* 'perverse'; with *fāh* 'hostile', *hēah* 'high', *nēah* 'near' we find in addition the doubling of the consonant in the inflexions *-ne*, *-re*, and *-ra*, and the

disappearance of the vowel from the remaining inflexions
hēanne, hēarre, hēas, hēa, etc., but we also find single consonant
forms (*hēane,* etc.) and analogical re-formations such as *hēahre,*
hēaum.

Frēo(h) 'free' has a variety of forms: a.sg.masc. *frēone, frigne,* a.sg.fem.
frēo, frige, and similar pairs.

53. We come now to the dissyllabic (and in a few cases tri-
syllabic) adjectives in *-ig, -en, -el, -ol, -er, -or* (§§ 170 ff). Where
the stressed syllable is *short* (as in *manig* 'many', *swutol* 'clear'),
the n.sg.fem. and n.a.pl.neut. are almost always uninflected;
in such adjectives, too, syncope is often resisted and one has
forms like *maniges, swutoles,* though with *micel* and *yfel* syncopated forms (*miclum, yflum,* etc.) are very frequent. Where
the stressed syllable is *long* (as in *lȳtel* 'little', *crīsten* 'Christian',
hālig 'holy'), the n.sg.fem. and n.a.pl.neut. are usually in *-u*
(*lȳtlu, hāligu*); syncope is usual before endings in or beginning
with a vowel (*lȳtles, hālge, hālgum*), except that it tends to be
resisted before *-u* (*hāl(i)gu, lȳt(e)lu*) and is not frequent with
adjectives in *-en* (*crīstenes*).

54. B. The Definite Declension

		masc.	*neut.*	*fem.*
sg.	n.	truma	trume	trume
	a.	truman	trume	truman
	g.d.i.	truman	truman	truman
pl.	n.a.	truman	truman	truman
	g.	trumra	trumra	trumra
	d.i.	trumum	trumum	trumum

Sometimes the g.pl. has *-ena,* and in late texts we sometimes
find *-an* in n.sg.masc.: *se forman dæg* 'the first day'. Adjectives
like *hēah* (§ 52) have one n.sg. for all genders (*hēa*), adding *-n*
etc. for oblique cases. Adjectives which have *-w-* in the indefinite paradigm (§ 51) or syncope before certain inflexions (§ 53)
have these throughout the definite declension except before
the *-ra* g.pl. where the conditions are the same as in the
indefinite declension.

Comparison of Adjectives and Adverbs

55. **Adjectives.** The comparative ends in *-ra* and is declined on the *definite* pattern (§ 54); the superlative ends in *-ost(a)*, *-(e)st(a)* and is also declined on the definite pattern except often for the n.sg.masc. and fem. and n.a.sg.neut.

The commonest pattern of comparison is as follows:

earm 'poor'	earmra 'poorer'	earmost 'poorest'
heard 'hard'	heardra	heardost
lēof 'dear'	leōfra	leōfost

Where the stem vowel of monosyllabic adjectives is *ǽ*, the superlative has *-a-* (see § 192):

glæd 'glad'	glædra	gladost

Adjectives like *gearu* are compared as follows:

gearu 'ready'	gearora	gearwost
nearu 'narrow'	nearora	nearwost

Adjectives like *rīce* drop the *-e* before the endings:

blīðe 'happy'	blīðra	blīðost
cēne 'bold'	cēnra	cēnost
rīce 'powerful'	rīcra	rīcost

Long-stemmed adjectives in *-en*, *-er*, *-ig*, *-ol*, etc. sometimes show syncope before the superlative ending and sometimes not (*cræftgost* 'strongest', *gesǽlgost* 'happiest', but also *gesǽligost*); with short-stemmed adjectives syncope is rare (*swutolost* 'clearest', *snoterost* 'wisest'). Syncope is extremely rare before the comparative ending (*cræftigra*, *snoterra*).

56. Several adjectives, which originally took different suffixes, show *i*-mutation in the comp. and superl. (§ 209); their superl. ending is generally recorded as *-(e)st(a)*:

eald 'old'	yldra	yldest
feorr 'far'	fyrra	fyrrest
geong 'young'	gingra	gingest
grēat 'large'	grȳtra	grȳtest
hēah 'high'	hȳrra	hȳhst
lang 'long'	lengra	lengest
sceort 'short'	scyrtra	scyrtest
strang 'strong'	strengra	strengest

Beside *brādra*, *-ost*, *brād* 'broad' has mutated forms *brǣdra*, *-est*; there are several variant forms for *hēah*, including *hȳhra*, *hīra*, *hēahra*, *hȳhst*, *hēah(e)st*; *nēah* 'near' has comp. *nēahra* or *nēarra*, but superl. with mutation, *nȳhst*.

57. With a small number of adjectives, the comp. and superl. have a different root from the positive:

gōd 'good'	{ betra	betst
	{ sēlra	sēlest
lȳtel 'little'	lǣssa	lǣst
micel 'great'	māra	mǣst
yfel 'evil'	wyrsa	wyrst

Beside *betra*, we find also *betera*, *bettra*; beside *betst(a)*, *wyrst(a)*, we find *betest(a)*, *wi(e)r(re)st(a)*.

58. Several other comp. and superl. adjectives have no positive forms at all but correspond to adverbs; the commonest are:

(ǣr 'before')	ǣrra 'earlier'	ǣrest 'first'
(ēast 'eastwards')	ēasterra 'more easterly'	ēastmest 'most easterly'
(inne 'inside')	innerra 'inner'	innemest 'inmost'

Like *ēast* are *norð* 'northwards', *sūð* 'southwards', *west* 'westwards'; like *inne* is *ūte* 'outside', except that it has alternative comp. and superl. forms with mutation, *ȳt-*. The examples in *-mest* are, as it were, double superlatives, since the *-m-* represents an old superl. suffix (cf Lat. *primus*, *optimus*) which survives in *forma* 'first' but of which there are few other OE examples.

59. **Adverbs.** The comp. ends in *-or*, the superl. in *-ost* or *-est*:

oft 'often'	oftor	oftost
hraðe 'quickly'	hraðor	hraðost
luflīce 'lovingly'	luflīcor	luflīcost

35

There are a few common exceptional forms (cf § 57):

lȳt 'little'	lǣs	lǣst
micle 'much'	mā	mǣst
wel 'well'	{ bet	betst
	sēl	sēlest
yfle 'ill'	wyrs	wyrst

Alternative forms include *betest* and *wi(e)r(re)st*. *Seldan* 'seldom' has comp. *seld(n)or*, superl. *seldost*. Examples with *i*-mutation (besides *bet*, *wyrs*, etc.) include *lange* 'long'—*leng*—*lengest*, *nȳr* (beside *nēar*) 'nearer', *sēft* 'more softly', *ȳð* 'more easily', and one or two others.

Numerals

60.

	Cardinal	Ordinal
1.	ān	forma, fyrsta, fyrmest
2.	twēgen	ōðer
3.	þrȳ	þridda
4.	feōwer	feōrða
5.	fíf	fífta
6.	syx	syxta
7.	seofon	seofoða
8.	eahta	eahtoða
9.	nigon	nigoða
10.	tȳn	teoða
11.	endleofan	endleofta
12.	twelf	twelfta
13.	þreōtȳne	þreōteoða
20.	twentig	twentigoða
21.	ān and twentig	ān and twentigoða
30.	þrītig	-oða
70.	hundseofontig	-oða
80.	hundeahtatig	-oða
90.	hundnigontig	-oða
100.	hundteōntig, hund(red)	hundteōntigoða
110.	hundendleofantig	-oða

	Cardinal	*Ordinal*
120.	hundtwelftig	-oða
200.	tū hund(red)	(not recorded)
1000.	þūsend	(„ „)

The numerals for 14-19 are formed as for 13; similarly, 22-29, 40-60, 130-190, 300, etc. may be inferred from the structure of 21, 30, 120, 200, etc. In place of ordinals corresponding to *hund* and *þūsend*, we find periphrases such as *æftemest on þām twām hundredum* 'last in the two hundred', i.e. 'two-hundredth'.

61. All ordinals follow the definite declension (§ 54), except *ōðer* which always has the indefinite inflexions (§§ 50, 53).

The first three cardinals are declined as follows. *Ān* can have both indefinite and definite inflexions (with the latter it means 'alone'), except that beside *ānne* there is an alternative a.sg. masc. *ǣnne*. In the plural, it means 'only, unique'. *Twēgen* is the n.a.pl.masc.; the n.a.pl.neut. and fem. is *twā* (with an alternative neut. form *tū*); g.pl. *twēg(r)a*, d.i.pl. *twǣm* or *twām*. *Þrȳ* is also the n.a.pl.masc., and the n.a.pl.neut. and fem. is *þrēo*, g.pl. *þrēora*, d.i.pl. *þrim*.

Like *twēgen* is *bēgen* 'both', n.a. neut. and fem. *bā* (*bū*), g. *bēg(r)a*, d.i. *bǣm*, *bām*.

62. The cardinals 4-19 are not usually declined when used attributively, but sometimes when they stand alone they take endings as follows: n.a. masc. and fem. *-e*, neut. *-u*, g. *-a*, d.i. *-um*. Thus *fīf menn* 'five men', but *ic sēo fīfe* 'I see five'. Numerals in *-tig* are sometimes declined as neuter nouns (thus with a g.sg., as in *þrītiges mīla brād* 'thirty miles wide'), more frequently with adjectival inflexions agreeing with the items counted, but frequently also with no inflexion at all. *Hund* and *þūsend* are either invariable or are declined as neuter nouns.

Some of the idioms involving numerals should be noted. Expressions such as *syxa sum* 'one of six' are special cases of the partitive genitive and are discussed in § 101, note; ordinals with *healf* are used as follows: *ōðer healf* 'one and a half', *þridde healf* 'two and a half', *fīfte healf hund* 'four hundred and fifty', etc.

Pronouns

63. Personal

First Person	sg.	dual	pl.
n.	ic	wit	wē
a.	mē	unc	ūs
g.	mīn	uncer	ūre
d.i.	mē	unc	ūs

Second Person			
n.	þū	git	gē
a.	þē	inc	ēow
g.	þīn	incer	ēower
d.i.	þē	inc	ēow

Third Person	sg.			pl.
	masc.	neut.	fem.	common
n.	hē	hit	hēo	hī
a.	hine	hit	hī	hī
g.	his	his	hire	hira
d.i.	him	him	hire	him

On the use of the personal pronouns as **reflexive**, see § 120c.

Early texts sometimes have distinctive a.sg. forms of the 1st and 2nd pers.: *mec, uncet, ūsic; þec, incit, ēowic; ēow*(-) often appears as *īow*(-), *ūre* as *ūser*; in the 3rd pers. there is considerable variety of form: for example, *hine, his, him, hit*, etc. often appear in lWS spelt *-y-*, and *hī, hire, hira* often appear as *hīe* (*hēo*), *hiere, heora*; so too we find *heom* for d.i.pl.

64. Possessive

The genitives of all the personal pronouns were used as possessives, and to a small extent also the general 3rd pers. form *sīn* 'his, her, their', an old reflexive. The possessives of the 1st and 2nd pers. and *sīn* took the indefinite adjective inflexion; *his, hire, hira* were not declined.

65. Demonstrative

On the distinction in usage between the following two demonstratives, see § 117:

	(a) se 'the, that'			(b) þes 'this'		
	masc.	*neut.*	*fem.*	*masc.*	*neut.*	*fem.*
sg.n.	se	þæt	sēō	þes	þis	þēos
a.	þone	þæt	þā	þisne	þis	þās
g.	þæs	þæs	þǣre	þisses	þisses	þisse
d.	þǣm	þǣm	þǣre	þissum	þissum	þisse
i.	þȳ	þȳ	þǣre	þȳs	þȳs	þisse

	common	common
pl.n.a.	þā	þās
g.	þāra	þissa
d.i.	þǣm	þissum

On the forms of **relative** pronoun, see §§ 120*b*, 153.

In pronominal functions (§ 120*a*), the n.sg.masc. *se* and *þes* had a long vowel. Alternative forms among the demonstratives included: *þām* for *þǣm*, *þon* for *þȳ*, *þisre* for *þisse*, *-y-* for *-i-*, etc.

66. Interrogative

Hwæðer 'which (of two)', *hwelc* (or *hwylc*) 'which (of many)' are declined with the indefinite adjective inflexion; *hwā* 'who' has only masc. and neut. sg. forms, which are as follows:

	masc.	*neut.*
n.	hwā	hwæt
a.	hwone	hwæt
g.	hwæs	hwæs
d.	hwǣm	hwǣm
i.	hwǣm	hwȳ

Beside *hwȳ* (or *hwī*), there exist the instr. forms *hwon* (in the phrases *for* or *tō hwon* 'why') and *hū* 'how'; other alternative forms are *hwām* for *hwǣm*, *hwæne* for *hwone*.

67. Indefinite

The interrogatives *hwā*, *hwæðer*, *hwelc* could be used indefinitely, 'any(one), any(thing)', and many other forms of indefinite pronouns were built around these three:

> āhwā, āhwæðer, āhwelc, 'anyone', etc.;
> gehwā, gehwylc, etc., 'each one', etc.;

æghwā, æghwylc, etc., 'each one', etc.;

swā hwā swā, etc., 'whoever', etc.;

hwæthwugu 'something', hwelchwugu 'someone';

nāthwā, nāthwelc 'someone' (lit. 'I don't know who').

Other indefinite pronouns include *ǣlc* 'each', *ǣnig* 'any', *man* or *mon* 'one' (see §§ 120*e*, 131), *swelc* (*swylc*) 'such', *þyllic* 'such', *wiht* (and its compounds and variants such as *āwiht*, *āuht*) 'anything', and several others.

Hwā, hwæðer, hwelc are declined as stated in § 66; *swelc* is like *hwelc*; *ǣlc, ǣnig*, and *þyllic* (or *þyslic*) take the indefinite adjective inflexions; the rest of the forms are invariable, though *wiht* has *-es* and *-e* endings in adverbial function, 'at all'.

Verbs

68. Almost three-quarters of the verbs that a student will meet in his OE reading will be of the **consonantal** conjugation, often called 'weak' conjugation. This was, and has remained, the productive and influential conjugation, and practically all new verbs that have been formed or adopted since the earliest OE times are in this category. From earliest OE times, too, verbs of the other main type of conjugation have tended to lose their distinctive inflexions and to take on those of the consonantal conjugation. This second type, which comprises about one-quarter of the verbs that the student will meet, is the **vocalic** (often called 'strong') conjugation. There remains a very small balance of **irregular** verbs, amounting only to about one-fiftieth of the verbs in the students' glossaries; these irregular verbs are of several types, and many display features both of the consonantal and of the vocalic conjugations.

Thus in order of *numerical* importance, we have consonantal, vocalic, and irregular verbs. From the point of view of *frequency*, however, these three main groups are of approximately equal importance. The numerical preponderance of the consonantal type is accounted for to a large extent by the fact that this type comprises very many verbs which are of rare occurrence (compare in Mod.E. the relatively rare verbs of this kind like *gesticulate, crystallise, signify,* beside the common ones like *love* and *hate*). On the other hand, the smaller total number of vocalic verbs are for the most part very common and are of high frequency in texts (compare in Mod.E. *sing, drink, write*). Above all, the very small number of irregular verbs (*be, will, can*, etc. in Mod.E.) must be learnt very carefully, since these are the commonest verbs in the language.

69. General Notes on Verb Inflexions

Person

(1) The pres. indic. sg. alone has distinctive forms for the first, second, and third persons; 1 p.sg. ends in *-e*, 2 p.sg. in *-st*, 3 p.sg. in *-ð*.

(2) The pret. indic. sg. has identical 1 and 3 p. forms (*-e* consonantal, no ending vocalic), but a distinctive 2 p. (*-est* consonantal, *-e* vocalic).

(3) The pres. indic. pl. and pret. indic. pl., and the pres. and pret. subj. sg. and pl. show no distinctions of person.

Tense

(4) The pres. indic. pl. almost always ends in *-að*, the pret. indic. pl. always in *-on*.

(5) Consonantal and most irregular verbs have a dental suffix in all preterite forms (*herian—herede*); vocalic verbs form the preterite with changes of stem-vowel (*bindan—band—bundon*).

Mood

(6) The pres. and pret. subj. sg. are in *-e*, pl. in *-en*.

(7) There are in general but two imperative forms, a 2 p.sg. in *-e, -a*, or without ending, and a 2 p.pl. in *-að*.

Non-finite forms

(8) Infinitives end in *-(i)an*, present participles in *-(i)ende*; past participles normally have the prefix *ge-* and end in *-ed* (consonantal) or *-en* (vocalic).

The whole paradigm of a given verb can be inferred from selected items (*principal parts*) as follows: infinitive (and pres. indic. 3 p.sg.), pret. indic. 1 and 3 p.sg., 1-3 p.pl. (vocalic verbs only), and past participle.

The pres. indic. 1 p.sg. is found in *-u*, later *-o* in Anglian texts; the 2 p.sg. in *-(e)st* is generally reckoned a development of *-es* before the initial dental of the pron. *þū*, and this earlier ending is found in some texts; instead of *-(e)ð*, the 3 p.sg. is found in *-es* in Nb texts. In WS the *-e-* of the 2 and 3 p.sg. endings has almost always been lost, with the result that the *-st*, *-þ* coming immediately after the stem occasion a number of assimilations; for example: *-(*d*)*dst*, *-(*d*)*dþ*, *-*tþ* > *-tst*, *-t*(*t*), *-t*(*t*) resp., thus we have, not *biddst, *lǣdst, *biddþ, *lǣdþ, *sitþ, but *bitst*, *lǣtst*, *bit*(*t*), *lǣt*(*t*), *sit*(*t*) from *biddan* 'pray', *lǣdan* 'lead', *sittan* 'sit'; **-sst*, **-sþ*, **-ðst* > *-st*, thus we have, not *lȳsst, *lȳsþ, *cȳðst, but *lȳst*, *lȳst*, *cȳst* from *lȳsan* 'loosen', *cȳðan* 'proclaim'. See also § 76, note. Syncope of the *-e-* in the pret. dental suffix of consonantal verbs (broadly speaking, after dentals and long syllables: see § 191) was likewise accompanied by assimilation; beside *cȳðde* we find *cȳdde* 'proclaimed', instead of *setde, we find *sette* 'set', etc. On assimilation, see further §§ 191, 197, and for individual verbs the student's attention is directed to the principal parts as listed in the paragraphs to follow.

There are alternative 1 and 2 p.pl. forms of all tenses and moods in *-e* when the pronouns (*wē*, *wit*, *gē*, *git*) immediately follow: *þurfe gē* 'do you need?'

There is a rare 1 p.pl. imperat. in *-an*, *-on*: *fremman* 'let us do', *lufian* 'let us love'.

The prefix *ge-* is not found with past participles which already have a prefix (such as *be-*, *for-*), and is not universal even with other verbs.

On voice and aspect, see §§ 131, 129 f.

70. **CONSONANTAL TYPE**

There are two main classes of consonantal verbs.

Class I. The stem of infinitives in this class almost always has a mutated vowel (see §§ 209, 163). We may broadly distinguish two sub-classes, according as the infinitive stem has (*a*) a short vowel followed by a double consonant or *-ri-*, or (*b*) a long vowel regardless of the following consonant, or a short vowel followed by a consonant cluster other than a doubling.

Class II. This class comprises almost all verbs with infinitives in *-ian* other than those which have *-r-* before this ending; the vast majority have unmutated stem vowels (see § 163).

The main distinctive features of these classes and sub-classes are illustrated in the paradigms of *fremman* 'perform', *nerian* 'save', *dēman* 'judge', *lufian* 'love':

Present	I(*a*)	I(*b*)		II
Indic.				
1 sg. ic	fremme	nerie	dēme	lufie
2 sg. þū	fremest	nerest	dēmst	lufast
3 sg. hē, hēo, hit	fremeð	nereð	dēmð	lufað
1-3 pl. wē, gē, hī	fremmað	neriað	dēmað	lufiað
Subj.				
1-3 sg. ic,þū,hē(&c)	fremme	nerie	dēme	lufie
1-3 pl. wē, gē, hī	fremmen	nerien	dēmen	lufien
Imperat. 2 sg.	freme	nere	dēm	lufa
2 pl.	fremmað	neriað	dēmað	lufiað
Participle	fremmende	neriende	dēmende	lufiende

Preterite				
Indic.				
1 & 3 sg. ic, hē(&c)	fremede	nerede	dēmde	lufode
2 sg. þū	fremedest	neredest	dēmdest	lufodest
1-3 pl. wē, gē, hī	fremedon	neredon	dēmdon	lufodon
Subj.				
1-3 sg. ic,þū,hē(&c)	fremede	nerede	dēmde	lufode
1-3 pl. wē, gē, hī	fremeden	nereden	dēmden	lufoden
Participle	ᵹefremed	ᵹenered	ᵹedēmed	ᵹelufod

The dual pronouns, *wit* and *git*, accompany the same verb forms as *wē* and *gē*. Between *i* and *e* we often find [j], spelt *g*; thus *nerige, lufigende; g(e)* may also replace *i* (*nerg(e)an, lufgende*), and *ge* may also come between *i* and *a* (*nerigean*).

71. Other common **Class I** verbs are as follows:

infin.	3 *sg.* pres. ind.	1, 3 *sg.* pret. ind.	*past pple*
(*a*)			
āswebban 'kill'	āswefeð	āswefede	āswefed
trymman 'strengthen'	trymeð	trymede	ᵹetrymed
Like *trymman* are *cnyssan* 'strike', *dynnan* 'resound'.			
settan 'set'	sett	sette	-sett

43

Like *settan* are *cnyttan* 'bind', *lettan* 'hinder'.

lecgan 'lay'	legð	legde	-legd (-lēd)
derian 'injure'	dereð	derede	-dered

Like *derian* are *erian* 'plough', *ferian* 'carry', *herian* 'praise', *spyrian* 'inquire', *werian* 'defend'.

(*b*)

bærnan 'burn up'	bærnð	bærnde	-bærned

Like *bærnan* are *ālȳsan* 'set free', *dǣlan* 'share', *drǣfan* 'expel', *fēdan* 'feed', *fēran* 'travel', *flȳman* 'rout', *gȳman* 'heed', *hǣlan* 'heal', *hȳran* 'hear', *lǣfan* 'leave', *lǣran* 'teach', *(ge)lȳfan* 'believe', *nȳdan* 'compel', *rǣran* 'raise', *rȳman* 'enlarge', *wēnan* 'expect'.

cȳðan 'proclaim'	cȳðð	cȳdde	-cȳdd

So too *cwiðan* 'lament'; both verbs have alternative pret. forms with *-ðd-*.

fyllan 'fill'	fylð	fylde	-fylled

So too *cennan* 'bring forth', *cyrran* 'turn', *fyllan* 'fell'.

sendan 'send'	sent	sende	-send

So too *andwyrdan* 'answer', *spendan* 'spend', *wendan* 'turn'.

nemnan 'name'	nemneð	nemde	-nemned
bētan 'make amends'	bētt	bētte	-bēted
ȳcan 'increase'	ȳcð	ȳcte	-ȳced

Like *bētan* and *ȳcan*, with pret. formed with *-t-*, are *grētan* 'greet', *mētan* 'meet', *swencan* 'molest', *wǣtan* 'moisten'.

cyssan 'kiss'	cysseð	cyste	-cyssed
(ge)lǣstan 'carry out'	-lǣst	-lǣste	-lǣsted

Like *-lǣstan* are *befæstan* 'secure', *þyrstan* 'thirst', *wēstan* 'lay waste'.

bytlan 'build'	bytleð	bytlede	-bytled

So too *frēfran* 'comfort', *timbran* 'build'.

gyrwan 'prepare'	gyreð	gyrede	-gyr(w)ed

So too *(be)syrwan* 'ensnare'; on the loss of *-w-*, see § 197.

tǣcan 'teach'	tǣcð	tǣhte	-tǣht

So too *geānlǣcan* 'unite', *rǣcan* 'reach'.

On the syncope and assimilation shown in many of the preterites, see § 191. There are a few fairly rare contracted verbs, *hēan* 'exalt', *pēon* 'perform', *tȳn* 'teach', *pȳn* 'press', with pret. *hēade, pēode, tȳde, pȳde* resp. Pret. forms *ȳhte, ihte* are also found for *ȳcan*.

72. Several Class I verbs have different vowels in the present and preterite since *i*-mutation is lacking in the latter; secondary changes including diphthongisation, lengthening, and assimilation increase the irregularity of these verbs (see §§ 184 f, 201, 211):

sellan 'sell'	selð	sealde	-seald

So too *cwellan* 'kill', *dwellan* 'hinder', *stellan* 'place', *tellan* 'count'.

reccan 'narrate'	recð	reahte	-reaht

So too *cweccan* 'shake', *dreccan* 'afflict', *leccan* 'moisten', *streccan* 'stretch', *peccan* 'cover', *weccan* 'awake'.

læccan 'catch'	læcð	lǣhte	-lǣht
bycgan 'buy'	bygð	bohte	-boht
wyrcan 'make'	wyrcð	worhte	-worht
bringan 'bring'	bringð	brōhte	-brōht
pencan 'think'	pencð	pōhte	-pōht
pyncan 'seem'	pyncð	pūhte	-pūht
sēcan 'seek'	sēcð	sōhte	-sōht

The short vowel in the present of *læccan* is difficult; cf also *reccan* 'care', pret. *rōhte*. After *c* in the infinitives *wyrcan, læccan, reccan*, etc. we often find an orthographic *-e-*. On the *o*∼*y* correspondence in *bycgan, wyrcan*, see §§ 207, 211. *Bringan* belongs historically to the vocalic Class III (see § 77), and a past pple *brungen* is recorded; the historically correct infinitive corresponding to *brōhte* is *brengan*, but this is rare. On the consonant alternations in these verbs, see §§ 179, 185, 197.

73. Common Class II verbs are as follows:

endian 'end'	endað	endode	-endod

So too *andswarian* 'answer', *āscian* 'ask', *bēotian* 'boast', *bismrian* 'insult', *blissian* 'rejoice', *bodian* 'preach', *clipian* 'call', *eardian* 'dwell', *ebbian* 'ebb', *fandian* 'test', *folgian* 'follow', *gaderian* 'gather', *geǣmetigan* 'empty', *heri(ge)an* 'ravage', *hȳrsumian* 'obey', *leornian* 'learn', *lōcian* 'look', *losian* 'be lost', *macian* 'make', *scēawian* 'look at', *trūwian* 'trust', *weorðian* 'honour', *wunian* 'dwell', *wundian* 'wound'.

Here belong also a few contracted verbs of which the commonest are *frēo(ga)n* 'love' (cf also *fēon* 'hate'), *smēagan* 'think', *twēo(ga)n* 'doubt', *þrēa(ga)n* 'reprove'; the preterites are *frēode, smēade, twēode, þrēade* resp.

Class II verbs frequently have pret. pl. in *-edon* instead of *-odon*. In lOE several verbs of Class I tended to be used with Class II inflexions, and we find new Cl. II vbs like *fremian* 'perform', *trymian* 'support', beside *fremman, trymman*; as might be expected, this process was particularly common with the Cl. I vbs in *-rian*.

74.   VOCALIC TYPE

There are seven classes of verbs in which tenses are distinguished by differences of stem-vowel. There is always a difference of stem-vowel between present and preterite, and in several classes the pret. pl. and past pple have each a different vowel from the pret. 1, 3 sg. The pret. indic. 2 sg. and pret. subj. sg. and pl. have always the same vowel and following consonant as the pret. indic. pl. The changes of vowel in Cl. VII are of obscure origin, but those in Cl. I-VI have arisen by **gradation**, on which see §§ 182f. The model paradigms given below, together with the *principal parts* in the paragraphs to follow, will give students the necessary equipment to recognise or reproduce any part of the commoner vocalic verbs. The verbs selected are *drīfan* 'drive' (a straightforward example), *cēosan* 'choose' (affected by the second cons. shift: §§ 180f), *hebban* 'raise' (an example of an otherwise vocalic verb with 'consonantal type' present), and *sēon* 'see' (a contracted verb: § 190):

Present
Indic.

1 sg. ic	drīfe	cēose	hebbe	sēo
2 sg. þū	drīfst	cȳst	hefst	syhst
3 sg. hē, hēo, hit	drīfð	cȳst	hefð	syhð
1-3 pl. wē, gē, hī	drīfað	cēosað	hebbað	sēoð
Subj.				
1-3 sg. ic,þū,hē(&c)	drīfe	cēose	hebbe	sēo
1-3 pl. wē, gē, hī	drīfen	cēosen	hebben	sēon

Imperat. 2 sg.	drīf	cēos	hefe	seoh
2 pl.	drīfaþ	cēosaþ	hebbaþ	sēoþ
Participle	drīfende	cēosende	hebbende	sēonde

Preterite
Indic.

1 & 3 sg. ic, hē(&c)	drāf	cēas	hōf	seah
2 sg. þū	drife	cure	hōfe	sāwe
1-3 pl. wē, gē, hī	drifon	curon	hōfon	sāwon
Subj.				
1-3 sg. ic,þū,hē(&c)	drife	cure	hōfe	sāwe
1-3 pl. wē, gē, hī	drifen	curen	hōfen	sāwen
Participle	ġedrifen	ġecoren	ġehafen	ġesewen

75. **Class I.** Apart from the contracted ones, verbs in this class have *i* as the stem-vowel of the infinitive; it should be noted that the *i* of the pret. pl. and past pple is *short*.

infin.	*3 sg. pres.*	*1,3 sg. pret.*	*pret. pl.*	*past pple*
drīfan 'drive'	drīfð	drāf	drifon	-drifen

So too *blīcan* 'shine', *hrīnan* 'touch', *mīðan* 'hide', *rīpan* 'reap', *scīnan* 'shine', *stīgan* 'ascend', *swīcan* 'deceive'.

rīsan 'rise'	rīst	rās	rison	-risen
bīdan 'wait'	bītt	bād	bidon	-biden
bītan 'bite'	bītt	bāt	biton	-biten

Also with 3 p.sg. in -*tt* are *gewītan* 'depart', *glīdan* 'glide', *rīdan* 'ride', *slītan* 'tear', *wlītan* 'look', *wrītan* 'write'.

Affected by the second cons. shift (§§ 180f) are:

līðan 'travel'	līðð	lāð	lidon	-liden
snīðan 'cut'	snīðð	snāð	snidon	-sniden

The contracted verbs are also so affected:

lēon 'lend'	lȳhð	lāh	ligon	-ligen

Other contracted verbs are *tēon* 'accuse', *þēon* 'prosper', *wrēon* 'cover'.

Verbs like *stīgan* have alternative 1 and 3 sg. pret. forms in -*h* (*stāh* beside *stāg*). The *s* of *rīsan* has been carried analogically into the pret. pl.

ɪ

and past pple; contrast *cēosan*, § 76. The *ēo* of the contracted infinitives caused verbs like *þēon* to be given alternative forms on the Cl. II model: *þēah, þugon, -þogen*; in fact, however, *þēon* belonged originally to Cl. III (**þinhan*), hence the occasional Cl. III forms of this verb, notably the past pple *geþungen* used as an adjective, 'excellent'.

76. Class II. The normal infinitive vowel is *ēo*, but there are a few 'aorist-present' verbs in which the infinitive and present forms have a lengthened form of the pret. pl. vowel.

    clēofan 'cleave'   clȳfð   clēaf   clufon   -clofen

So too *brēowan* 'brew', *hrēowan* 'rue', *smēocan* 'smoke'; *drēogan* 'endure', *flēogan* 'fly', *lēogan* 'lie' have I and 3 sg. pret. in both -*g* and -*h*.

    bēodan 'offer'   bȳtt   bēad   budon   -boden
    brēotan 'break'   brȳtt   brēat   bruton   -broten

Also with 3 sg. pres. in -*tt* are *flēotan* 'float', *gēotan* 'pour', *grēotan* 'weep', *scēotan* 'shoot'.

Affected by the second cons. shift (§§ 180f) are:

    sēoðan 'boil'   sȳðð   sēað   sudon   -soden
    cēosan 'choose'   cȳst   cēas   curon   -coren

Like *cēosan* are *drēosan* 'fall', *(for)lēosan* 'lose', *frēosan* 'freeze', *hrēosan* 'fall'.

Contracted verbs are also affected by the second cons. shift:

    flēon 'flee'   flȳhð   flēah   flugon   -flogen

So too *tēon* 'draw'.

The aorist-present pattern is as follows:

    brūcan 'enjoy'   brȳcð   brēac   brucon   -brocen

So too *būgan* (*bēag, bēah*) 'bend', *dūfan* 'dive', *lūcan* 'lock', *lūtan* 'bow', *scūfan* 'push'.

In *ābrēoðan* 'perish', unlike *sēoðan*, the *ð* has been extended to the pret. pl. and past pple. The I and 3 sg. pret. of *ofhrēowan* 'pity' is *ofhrēow*. In this class, as in all except Cl. I where the vowel is not subject to the change, the vowel of the stem undergoes raising of *e* to *i* or *i*-mutation (§§ 207 ff) in the 2 and 3 sg. pres. indic.; thus with the foregoing verbs we have 3 sg. *cȳst* and *flȳhð*, from *cēosan* and *flēon* respectively. These changes do not affect consonantal verbs, since Cl. I verbs already have mutated vowels (compare *dēman* 'judge' with *dōm* 'judgment') and Cl. II verbs were not subject to the mutations because they had different personal endings. In Angl. texts and sometimes also in lWS we find vocalic verbs with 2 and 3 sg. pres. indic. in *-est* and *-eð*, preceded by the unchanged infinitive vowel, as *cēoseð*.

77. Class III. The majority of verbs in this class have in the infinitive either (*a*) *i* followed by a nasal plus another consonant (past pple *-u-*), or (*b*) *e* or *eo* followed by a liquid plus another consonant (past pple *-o-*).

(*a*)

drincan 'drink'	drincð	dranc	druncon	-druncen

So too *climban* 'climb', *gelimpan* 'happen', *onginnan* 'begin', *sincan* 'sink', *singan* 'sing', *springan* 'spring', *swimman* 'swim', *swincan* 'toil', *þringan* 'press', *winnan* 'strive'.

bindan 'bind'	bint	band	bundon	-bunden

With similar 3 sg. pres. are *findan* 'find', *windan* 'wind'.

Two verbs, *byrnan* (*birnan*) and *yrnan* (*irnan*) have been affected by metathesis (§ 193; compare the Gothic forms *brinnan, rinnan*):

byrnan 'burn'	byrnð	barn	burnon	-burnen
yrnan 'run'	yrnð	arn	urnon	-urnen

The 1 and 3 sg. pret. may have *-o-* instead of *-a-* (§ 188), or alternatively *-ea-* (§§ 193, 201). An unmetathesised verb (*ge*)*rinnan* in the sense of 'flow' has forms like *-ginnan*. We sometimes find *funde* throughout the pret. sg. of *findan*.

78. (*b*)

helpan 'help'	hilpð	healp	hulpon	-holpen

For the *-ea-*, see §§ 201ff; so too *belgan* 'be angry', *delfan* 'dig', *swelgan* 'swallow', *swellan* 'swell'; *meltan* 'melt' and *sweltan* 'die' have 3 sg. pres. in *-ilt*.

gylpan 'boast'	gylpð	gealp	gulpon	-golpen

With infinitive similarly affected by palatal consonant diphthongisation (§ 204) are *gyldan* 'pay' (3 sg. pres. *gylt*), *gyllan* 'yell'; these verbs occur also with *-ie-* in the infin. and pres. forms.

weorpan 'throw'	wyrpð	wearp	wurpon	-worpen

Also with diphthongisation (§§ 201ff) in infin. are *beorgan* 'protect' (1,3 sg. pret. *bearg, bearh*), *ceorfan* 'cut', *feohtan* 'fight' (3 sg. pres. *fyht*), *hweorfan* 'turn', *steorfan* 'die'. Two aorist-presents belong here, *murnan* 'mourn' (with an alternative consonantal pret. *murnde*, beside *mearn*) and *spurnan* 'spurn'; both have 3 sg. pres. in *-yrnð*.

Affected by the second cons. shift (§§ 180f) is:

weorðan 'become' wyrð wearð wurdon -worden

Fēolan 'enter' has Cl. III forms *fealh, fulgon*, etc. beside the more usual Cl. IV pret. pl. *fǣlon*, past pple *-folen*.

79. There is a small group of irregular verbs, all of which have *æ* in 1 and 3 sg. pret. In two, there has been metathesis (§ 203), which occurred after the period of diphthongisation before velarised consonants:

berstan 'burst' byrst bærst burston -borsten

So too *perscan* 'thresh'. With forms similar to these are a further two verbs with stems ending in *-gd*: *bregdan* 'pull, brandish', *stregdan* 'strew'; these have alternative forms with loss of *g* and lengthening (§ 197): *brēdan, brǣd, brūdon*, etc. With *frignan* (*frīnan*) 'ask', there are several variant forms, including 1 and 3 sg. pret. *frægn, frān, fræng*; pret. pl. *frugnon, frūnon, frungon*; past pple *-frugnen, -ū-, -frugen*; from the same root, there was also an infin. *fricgan* and past pple *-frigen* on the Cl. V model (compare *licgan*, § 81).

80. **Class IV** contains only a few verbs; most have *e* in the infin., followed by *r* or *l*:

beran 'bear' birð bær bǣron -boren

So too *brecan* 'break', *helan* 'conceal', *stelan* 'steal', *teran* 'tear'; *sceran* 'cut' has in addition forms affected by palatal consonant diphthongisation (§ 204): *scieran, scear, sceāron*.

The following two are irregular, the first being an aorist-present:

cuman 'come' cymð cōm cōmon -cumen
niman 'take' nimð nōm nōmon -numen

In addition the latter pair have the pret. forms *cwōm(on), nam, nāmon*, resp. (see §§ 186d, e, 187).

81. **Class V** verbs mainly have infinitives with *e* followed by a single consonant other than a liquid or nasal:

sprecan 'speak'   spricð   spræc   sprǣcon   -sprecen

So too *drepan* 'strike' (with alternative past pple *-dropen*), *metan* 'measure', *swefan* 'sleep', *tredan* 'tread', *wefan* 'weave', *wrecan* 'avenge'; *(fr)etan* 'eat' has 1 and 3 sg. pret. *(fr)ǣt.*

Two verbs, *gifan* 'give' and *(on)gytan* 'catch, perceive', have variant forms of infin. and past pple with *-i-, -y-, -ie-* (§ 193) and are affected throughout by palatal consonant diphthongisation (§ 204):

gifan   gifð   geaf   gēafon   -gifen
-gytan   -gytt   -geat   -gēaton   -gyten

The following verb is affected by the second cons. shift (§§ 180f):

cweðan 'say'   cwiðð   cwæð   cwǣdon   -cweden

So too the defective verb *wesan* 'be' (see § 87).

Contracted verbs, affected both by the second cons. shift and by velarised consonant diphthongisation (§§ 180f, 201ff) include:

gefēon 'rejoice'   gefyhð   gefeah   gefǣgon   (gefǣgen, *adj.*)
sēon 'see'   syhð   seah   sāwon   -sewen

A few verbs have present forms of the consonantal type:

biddan 'pray'   bitt   bæd   bǣdon   -beden
licgan 'lie'   lið   læg   lǣgon   -legen

So too *sittan* 'sit', *fricgan* (cf *frignan*, § 79) 'ask' (past pple *-frigen* or *-frægen*), *þicgan* 'receive' (3 sg. pres. *þigeð*, 1 and 3 sg. pret. *þeah*; cf *gefēon*).

Licgan has an alternative pret. pl. *lāgon*; on the *-ā-* in this form and in *sāwon*, see § 187c; *sēon* has another common past pple form *-sawen*; in addition, there are forms with *-g-* in the pret. pl. (*sǣgon, sēgon*) and past pple (*-segen*): see § 180.

82. **Class VI.** The typical verbs in this class have *a* in the infinitive.

faran 'go'   færð   fōr   fōron   -faren

So too *bacan* 'bake', *dragan* 'draw', *galan* 'sing', *grafan* 'dig', *hladan* 'load', *wadan* 'go', *wascan* (*waxan*) 'wash', *scacan* 'shake' and *scafan* 'shave' sometimes have *e* after *sc* (§ 17, note); the verb 'stand' has *-n-* throughout the pres. and in the past pple.:

standan	stent	stōd	stōdon	-standen

The verb *wæcnan* 'awake' has pret. *wōc, wōcon*.

Contracted verbs, affected by the second cons. shift (§§ 180f), include:

slēan 'strike'	slyhð	slōg	slōgon	-slagen

So too *lēan* 'blame', *þwēan* 'wash'; the 1 and 3 sg. pret. may have an alternative form in *-h*.

A few important verbs have present forms of consonantal type:

swerian 'swear'	swereð	swōr	swōron	-sworen
hebban 'raise'	hefð	hōf	hōfon	-hafen

Similarly, *hlihhan* 'laugh' has 1, 3 sg. pret. *hlōg* (or *-h*), *sceððan* 'injure' has *scōd*, *scyppan* 'create' *scōp*, and *steppan* 'step' *stōp*.

The past pple vowel in this class is *-æ-* almost as often as *-a-*, and in addition the contracted verbs frequently have *-e-* (e.g. *-slegen*). Some of the consonantal-type presents have consonantal preterites also: *hebban—hefde, swerian—swerede*.

83. Class VII. The infinitive vowels in this class are various and provide little guide; the verbs are best considered according as their preterite vowel is *ēo* or *ē*. Although this class is often described as containing 'reduplicating' verbs (compare Lat. *currō—cucurrī*), the signs of reduplication are meagre in OE; *leolc* 'played' (*lācan*), *heht* 'called' (*hātan*) are among the few vestiges recorded and even in these the phenomenon is scarcely recognisable without comparing the Gothic cognates *laílaik, haíháit*.

(*a*)

feallan 'fall'	fylð	fēoll	fēollon	-feallen
healdan 'hold'	hylt	hēold	hēoldon	-healden

So too *fealdan* 'fold', *wealcan* 'roll', *weallan* 'boil', *weaxan* 'grow' (with alternative pret. *wōx* by Cl. VI to which it originally belonged).

cnāwan 'know' cnǣwǒ cnēōw cnēōwon -cnāwen

So too *blāwan* 'blow', *māwan* 'mow', *sāwan* 'sow', and several others.

grōwan 'grow' grēwǒ grēōw grēōwon -grōwen

So too *blōtan* 'sacrifice', *blōwan* 'blossom', *flōwan* 'flow', *rōwan* 'row' (pret. pl. *rēō(wo)n*).

wēpan 'weep' wēpǒ weōp weōpon -wōpen
hlēapan 'leap' hlȳpǒ hleōp hleōpon -hleāpen

Like *hlēapan* are *beātan* 'beat', *heāwan* 'hew'.

bannan 'summon' benǒ beōn(n) beōnnon -bannen

So too *spannan* 'fasten' and *gangan* 'go', but besides -*eō*- the latter has as pret. vowels -*ē*-, -*īe*- and (in *Beowulf* only) -*a*-.

84. (*b*)

lǣtan 'let' lǣtt lēt lēton -lǣten

So too *ondrǣdan* 'fear', *rǣdan* 'advise', *slǣpan* 'sleep' (3 sg. pres. *slǣpǒ*); these three also had consonantal preterites in -*dde*, -*pte*.

hātan 'call' hǣtt hēt hēton -hāten

So too *lācan* 'play' (3 sg. pres. *lǣcǒ*), *sc(e)ādan* 'divide'.

blandan 'mix' blent blēnd blēndon -blanden

Contracted verbs, affected also by the second cons. shift (§§ 180f), are as follows:

fōn 'seize' fēhǒ fēng fēngon -fangen
hōn 'hang' hēhǒ hēng hēngon -hangen

Sc(e)ādan has an alternative pret. *sceād*; on *hātan, lācan* see also § 83.

85.   **IRREGULAR VERBS**

Most of the verbs presented under this head are of high frequency and should be learnt completely. We may consider them in three groups: (1) the 'have' group (usually presented as the third class of consonantal verbs), (2) anomalous verbs, 'be', 'will', 'do', 'go', (3) preterite-present verbs, such as 'can'. With the single exception of 'be', all the verbs in these groups have consonantal preterites.

86. Group I comprises *habban* 'have', *libban* 'live', *secgan* 'say', and *hycgan* 'think'. Their forms are as follows:

Present

Indic.

1 sg. ic	hæbbe	libbe	secge	hycge
2 sg. þū	hæfst	leofast	sægst	hogast
3 sg. hē, hēo, hit	hæfð	leofað	sægð	hogað
1-3 pl. wē, gē, hī	habbað	libbað	secgað	hycgað

Subj.

1-3 sg. ic,þū,hē(&c)	hæbbe	libbe	secge	hycge
1-3 pl. wē, gē, hī	hæbben	libben	secgen	hycgen

Imperat. 2 sg.	hafa	leofa	sæge	hyge, hoga
2 pl.	habbað	libbað	secgað	hycgað

Participle	hæbbende	libbende	secgende	hycgende

Preterite

Indic.

1, 3 sg. ic, hē(&c)	hæfde	lifde	sæde	hog(o)de
			(&c, like *dēman*, § 70)	
Participle	-hæfd	-lifd	-sæd	-hogod

Many variant forms are found; *hafast*, *hafað* for *hæfst*, *hæfð*; *lifge*, *-að*, etc. for *libbe*, *-að*, etc.; *lifast*, *-að*, *-a* for *leofast*, *-að*, *-a;* *leofode* for *lifde* (thus a Cl. II consonantal vb *lifian* is evolved beside *libban*); *sagast*, *-að*, *-a* for *sægst*, *-ð*, *-e;* *sægde*, etc. for *sæde*, etc.; *hygst*, *hygð* for *hogast*, *-að*. There is a negative form of *habban*: *nabban*, *næbbe*, *næfde*, etc.

87. Group 2

(*a*) *bēon, wesan* 'be'. There are two forms for the pres. indic. and subj. (from two distinct roots, resp. cognate with Lat. *esse* and *fui*) and for the imperat. (one from *wesan*, the other from *bēon*). The pret. indic. and subj. are from *wesan* (vocalic Cl. V; § 81).

	Present		*Preterite*
Indic. 1 sg. ic	eom *or*	bēo	wæs
2 sg. þū	eart	bist	wære
3 sg. hē, hēo, hit	is	bið	wæs
1-3 pl. wē, gē, hī	sind(on)	bēoð	wæron

Subj.1-3 sg. ic, þū, hē (&c)	sȳ *or*	bēo	wǣre
1-3 pl. wē, gē, hī	sȳn	bēon	wǣren
Imperat. 2 sg.	wes	bēo	
2 pl.	wesað	bēoð	
Participles	wesende	bēonde	gebēon

Mercian and Nb texts show a pres. indic. pl. (*e*)*arun*. Negative forms (*neom, næs*, etc.) occur for all parts which begin with *w* or with a vowel. Beside *sind*(*on*), *-y-*, we also find *sint*, *-y-*. On a distinction in usage between *eom* etc. and *bēo* etc., see § 127.

88. (*b*) *willan* 'will, wish', *dōn* 'do', *gān* 'go':

Present

Indic. 1 sg. ic	wille	dō	gā
2 sg. þū	wilt	dēst	gǣst
3 sg. hē, hēo, hit	wile (wille)	dēð	gǣð
1-3 pl. wē, gē, hī	willað	dōð	gāð
Subj. 1-3 sg. ic, þū, hē (&c)	wille (wile)	dō	gā
1-3 pl. wē, gē, hī	willen	dōn	gān
Imperat. 2 sg.		dō	gā
2 pl.		dōð	gāð
Participles	willende	dōnde	

Preterite

Indic. 1, 3 sg. ic, hē (&c)	wolde	dyde	ēode
		(etc., like *dēman*, § 70)	
Participles		gedōn	gegān

There is confusion between *wile* and *wille*, the former (used in OE as 3 sg. pres. indic.) being originally an optative, the latter being a later formation. Negative forms of *willan* occur frequently, usually spelt in WS with *-y-* in the present: *nylle* (etc.), *nolde* (etc.); the negative forms include a 2 sg. and pl. imperative: *nelle, nellað*. The pret. forms corresponding to *gān* are from a different root which itself is not recorded with present forms.

89. **Group 3.** For a number of common verbs a new consonantal preterite was formed in Gmc because the old vocalic preterite had assumed a present meaning. Thus (*ic*) *wāt* (from *witan*, cognate with Lat. *vidēre*) is in form a preterite, parallel

55

with that of *drīfan* (§§ 74-5), and the meaning 'I know' is derived from the old perfective meaning 'I have seen'. A new preterite (OE *ic wiste*) was therefore necessary to express the past of the new meaning, 'know'.

While *wāt* itself is easy to relate to the OE system of vocalic preterites, and while this is true also of Class III examples like *cann—cunnon, þearf—þurfon*, several of the preterite-present verbs are but obscurely related to the vocalic series presented in §§ 75-84. For this reason, no very useful purpose is served by identifying each example with its historically appropriate vocalic class.

The more important verbs will be dealt with in more detail than the others, but it must be remembered in any case that the paradigms of several are defective since they are incompletely recorded.

90. (*a*) **witan** 'know':

	Present	Preterite	
Indic.1 & *3 sg.* ic, hē (&c)	**wāt**	**wiste** *or*	wisse
2 sg. þū	**wāst**	**wistest**	wisses(t)
1-3 pl. wē, gē, hī	**witon**	**wiston**	wisson
Subj. *1-3 sg.* ic,þū,hē (&c)	**wite**	**wiste**	wisse
1-3 pl. wē, gē, hī	**witen**	**wisten**	wissen
Imperat. *2 sg.*	**wite**		
2 pl.	**witað**		
Participles	**witende**	**ġewiten** (gewiss, *adj.*)	

Negative forms occur freely: *nāt, nyton, nyste,* etc.

(*b*) **sculan** 'to have to, be obliged to':

Indic. 1 & *3 sg.* ic, hē (&c)	**sceal**	**sceolde**
2 sg. þū	**scealt**	**sceoldest**
1-3 pl. wē, gē, hī	**sculon** (sceo-)	**sceoldon**
Subj. *1-3 sg.* ic,þū,hē (&c)	**scyle** (-i-, -u-)	**sceolde**
1-3 pl. wē, gē, hī	**scylen** (-i-, -u-)	**sceolden**

Beside *sceolde*, etc., forms with *sco-* are common.

56

91. (a) **cunnan** 'know, be able'; **unnan** 'grant':

Indic.	*1 & 3 sg.* ic, hē (&c)	**can(n)**	**cūðe**
	2 sg. þū	**canst**	**cūðest**
	1-3 pl. wē, gē, hī	**cunnon**	**cūðon**
Subj. sg. & pl.		**cunne(n)**	**cūðe(n)**
Participle			**-cunnen** (cūð, *adj.*)

So too *unnan*, except that there is no adjective form corresponding to *cūð*.

On the loss of *n* in *cūðe*, etc., see §§ 180*f*, 188.

(b) **magan** 'be able':

Indic.	*1 & 3 sg.* ic, hē (&c)	**mæg**	**meahte**	*or*	**mihte**
	2 sg. þū	**meaht** (miht)	**meahtest**		-i-
	1-3 pl. wē, gē, hī	**magon**	**meahton**		-i-
Subj. sg. & pl.		**mæge(n)**	**meahte(n)**		-i-
Participle		**magende**			

On the variant forms with *-ea-* and *-i-*, see § 205, note.

92. **þurfan** 'to need'; **ic dear(r)** 'I dare'; **(ge)munan** 'remember':

Present

Indic.	*1 & 3 sg.* ic, hē (&c)	**þearf**	**dear(r)**	**-man**
	2 sg. þū	**þearft**	**dearst**	**-manst**
	1-3 pl. wē, gē, hī	**þurfon**	**durron**	**-munon**
Subj. sg. & pl.		**þurfe(n)**	**durre(n)**	**-mune(n)**
Participle		**þearfende**		**-munende**
Preterite		**þorfte**	**dorste**	**-munde**
			(etc., like *dēman*, § 70)	
Participle				**-munen**

All three verbs have fairly common forms of pres. subj. with -y-; beside *þearfende*, we find forms with stem vowel -y- and -u-.

93. **dugan** 'avail, be profitable'; **āgan** 'have'; **ic mōt** 'I am allowed':

Present

Indic.	*1 & 3 sg.* ic, hē (&c)	**dēah**	**āh**	**mōt**
	2 sg. þū		**āhst**	**mōst**
	1-3 pl. wē, gē, hī	**dugon**	**āgon**	**mōton**

Subj. sg. & pl.	duge(n)	āge(n)	mōte(n)
Participle	dugende	āgende	
Preterite	dohte	āhte	mōste
		(etc., like *dēman*, § 70)	
Participle		āgen, āgen	

Beside *dēah*, *āh*, we commonly also find *dēag*, *āg*; an imperat. form *āge* is recorded. A further pret.-pres. verb, *-neah* 'is ample' (found with the prefixes *be-*, *ge-*), is recorded only in the 3 sg. pres. indic. with a corresponding pl. *-nugon*, a pres. subj. *-nuge*, and a pret. *-nohte*.

III

SYNTAX

94. **General.** The notes on syntax that follow are written with the aim of providing the student of our earliest literature and language with a guide to the outstanding features of OE usage. We are not therefore attempting a systematic description of OE syntax as a whole. Many relatively minor features must be ignored in order to leave room for major ones and in order that these major patterns should not be obscured and overshadowed by a plethora of minor ones which certainly co-existed with them; these, for the purposes of the ordinary student, may be treated as *ad hoc* exceptions when he meets them in his texts and reads an editor's notes on them. Much must be omitted too that shows little difference from present-day usage, in order to leave room for that which shows a great deal. On the other hand, in the constructions dealt with, we shall seek to explain OE structure from time to time by reference to the parallelism existing with Mod.E. structure. As occasion arises, attention is also drawn to the possibility of Latin influence and to the differences in usage between poetry and prose in OE.

An excellent synopsis of OE syntax appears in N. Davis, *Sweet's Anglo-Saxon Primer* (Oxford 1953); see also P. S. Ardern, *First Readings in Old English* (Wellington, N.Z. and London 1951); a fuller treatment is given in F. Mossé, *Manuel de l'Anglais du Moyen Âge* (Paris 1945). For OE syntax viewed in the light of subsequent usage, the student is referred to K. Brunner, *Die Englische Sprache* II (Halle 1951).

Functions of the Cases

NOMINATIVE

95. The nominative might be loosely defined as the case of *activity*; thus it is the case for the subjects of verbs: *hē sǣde* 'he said', *se cyning ofslægen wæs* 'the king was slain'; it is also used for the subject of verbs omitted by ellipsis after *than* and

AN OLD ENGLISH GRAMMAR

for the complement of the subject with verbs like 'be', 'call': *sē wæs betera ðonne ic* 'he was better than I', *þū eart fruma* 'thou art the beginning', *God is gehāten sīo hēhste ēcnes* 'God is called the highest eternity'. The nominative is used in direct address, there being no vocative inflexion: *Ðū iunga man* 'You, young man', *Ēalā lēof hlāford* 'Oh, dear master'.

Hātan often takes the nominative also when its subject is distinct from what is named: *on þǣm dæge þe wē hātað hlāfmæsse* (accus. would be *-an*) 'on the day that we call Lammas'.

ACCUSATIVE

96. In direct antithesis to the nominative, the accusative might be called the *passive* case, indicating that something is done to the referent of the word so inflected. It is above all else an inflexion showing a relationship to a verb.

Direct Object. The accusative is used for the sole object of the majority of OE verbs: *hē ofslōg þone aldormon* 'he killed the governor'. This object is sometimes a reflexive pronoun: *hiene bestæl se here* 'the raiders stole away'; other verbs taking an accusative reflexive include *onmunan* 'care for', *onscunian* 'be afraid', *restan* 'rest', *war(e)nian* 'take warning', *wendan* 'go'.

Some impersonal verbs are construed with an accusative object: *hine nānes ðinges ne lyste* 'he desired nothing'. The object of a verb may be cognate with it (*singað . . . song nēowne* 'sing a new song'), or it may be an infinitive with its own subject (which is in the accus.): *ne hȳrde ic snotorlīcor . . . guman þingian* 'I have not heard a man speak more wisely'. A few OE verbs take two accus. objects: *þā ācsode man hine hwylcne cræft hē cūðe* 'then someone asked him what skill he professed', *ne meahton wē gelǣran lēofne þēoden . . . rǣd ǣnigne* 'we could not persuade the dear prince of any good counsel'.

Usually however two objects with a single verb appear in different cases. Verbs of depriving, requesting, accusing often have accus. of the person and gen. of the thing: *Ic ðē . . . Bearn Alwaldan, biddan wylle miltse þīnre* 'I would pray thee for thy mercy, Son of the Almighty'. Verbs of telling, answering, giving usually have accus. of the thing and dat. of the person: *Hē þǣm bātwearde . . . swurd gesealde* 'he gave the boatguard a sword'. On this type of verb and others which are construed with cases other than the accus., see §§ 95, 103, 106, 107. 'Double

60

objects', as in Mod.E. 'they crowned her queen', are expressed in OE as an accus. and a *tō*-phrase: *hine hālgode tō cyninge* 'consecrated him king'.

97. **Adverbial.** The accus. is used to state extent of space or time. Space: *ic heonan nelle fléon fótes trym* 'I will not flee from here as much as a foot', *him wæs ealne weg wēste land on þæt stéorbord* 'there was waste land all the way to his starboard'. Time: *ealle þā hwīle þe þæt līc bið inne* 'the whole time that the body is inside', *ic wolde ðætte híe ealneg æt ðǣre stówe wǣren* 'I should like them to be always in that place', *þā sǣton híe þone winter æt Cwātbrycge* 'they then stayed that winter at Bridgnorth'.

In *hām*, we find the accusative used for direction: *ārīs, and gecyrr hām* 'arise and go home'.

98. **Prepositional.** As in other IE languages, many prepositions implying movement or destination in space or time are used with the accusative: *fore* 'before', *geond* 'throughout', *in* 'into', *ofer* 'beyond', *on* 'into, against', *ongēan* 'towards', *þurh* 'through', *wið* 'against, towards, along', *ymbe* 'around'; *for* takes the accus. when it means 'as, in place of': *hiora cyningas hī weorþodon for godas* 'they worshipped their kings as gods'.

Again as in other IE languages, many of these prepositions were used also with the dative when the situation is static, though the selection of case with these prepositions does not consistently rest on this mobile-static distinction.

GENITIVE

99. The genitive is a case of very complex functions in OE and none of the many attempts to classify these functions has been wholly successful. This is partly because many actual examples of the genitive may be interpreted in more than one way, and partly because by the very act of classifying, of naming categories and of inevitably forcing them into a genetic relationship we erect artificial barriers between functions which are intimately related, and make the distinction between others seem greater than it is. However, some kind of schematisation

of the complexity seems necessary, and provided we always remember that most of the categories shade off into others, it may be helpful to study the genitive in the following classification.

There are two primary groups of usage: subjective (or active), and objective (or passive); thus *his* in *his murder* may be subjective or objective according to whether the male person referred to did the killing or was himself killed:

He might have got off but for his murder of the other girl.

He was a fine man and it is hoped that his murder will be avenged.

100. The **subjective** genitive is common and idiomatic in OE; for example: *Grendles dǣda* 'Grendel's deeds', *þæs bisceopes bodung* 'the bishop's preaching'. Closely associated with it are the **possessive** genitive (as in *hiora scipu* 'their ships') and the genitive of **origin**: *ides Scyldinga* 'the lady of the Scyldings', *Bēowulf Gēata* 'B. of the Geats'. Here too belongs the **instrumental** genitive, as in *nīða ofercumen* 'overcome by afflictions'.

101. The **objective** genitive is illustrated by *folces weard* 'protector of the people', *tō his fēonda slege* 'to the defeat of his foes', *tōeācan þæs landes sceāwunge* 'besides the surveying of the land'. The following are associated with it:

genitive of **measure**: *fōtes trym* 'the space of a foot', *sē wæs fīftiges fōtgemearces lang* 'it was fifty feet long', *ānes mōnðes fyrst* 'the space of one month';

descriptive and **defining** genitive: *in Myrcna mǣgðe* 'among the people of the Mercians', *mǣres līfes man* 'a man of glorious life', *ār wīcinga* 'the messenger of the Vikings', *ic wæs . . . miccles cynnes* 'I was of great lineage', *wīges heard* 'brave in war', *earfeþa gemyndig* 'mindful of hardships', *frōd feores* 'advanced in age';

partitive genitive: *wundres dǣl* 'small wonder', *sum hund scipa* 'a hundred ships', *fela tācna* 'many signs', *hūsa sēlest* 'best of houses', *ānra gehwelc* 'each one', *ān heora* 'one of them'.

Sometimes *fela* and often *sum* appear without the genitive: *fela pearfan sǣtan geond þā strǣt* 'many poor people sat in the street', *sume hi sǣdon* 'some of them said'; moreover, even during the OE period, some of these relationships were coming to be expressed by *of* (with the dative) instead of by the genitive: *sume of ðām cnihtum* 'some of the men'. A special case of the partitive genitive consists of *sum* preceded by a numeral; this idiom was much used to express the numbers of a man's followers: *Gewāt þā twelfa sum* '(he) then departed, one of twelve', i.e. 'with eleven companions'.

102. **Adverbial.** Related to one or other of these forms of the objective genitive is the adverbial use of the genitive: *dæges ond nihtes* 'by day and night', *Godes þonces* 'through God's grace', *wordes oððe dǣde* 'by word or deed', *ealles* 'entirely', *þæs* 'so much, thereafter', *þā hē þā wæs þiderweardes ond sīo operu fierd wæs hāmweardes* 'when he was going there and the other levy was on the way home', *rīdeð ǣlc hys weges* 'each rides on his way'.

Hence the use of the genitive inflexion (particularly *-es*) in the formation of adverbs; see § 166; in *nihtes* 'by night', *-es* shows a generalisation of the masc. and neut. gen. sg. for adverbial purposes: the normal gen. sg. of this fem. noun has *-e*.

103. A number of verbs take a genitive which is also closely related to the categories of the objective genitive. Many examples can be classed according to the function of the genitive (thus *brūcan* 'enjoy' may be said to take a partitive genitive, *fægnian* 'rejoice' a descriptive genitive) or according to the meaning of the verbs (thus the genitive may be said to accompany verbs of depriving, rejoicing, and using): but neither method can be applied simply, still less exhaustively. In the end, the student is probably best served by noting all the common verbs which regularly or in a special context behave in this way:

āmyrran 'hinder (from)', *bedǣlan* 'deprive (of)', *belīðan* 'deprive (of)', *āgēotan* 'drain (of)', *benǣman* 'deprive (of)', *beneah* 'enjoys' (§ 95, note), *berȳpan* 'despoil', *bestrȳpan* 'strip', *beþurfan* 'need', *bīdan* 'wait for', *blissian* 'rejoice (at)', *brūcan* 'enjoy', *(ge)cunnian* 'try', *ēhtan* 'pursue', *fægnian* 'rejoice', *fan-*

ꟻ 63

dian 'try', *gefēon* 'rejoice', *gȳman* 'notice', *gyrnan* 'desire', *hēdan* 'look after', *helpan* 'help' (see also § 107), *hogian* 'intend', *latian* 'delay', *gelȳfan* 'believe', *nēos(i)an* 'visit', *nēotan* 'use', *ofhrēowan* 'pity', *onfōn* 'receive', *onmunan* 'care for', *reccan* 'care', *strȳnan* 'beget', *swīcan* 'cease', *twēo(ga)n* 'doubt', *þurfan* 'need', *þyrstan* 'thirst (for)', *wealdan* 'rule', *wēnan* 'expect', *wilnian* 'desire', *wundrian* 'wonder (at)', *gewyrcan* 'strive after'.

Some verbs, governing two objects, may take genitive and accusative; thus *geǣmeti(gi)an* 'free, empty', *biddan* 'ask', *lettan* 'hinder', *gelystan* (impers.) 'desire', *sc(e)amian* (impers.) 'shame'; others may take genitive and dative; thus *geunnan* 'grant', *forwyrnan* 'refuse', *ofþyncan* (impers.) 'be displeased with', *onlēon* 'lend', *gestȳran* 'restrain', *tilian* 'gain', *tīðian* 'grant', *þancian* 'thank', *gewanian* 'deprive', *wyrnan* 'withhold'.

104. **Prepositional.** No preposition in OE takes the genitive exclusively and only a few take this case at all; note however: *andlang þæs fūlan brōces* (~*ealdan weges*) 'along the dirty stream (~old road)'; *tō*, especially with reference to time, as in *tō þæs þe* 'until', *tō hwilces tīman* 'at what time'; *wið*, meaning 'towards', as in *þā spearcan wundon wiþ þæs hrōfes* 'the sparks flew towards the roof'.

DATIVE (AND INSTRUMENTAL)

105. The functions of the OE dative, like those of the genitive, are very complex. This is partly because this case had largely come to express the functions of the old instrumental in addition to those of the dative proper. In the following outline the term 'instrumental' will, unless otherwise stated, be used to describe not an inflexion but a function, which was expressed with the instrumental case insofar as distinctive forms remained (see §§ 48, 50, 65f) but more generally with the dative.

106. **Dative object.** The dative is frequently concerned with *sharing*, and this can be most clearly seen where the dative is used for the 'indirect' (personal) object with transitive verbs: *þe him hringas geaf* 'who gave him rings', *þīnum māgum lǣf folc ond rīce* 'bequeath people and kingdom to your kinsmen',

sege þīnum lēodum miccle lāþre spell 'report to your people a much more disagreeable message'.

In late OE, *tō* came to be used with the indirect object just as in Mod.E.; thus *gyfan (tō) ǣnigum* 'give (to) anyone'. With a few verbs, notably *cweðan* and *sprecan*, *tō* was normal OE practice: *hē cwæþ tō mē (mihi dixit)* 'he said to me'.

107. The dative was used for the sole 'object' of many intransitive verbs, the cognates of which in Mod.E. are regarded as transitive (for example, 'help', 'answer', 'follow'), and it was used also with several common impersonal verbs and with other verbs used reflexively. The following list comprises the commoner OE verbs which were construed with a dative:

ætwindan 'escape (from)', *ætwītan* 'reproach', *andswarian* 'answer', *ārian* 'honour', *bedrēosan* 'deprive (of)', *bēodan* 'offer', *beorgan* 'save', *betǣcan* 'entrust', *bodian* 'announce', *gebiddan* (reflex.) 'pray', *bregdan* 'pull', *cyrran* (reflex.) 'submit', *(ge)dafenian* 'suit', *dēman* 'judge', *derian* 'harm', *gefēon* 'rejoice', *fylgan* 'follow', *gefremman* 'benefit', *fulgān* 'accomplish', *fylstan* 'help', *helpan* 'help', *hȳrsumian* 'obey', *līcian* 'please', *gelȳfan* 'believe', *linnan* 'cease (from)', *losian* 'be lost', *miltsian* 'pity', *mislimpan* (impers.) 'go wrong', *genēalǣcan* 'approach', *genyhtsumian* 'suffice', *oftēon* 'withhold', *ōleccan* 'flatter', *onfōn* 'receive', *sǣlan* 'happen', *sceððan* 'injure', *gespōwan* (impers.) 'succeed', *þegnian* 'serve', *þēow(i)an* 'serve', *þingian* 'intercede', *þīwian* 'serve', *geþwǣrian* 'allow', *geþwǣrlǣcan* 'agree to', *þyncan* (impers.) 'seem', *wealdan* 'rule', *wīsian* 'guide', *gewītan* (reflex.) 'go', *wiðstandan* 'resist'. Verbs construed with a dative and an accusative include: *ālēogan* 'deny', *ālȳfan* 'allow', *becweðan* 'bequeath', *oðþringan* 'deprive', *oðwendan* 'deprive', *þingian* 'mediate'.

For verbs taking gen. and dat., see above, § 103. Both *weorðan* and *wesan* appear on occasion with dative pronouns, usually classed as reflexive: *hē wearð him on ānon scipe* 'he got aboard a ship', *hē wearð him aweg* 'he went away', *Ādām sceal . . . wesan him on wynne* 'Adam shall live in joy'. Before the end of the OE period, there are many signs that accus. and dat. were no longer sharply distinguished in verb ~ (pro)noun relationships; on this see K. Brunner, *Die Englische Sprache* II.39-40 (Halle 1951) and C. L. Wrenn, *Trans. Phil. Soc.* 1943, pp. 29-30.

108. **Possessive.** In a frequently recurring pattern where we have (though not necessarily in this order) *subject—verb—(object)—preposition—noun*, the *noun* is defined by a noun or pronoun in the dative; this use of the dative is usually called 'possessive': *hē ... sette his ... hond him on þæt hēafod* 'he placed his hand on his head', *Dyde him of healse hring gyldenne* '(he) took from his neck a gold ring'. A special case of this idiom occurs with the preposition *tō*: *þone God sende folce tō frōfre* 'whom God sent as the people's comfort', *hæleþum tō helpe* 'as the heroes' aid' (*Beowulf* 1961; but note the use of the genitive instead in line 1830: *hæleþa tō helpe*), *fremdum tō gewealde* 'into the hands of foreigners'.

109. **Locative.** Even in OE, place is rarely indicated by the dative without a preposition; there are however examples in *Beowulf*, such as *wīcum wunian* 'to live in the dwelling' (l. 3083, but cf l. 3128: *on sele wunian* 'to live in the hall').

110. **Temporal.** The temporal use of the dative can be seen in expressions like *hwīlum* 'at times', *sumum dæge* 'on a certain day' (or, with the instrumental inflexion, *sume dæge*; *þȳ dōgore* 'on that day'). This usage is frequent, but at the same time prepositional phrases are also common: *æt sumum cirre* 'at a certain time', *on þysum* (or, with the instr. form, *þȳs*) *gēare* 'in this year'.

111. **Dative Absolute.** This idiom, not very frequent in OE, is modelled directly on the Latin ablative absolute; the notional relationship involved is usually temporal or modal (see §§ 152ff). Thus, *gefultumigendum Gode* (L. *deō favente*) 'with God helping', *him sprecendum hī cōmon* (L. *eō loquente veniunt*) 'while He was speaking, they came', *gewunnenum sige* 'victory having been won', *āstrehtum handbredum tō heofenlicum rodore* 'having stretched out his palms to the heavenly sky'. For further reading on participial constructions, see § 159, note.

112. **Instrumental.** This function, expressed through the dat. or instr. inflexion, was very important in OE and at the same time is among the most difficult for present-day English speakers to understand. The instrumental can be defined in

SYNTAX

several ways since its range is considerable, but broadly speaking it has to do with the *means* or manner of an action: *hondum
gebrōden* 'hand-woven', *mundum brugdon* 'you brandished
(with) your hands', *hine þā hēafde becearf* 'then (he) cut his
head off (cut him off as regards the head)', *wearð ðā him . . .
gelufod* '(he) then became beloved by Him', *fȳrbendum fæst* 'firm
with forged bands', *wundum wērig* 'exhausted through wounds',
dōme gedȳrsod 'made precious through glory'. It includes the
characteristic **comitative** function seen in expressions like the
following: *worhte Ælfred cyning lȳtle werede geweorc* 'King A.
built a defence-work with a small force'.

Prepositions are also used: *erede mid horsum* 'ploughed with horses',
hē wæs bepǣht fram ðām tungelwitegum 'he was deceived by the astro-
logers'; similarly, *mid* with the dative came to be used for the comitative
function: *him cēnlice wið feaht mid lȳtlum werode* 'he fought boldly
against him with a small force'.
Through their ready acceptance as indications of means and manner,
the endings *-e* and *-um* (usually with adjectives and nouns resp.) came
to be widely used in the formation of adverbs: *hlūde* 'loudly', *wide*
'widely', *miclum* 'greatly', *styccemǣlum* 'piecemeal', *unwearnum* 'irresistibly' (see also § 166).

113. Two uses of the instrumental inflexion are worthy of
special mention. Causal expressions involving *þȳ* (*þon*), *hwȳ*
(*hwon*) are very common: *ðȳ hē þone feōnd ofercwōm* 'therefore
he overcame the enemy', *Hwȳ sceal ic . . . ðeōwian?* 'Why must
I serve?'; compare also, with prepositions, *forðon* (*forðȳ*) 'for
this reason', *tō hwon* 'why'. Secondly, we have the expressions
of comparison which survive in the Mod.E. pattern 'the more
the merrier': *Hige sceal þē* (= *þȳ*) *heardra . . . þē* (= *þȳ*) *ūre
mægen lȳtlað* 'mind must be the sterner as our strength lessens',
sege þīnum leōdum miccle lāþre spell 'give your people a much
more disagreeable message (a message more disagreeable *by
far*)', *mǣrða þon mā* 'the more glories', *þȳ læs ðe hit eōw ǣðrȳt
þince* 'lest (by that much less) it may seem tedious to you'.

114. **Adjectival.** Numerous adjectives (generally signifying
nearness or an emotional relationship) are used with the dative:
gelic wæs hē þām leōhtum steorrum 'he was like the bright stars',
him wæs lāð 'it was disagreeable to him (he was reluctant)'.

67

So also, *nēah* 'near', *lēof* 'dear', *hold* 'loyal', *nȳdbeðearf* 'necessary', and several others.

Comparatives sometimes take the dative but are more usually followed by *þonne* and the nominative; within a few lines in the Alfredian translation of Bede we find *mihtigra þē* and *cræftigra . . . þonne þū*, both meaning 'mightier than thou' (cf above, § 95).

115. Prepositional. The dative is the chief case used with prepositions. For example, *æfter* 'after', *ǣr* 'before', *æt* 'at', *bī, be* 'beside', *betwēonan* 'between', *būtan* 'without', *for* 'before', *fram* 'from, by', *mid* 'with', *of* 'from', *tō* 'to, for'. Several prepositions, taking the accusative when there is motion, have the dative when there is none; for example, *ofer* 'beyond', *on* 'in, on', *under* 'under', *wið* 'opposite, against, with'.

In some frequently recurring phrases, notably *æt hām* 'at home', *tōdæg* 'today', the dative inflexion was to a large extent dropped quite early in the OE period.

Noun Modifiers and Pronouns

116. Adjectives. The *indefinite declension* (§ 50ff) was that in general use. It is found when the adjective is predicative (*ðā wurdon hī . . . drēorige* 'then they became sad') and when no attempt is being made to specify and particularise the item modified (*þǣr sint swīðe micle meras fersce* 'there are very large fresh-water lakes'). In practice, we may say that it is used when not preceded by one of the demonstratives or when no other reason calls for the definite declension.

By contrast, the *definite declension* (§ 54) is the specifying and particularising form, usually signifying that the item modified is the one expected in that context or the one referred to just previously (*se foresprecena here* 'the above mentioned force'). Thus it is regularly used after demonstratives, whether the adjective precedes or follows the noun or is being used substantively: *on þisum lǣnan stoclīfe* 'in this fleeting dwelling-place', *under þām cealdan wætere ond þām wǣtan* 'under the cold and wet water', *þām ādligan* 'to the sick one'. It is also used with ordinal numerals except *ōðer* (*ōðer wæter, ðridde lyft, fēorþe fȳr* 'the second water, the third air, the fourth fire', *sīo ōþeru fierd* 'the other levy'), and with comparative adjectives (*þā wǣron ǣgðer ge swiftran ge unwealtran* 'they were both faster and steadier'). The superlative is also associated with the definite inflexion, but to a large extent this is in any case already provided for under the first rule given above, since the superlative is most frequently found following a demonstrative: *þone mǣstan dǣl* 'the largest part'; when this is not so (usually in predicative function after a copula verb and hence in the nominative case), the indefinite inflexion is generally found: *þæt ... land is ... brādost* 'the land is widest'. The definite inflexion is frequently found after possessives (*mid his micclan werode* 'with his large force') and in expressions of direct address (*Bēowulf lēofa* 'dear B.', *snottra fengel* 'wise king', *lēofan men* 'beloved people'). It is also used to some extent in early verse in environments where none of these conditions obtain; for example, *wīsa fengel geatolic gende* 'the wise king rode well-equipped'.

There are some irregularities in the recorded usage even after demonstratives, but it is likely that cases like *fram þissum wrǣcfullum life* 'from this miserable life' (Ælfric) display reverse spellings after the lOE weakening of inflexions (cf § 13). It should be noted that *ān*, standing alone or following the item it modifies, appears with definite inflexion when it has the meaning 'alone' (*Apollonius āna swigode* 'A. alone was silent'), but is found with indefinite inflexion, even after a demonstrative, in the sense 'one': *on þǣre ānre mīle* 'in that one mile'; compare in succeeding lines in Ælfric: *būton þām ānum poste* 'except that one post', *se post āna* 'that post alone'.

117. Demonstratives and Articles. The functions of the two OE demonstratives (§ 65), *se* (*þæt, sēo*) and *þes* (*þis, þēos*), may be defined respectively as specifying and deictic. The first merely particularises, singles out from the generality, indicates and identifies the known and expected. The latter (which is much less frequently used in OE as a whole) points to and singles out a part of a series, the whole of which may already be specific. One line from the AS Chronicle will illustrate the distinction: *on þysum gēare fōr se micla here þe wē gefyrn ymbe sprǣcon* 'in this year (this one, of a chronicled series of equally specific years), that (*or* the) large enemy force (i.e., not simply a force of unidentified enemies not previously encountered, but the particular one) of which we spoke earlier went . . . '. In this example, *se* has been translated as 'that *or* the', and it must be emphasised that until the very close of the OE period *se* (rarely *þe* until very late) was simply an inflexional variant of *þæt*, in complementary distribution with it, and not contrasted with it as Mod.E. *the* is with *that*. The existence of a 'definite article' in OE is a vexed question, but it seems to be one which has been raised largely by our desire to impose upon OE a terminology familiar in and suitable for Mod.E.: where today we have three contrastive and formally distinct defining words, *the*, *that*, *this*, each with a name, in OE there were but two, *se* and *þes*, and we are left as it were with a name to spare. The problem partly disappears when we reflect that in many instances of their use today, *the* and *that* are interchangeable ('Do you remember the/that man I was speaking to last night?'); in OE *se* (*þæt*, *sēo*) embraced practically the whole range of functions performed today, jointly or separately, by *the* and *that*. Thus we have contexts in which *þes* and *se* are in contrast simply as deictic and identifying words respectively: *ic tōwurþe ēower templ . . . On Godes naman āhrēose þis templ . . . Hwæt ðā færlīce āhrēas þæt templ* 'I shall destroy your temple . . . In God's name, let this temple fall . . . Lo then suddenly the temple fell'. We have other contexts (though few of them and fairly late) in which *þes* and *se* are in partial contrast also as 'near' and 'far' deictics respectively: *þis lēoht wē habbaþ wiþ nȳtenu gemǣne, ac þæt lēoht wē sceolan sēcan þæt wē mōtan habban mid englum gemǣne* 'this light we have in common with beasts, but that light must we seek which we may have in common with angels'.

118. Although there are numerous points in which poetry and prose differ to some extent over the use of *se*, the most important difference seems to be the relative infrequency of *se* before a noun in the poetry. Where it does occur, it seems to have precisely the same function as in the prose: *Wæs se gryre lǣssa efne swā micle swā bið mægþa cræft . . . be wǣpnedmen* 'the horror (of the entry of Grendel's mother, just described)

was just so much less as is women's strength compared with a man', *Ne wæs þæt gewrixle til* 'the exchange (just mentioned) was not a good one'. But in many cases where the prose, particularly the late prose, would have *se*, there is nothing in the verse: *Næs Bēowulf ðǣr, ac wæs ōþer in ǣr geteohhod æfter māþðum-gife mǣrum Gēate* 'B. was not there, another lodging having been assigned to *the* glorious Geat after *the* treasure-giving'.

In prose generally, as well as verse, there are many environments in which Mod.E. usage requires *the* but in which no corresponding form is necessary in OE; thus for example in many prepositional phrases and in set expressions of all kinds: *āhton wælstōwe gewald* 'had (*the*) mastery of *the* battlefield'. Since however *se* embraced the functions of Mod.E. *the* and the deictic demonstrative, the reverse is also true, and we find *se* used where 'the' is not a possible translation: *se Cyneheard wæs þæs Sigebryhtes brōþur* '(*this*) C. was the brother of (*this*) S.'.

119. If anything corresponding to the 'definite article' is rare in OE verse, an 'indefinite article' is rarer still; *ān* is usually a numeral, and when it is not it shares for the most part with *sum* a 'strong indefiniteness' akin to Mod.E. 'a certain' rather than the 'weak indefiniteness' of Mod.E. 'a(n)': *Ðā ic . . . gefrægn hord rēafian . . . ānne mannan* 'Then I heard of some man robbing the hoard', *Þæt wæs ān cyning* 'There was a (unique) king', *sume worde hēt, þæt ic his ǣrest ðē ēst gesægde* 'commanded, in a specific message, that I should first tell you the quality of it'. In the earlier prose too, *ān* (when it is not purely a numeral) and *sum* have 'strong indefiniteness': *þǣr is mid Estum ān mǣgð* 'among the Estonians there is a certain tribe', *þā stōd him sum mon æt* 'then there stood by him a certain man'. For the bulk of OE usage, in fact, the function of 'indefinite article' (as contrasting with *se, þæt, sēō*) was expressed by zero, just as it is with plurals in Mod.E.: 'I like reading books but the books must be readable'. Thus: *On frymðe wæs word and þæt word wæs mid Gode and þæt word wæs God* 'In the beginning there was word, and the word was with God and the word was God'. There are however cases,

especially in lOE (in *Apollonius*, for example: *hig worhton . . . āne anlīcnesse of āre* 'they made a statue of brass'), where we seem indeed to have *an* in simple indefinite function, but such cases are rare.

120. **Pronouns.** (*a*) The two **demonstratives** *sē* (*þæt, sēo*) and *þēs* (*þis, þēos*) were used pronominally as deictics and sometimes (as in Mod.E.) as contrastive deictics: *ān ðǣra wæs* 'one of these was . . .', *þæs oferēode: þisses swā mæg* 'Things passed over so far as *that* was concerned: so it may be with *this*'. The series *sē, þæt, sēo* appear also to have been used exactly as personal pronouns: *and sē unrihtlīce ofslegen wæs* 'and he was unjustly slain', *þā sē forðfērde* 'when he died', *and sē hæfde vii winter rīce* 'and he held the kingship for seven years'. But the chief pronominal function of *sē* is in relative constructions: *þæt lȳtle þæt hē erede* 'the little that he ploughed', *understande sē ðe wille* 'let him understand who will'.

Despite examples like *and sē . . . ofslegen wæs*, which he quotes, S. O. Andrew contends that we are here dealing with relative and not personal pronouns; see *Syntax and Style in Old English* (Cambridge 1940), pp. 36 ff. As a pronoun, *sē* had a long vowel.

(*b*) The most frequent **relative** pronoun was the invariable particle *þe*, sometimes preceded by the relevant form of the *sē* series (though, as we have seen above, a form of *sē* could be the sole relative pronoun), with the antecedent often preceded and defined by the same form of the *sē* series. For examples, see below, § 153. Sometimes, too, the relative could be zero, as in the Mod.E. expression 'There's a man stands at that corner every night': *on þȳs gēare gefōr Ælfred, wæs æt Baðum gerēfa* 'in this year Æ. died, who was sheriff at Bath'.

(*c*) The **reflexive** function was performed by the simple personal pronouns: *se cyning hine . . . wende* 'the king went (lit. turned himself)', *wit unc . . . werian þōhton* 'we-two intended to defend ourselves'.

See also § 107. For the most part, *self* was used in OE simply to emphasise and was not, as in Mod.E., associated with being a reflexive sign or a pronoun-enclitic: *wē hit . . . ne selfe ne lufodon* 'we ourselves did not love it'.

(*d*) Apart from serving as reflexives, the **personal** pronouns have little that is distinctively OE when they are present; it is their absence that is striking. In the second of two parallel constructions we can in Mod.E. often omit the pronoun: 'we work and slave'; in OE considerably greater freedom obtained in this connexion: *hīe þā swā dydon, worhton* ... 'they then did so, built ...', *Wǣre ðū on wǣdle, sealdest mē* 'Even though you were poor, (you) gave me ...', *Hǣfdon swurd nacod, þā wit on sund rēowon* '(We) held bare swords, when we-two swam to sea', *gif ic wiste hū wið ðām āglǣcean elles meahte ... wið-grīpan* 'if I knew how else (I) could grapple with the monster', *inne on þǣm fæstenne sǣton fēawe cirlisce menn on, ond wæs sāmworht* 'within the stronghold there remained a few working-men, and (it) was half-built'. The pronoun object could similarly be omitted: *hīe him āsetton segen gyldenne hēah ofer hēafod, lēton holm beran, gēafon on gār-secg* 'they set a golden banner high above his head, let the sea carry (him), released (him) unto the ocean'.

(*e*) An OE construction all but unparalleled in Mod.E. is the **impersonal** verb with which regularly there was no subject expressed: *hine nānes ðinges ne lyste* '(it) desired him of nothing, *i.e.* he desired nothing', *ǣlcum menn þūhte* '(it) seemed to each man'. In lOE however we find *hit* coming to be used as the subject in such expressions (Wulfstan has *swā hit þincan mæg* 'as it may seem'), and we find *hit* also with the increasingly used periphrastic passive (§ 131) in **indefinite** expressions: *Ys hyt ālȳfed* ... ? 'Is it allowed ... ?' Instead of this periphrastic passive in general OE usage, however, we find the indefinite pronoun *man* as in *þe mon hǣt* 'which is called', a formula often used to translate Latin *vocātur*, *dīcuntur*, and other passives.

(*f*) The **indefinite** pronouns, *gehwā, gehwylc* 'every, each', *hwylc* 'any', etc., commonly take the gen. pl.: *on mǣgþa gehwǣm* 'in every tribe', *ūhtna gehwylce* 'every dawn', *Frȳsna hwylc* 'any Frisian'; 'each one' is frequently rendered in OE by *gehwylc* followed or preceded by the gen. pl. *ānra*: thus, *ānra gehwylc*. See also § 101.

73

Concord

121. Grammatical agreement was of great importance in OE structure in indicating the relationship between words which showed inflexional distinctions of number, person, case, and gender. Concord existed between the following items:

(a) Subject and verb (number and person): ðā Deniscan cōmon 'the Danes came', Eart þū se Bēowulf, sē þe wið Brecan wunne? 'Are you the Beowulf that strove (2 sg.) against Breca?'

(b) Demonstratives, adjectives, and nouns (number, case, and gender): æfter þǣm gedrynce 'after the drinking', mid fullum wǣstme and heofenlicere snoternysse 'with full stature and heavenly wisdom'.

(c) Pronouns and their designata (number, case, and gender): of ðǣre ... rōde sumne dǣl þæs mēoses þe hēo mid beweaxen wæs 'from the cross a certain amount of the moss with which it (fem. sg., agreeing with rōd) was overgrown', hē ... wolde Grendle forgyldan gūðrǣsa fela ðāra þe hē geworhte 'he wanted to repay Grendel for the many attacks that (g.pl., agreeing with gūðrǣsa) he had made'.

(d) Pronouns and their modifiers (number, case, and gender): æt his selfes hām 'at his own home', ūre ealra 'of us all', ūs eallum 'to us all', gesǣlige hī wurdon geborene 'they were born blessed'.

With regard to (a), (c), and (d), it should be noted that the *dual* number (1st and 2nd pers. pron. only; see § 63) corresponds to *plural* in concord with other items: *wit þæt gecwǣdon* 'he-and-I agreed upon this'.

122. It is necessary to amplify the above statement of the norm. In the first place, the strict case agreement in appositive expressions should be noted: *wæs hē se mon ... geseted* 'he, this man, was placed ...', *hē wrǣc þone aldormon Cumbran* 'he avenged Cumbra, the governor', *feredon Aidanes sāwle þæs hālgan bisceopes* '(they) bore the soul of Aidan, the holy bishop', *æt Plegmunde mīnum ærcebiscepe* 'from P., my archbishop'. But appositive phrases of the pattern 'called X' do not require concord: *fram Brytta cyninge, Ceadwalla gecīged* 'from the king of the Britons, called C.', *tō Westseaxena kyninge, Cynegyls*

74

gehāten (not **Cynegylse gehātnum*) 'to the king of the West Saxons, called C.'. Nor, in other cases, is concord invariable: *Ic on Higelāce wāt, Gēata dryhten* 'I know as to H., the lord of the Geats'.

123. Past participles display some variety of usage. With copula verbs ('be', 'become') they often agree with the subject (*wǣron hātene* 'were called', *ofslægene wǣrun* 'were slain'), but more usually they are invariable: (*rāpas*) *bēoð of hwæles hȳde geworht* '(the ropes) are made of whale's hide'. With forms of *habban*, the participle is normally invariable (*hæfdon . . . āþas geseald* '(they) had given oaths'), but sometimes it agrees with the object: *hīe hine ofslægenne hæfdon* 'they had slain him'; here, no doubt, we see a survival of the normal use of this construction before it came to be used as a 'pluperfect tense' (§ 128),—'they had him dead'.

124. Strict concord in grammatical gender is the rule in OE. It is particularly regular with demonstratives and adjectives (*þæs wīfes* 'the woman's'), though adjectives tended to have a one-gender plural: *wurdon hiora wīf . . . sārige* 'their wives became sad', *earme wīf* 'wretched women'. A mixture of genders requires neuter concord in the modifiers: *Ādām gemǣlde, and tō Ēuan spræc: '. . . wit hēr baru standað'* 'Adam spoke, and addressed Eve: "You-and-I stand here naked".' Grammatical gender is on the whole regular also with pronouns: *se hwæl~hē* 'the whale (m.)~it', *mycel sǣ ~ sēo is brādre* 'great sea (f.) ~ it is broader', *mycel ēa ~ hīo tōlīð* 'great river (f.) ~ it separates', *weall ~ hē is geworht of tigelan* 'wall (m.) ~ it is made of tile'. But pronouns, particularly when relating to human beings, are sometimes used with natural gender in spite of the normal requirements of grammatical concord: *þæt mǣden ~ hēo wearð* 'the maiden (n.) ~ she was'.

125. Analogous to the use in late OE of *hit* as the subject of impersonal verbs (§ 120e) is the widespread use of neuter singulars (*hit, þæt, þis, hwæt*), without regard to gender or number, before the verb 'to be' or in contexts where the designatum is a statement, fact, or event: *þæt wǣron . . . Finnas* 'they were Lapps', *þæt wǣron gesweostor* 'who were sisters', *Hwæt bēoð . . . ?*

'What are ... ?', *hē nyste hwæt þæs sōþes wæs, for þæm hē hit self ne seah* 'he did not know how much of this was true, because he himself did not see it', *þis wearð þā Harolde cyninge gecȳdd* 'This was then made known to King Harold', *hwæt sindon gē?* 'who are you (pl.)?'.

Note also *hit man hāt Wislemūða* 'it is called (lit. one calls it) Vistula-mouth', *Hwæt gif hit unclǣne bēoþ fixas?* 'What if they are unclean fish?', though *bēoþ* in the latter example may be explained as a scribal error (cf G. N. Garmonsway, *Ælfric's Colloquy*, London 1939, pp. 26-7). It is the use of neut. sg. for 'facts' and 'events' that leads to the evolution of the conjunctions *þæt, oð þæt, forþæm,* etc.: *God sylf wāt ... þæt wē winnað rihtlice* 'God Himself knows (this fact, namely) that we struggle righteously', *oþ þæt man him fette* 'until (this event, namely that) someone fetched for him ... ', *him wearð þæs tiþod* 'he was granted this', lit. 'it was granted to him of this (matter)', *forþon* 'therefore, on account of this (fact)'.

126. Number-concord between subject and verb shows in two respects some variation in usage. First, a verb is often singular when it precedes a plural, especially compound, subject: *þǣr sceal bēon gedrync and plega* 'there must be drinking and merrymaking', *gefeaht Æþered cyning ond Ælfred* 'King Æ. and Æ. fought' (but three lines earlier, *Æþered cyning ond Ælfred ... gelǣddon* 'King Æ. and Æ. led'), *þā gegaderode Æþered ... ond Æþelm ... ond þā cinges þegnas* 'then Æ. and Æ. and the king's thanes assembled' (an interesting example, since the meaning of this intransitive verb itself suggests plurality), *ætsomne cwōm syxtig monna* 'sixty men came together'. The verb is not always singular in this position however: *wurdon viiii folcgefeoht gefohten* 'nine engagements were fought'. There are also cases (see *Beowulf* 905, 2164) in which a plural subject precedes a singular verb, but instances of this are rare.

Secondly, indefinite pronouns and collective nouns caused much conflict between grammatical and logical concord: *rīdeð ǣlc ... and hyt mōtan habban* 'each rides and can (pl.) have it', *þider urnon swā hwelc swā þonne gearo wearþ* 'whoever was then ready ran (pl.) there', *ān mǣgð þæt hī magon* 'one tribe who (pl.) can (pl.)', *þone here* ～ *hīe* 'that raiding force ～ they', but a few lines below *þone here* ～ *hine* 'that raiding force ～ it', *sīo fierd ... þone here geflīemde, ond þā herehȳþa āhreddon* 'the militia routed (sg.) the raiding force and recaptured (pl.) the plunder', *mid þǣre scīre þe mid him fierdedon* 'with the shire that *were* campaigning with him', *se dǣl þe þǣr aweg cōm wurdon . . . generede* 'the part that escaped (sg.) *were* saved', *sēo buruhwaru hine underfēngon* 'the township received (pl.) him'.

Tense, Aspect, Voice

127. Tense

As pointed out in § 3, the OE verbs had only two tense-inflexions, present and preterite; for the most part, time-relationships other than present and past were either implicit in the context or were expressed with the help of contextual features such as adverbs of time. The present inflexion expressed present (*þā þēowan drincað medo* 'the slaves drink mead') and future time (*ic ārīse and ic fare tō mīnum fæder*, which corresponds to the Latin *surgam et ībō ad patrem meum*; *ic mē mid Hruntinge dōm gewyrce, oþðe mec dēað nimeð* 'I shall achieve fame for myself with Hrunting, or death will take me'). To some extent, a distinction in function is to be observed between the two present forms of 'to be', inasmuch as the *bið*, *bēoð* forms seem to have been used more frequently to denote future than *is, sint*: *bēoþ þā fyrmestan ȳtemeste* 'the first shall be last'; Ælfric's Latin Grammar equates *eom, eart, is* to Lat. *sum, es, est*, and *bēo, bist, bið* to *erō, eris, erit*. At times a present form alternates with a preterite (*næs him feor þanon tō gesēcanne . . . Higelāc Hrēþling, þǣr æt hām wunað* 'it *was* not far from there for him to find Higelac, son of Hreþel, where he *sits* at home'), but a historic present properly so called is of rare and even dubious occurrence in OE.

The preterite inflexion expressed both past (*hī fēollon* 'they fell') and 'past-in-the-past' (pluperfect) time: *wolde Grendle forgyldan gūðrǣsa fela, ðāra þe hē geworhte . . . oftor micle ðonne on ǣnne sīð* '(he) wanted to repay Grendel for the many attacks which he (had) carried out much more often than on one occasion'. The pluperfect time-relation is often implicit by reason of the type of clause: *siððan hīe hīe geliornodon, hīe hīe wendon . . . on hiora āgen geðīode* 'after they (had) studied them, they translated them into their own language'; often too it is assisted by the presence of *ǣr*: *Ne mētte hē ǣr nān gebūn land, siþþan hē from his āgnum hām fōr* 'He had not found any inhabited land, since he had left his own place'.

128. In addition, OE saw the rise of the complex verbal forms usually called 'compound tenses'. Thus, although *willan* and *sculan* with an infinitive usually imply volition or obligation respectively, these constructions are found occasionally translating Latin futures: *ic wille wyrcean mīn setl* (*pōnam sēdem meam*) 'I shall make my throne', *forðǣm gē sculon . . . wēpan* (*quoniam flēbitis*) 'because you will weep'. So, too, the preterite forms of these verbs could indicate reported future: *Hīe ne wēndon ðætte ǣfre menn sceolden swǣ reccelēase weorðan* 'They did not expect that people would ever become so careless'. But for the most part *willan* and *sculan* are overlaid with their other functions even when partly indicating future: *Hīe willað ēow . . . gāras syllan* 'They are about to (*and* want to) give you spears'.

The pluperfect was widely expressed by the preterite of *habban* together with the past participle of transitive verbs, and the preterite of *wesan* with the past participle of intransitive verbs: *Siððan ic hīe ðā geliornod hæfde . . . ic hīe on Englisc āwende* 'Then when I had studied them, I translated them into English', *se hālga fæder wæs inn āgān* 'the holy father had gone in'. Where the participles agree—in the one case with the object, and in the other case with the subject—we have a survival from the time when they had predicative adjectival function rather than a tense function (see § 123): *hī hæfdon þā heora stemn gesetenne and hiora mete genotudne* 'they had finished their tour of duty and used up their food', (*lār*) *wæs oðfeallenu* '(learning) had declined'. Of the two pluperfect auxiliaries, *habban* shows signs of becoming the preferred one even within the OE period, when it is to be found occasionally with intransitive verbs: *wē tō symble geseten hæfdon* 'we had sat down to the feast'.

129. Aspect

In speaking of the present tense of 'have' (*habban*, rarely *āgan*) and 'be' with a past participle, we pass from the consideration of tense (the expression of the *time* of an action) to the consideration of aspect (the expression of the *manner* or *quality* of an action). For ordinary purposes, we need distinguish only 'perfective' aspect (relating to momentary actions, such as inception or completion) and 'durative' aspect (relating to both habitual and continuous actions).

The perfect of transitive verbs expressed with 'have' (*hē hafað onfunden* 'he has found') and the perfect of intransitive verbs expressed with 'be' (*is nū geworden* '(it) has now happened') do not refer to a different time from the simple preterites (*hē onfand, nū gewearð*) but to the same time regarded more specifically as perfective. In OE the perfective aspect could equally well be expressed with the simple preterite form: *Hine hālig God ... ūs onsende* 'Holy God has despatched him to us'. In other cases, the function was assisted by adverbs: *nȳdþearf ... þæt hē Godes lage gȳme bet þonne hē ǣr dyde* 'necessary that he should heed God's law better than he has done formerly'. Some verbs (such as *cuman* 'come', *feallan* 'fall', *weorðan* 'become') are, as it were, inherently perfective and need no formal indication of aspect; for a larger number, perfective aspect was expressed not by means of an inflexion but by prefixing elements such as *ā-, be-, for-, ge-, of-, tō-* (see §§ 168, 170f): *siglde hē ... swā swā hē mehte on fīf dagum gesiglan* 'he kept sailing as far as he could (manage to) sail in five days'.

130.
The durative aspect is inherent in the meaning of most verbs ('be', 'live', for example) and it is therefore not surprising that special forms and constructions were used only to a minor extent in OE to express it: *ðēos woruld ... nēalǣcð þām ende* 'this world is approaching the end', *wē forhealdað ǣghwǣr Godes gerihta ealles tō gelōme* 'we (repeatedly) withhold God's dues everywhere all too frequently', *wæs se cyng ... on fære mid þære scīre þe mid him fierdedon* 'the king was on his way with the shire-men that were campaigning with him'. We find *wolde* with an infinitive quite frequently expressing habitual

79

(as opposed to continuous) action: *wildu dēor ðǣr woldon tō irnan* 'wild animals were wont to run there', *Hē wolde æfter ūhtsange oftost hine gebiddan* 'It was usually after Matins that he would pray'. When verbs naturally perfective in meaning were intended to have durative force, they were accompanied by an infinitive or present participle: *Ðā cōm . . . Grendel gongan* 'Then came Grendel travelling', *flēogende cōm* 'came flying'.

We also find the verb 'be' with a present participle expressing durative aspect: *ic mē gebidde to ðǣm Gode þe bīo eardigende on heofonum* 'I pray (at this moment) to the God who is dwelling (not only at this moment) in the heavens', *Ðǣr wǣron sume of ðǣm bōcerum sittende, and on hiera heortum ðencende (Erant . . . sedentes . . . cogitantes)* 'There were some of the scribes sitting there and thinking in their hearts'. Many cases of this construction, however, have no durative function, and it is often difficult to say in what way the expression differs from the simple tense form; at times it seems ingressive: *þætte nǣnig . . . wǣre āwendende þās ūre dōmas* 'that no one should set about changing these our decrees'.

131. Voice

With a single exception, OE verbs showed only active voice inflexions. The exception is *hātan* 'call' which, besides having a vocalic active preterite *hēt*, had a consonantal preterite *hātte* which was passive and which was used both for present and past: *sēo ēa hātte Temese* 'the river is called Thames', *hwæt hātton þāge* 'what are those called?', *Rachel hātte Iācobes wīf* 'Jacob's wife was called Rachel'. For the rest, the notional passive was expressed in one of two principal ways: a copula verb with the past participle, or the indefinite pronoun *man* with the ordinary active verb-form. In the periphrastic expression just mentioned there were two auxiliaries: *bēon/wesan* and *weorðan*. To some extent there was a distinction of aspect involved, the former being used in durative expressions (*ne bið ðǣr nǣnig ealo gebrowen* 'no ale is (ever) brewed there'), the latter in perfective expressions (*þæt hūs wearð ðā forburnen* 'the house was then burnt down'). But there was much free variation, ignoring aspect, and writers seem often simply to have preferred one or the other auxiliary. The OE verb 'to be' did not develop a past participle until very late, and the 'pluperfect passive' was not distinguished from the preterite: *þe þæt hālige dūst on āhangen wæs* 'on which the holy dust had been hung'. A passive infinitive was usually expressed with the active form: *þās þing sint tō dōnne* 'these things are to be done', *hēht hine lǣran* (Lat. *iussit illum . . . doceri*) 'commanded him to be taught'; but periphrastic expressions were available where the active form might be ambiguous: *sceal wesan Ismāhēl hāten* 'shall be called I'.

The use of *man* calls for no comment: *mon mæg gīet gesīon hiora swæð* 'one can still see their track (*or* their track can still be seen)', *worhte man hit him tō wīte* 'it had been made as a punishment for them', *Ēadwerd man forrǣdde and syððan ācwealde* 'E. was betrayed and then killed'.

It is to be noted that, despite its distinctive passive inflexion, *hātan* was often used with the periphrastic construction and also with *man*: *hī sind gehātene* 'they are called', *tō þæm porte þe mon hæt æt Hæþum* 'to the trading place which is called Hedeby'.

For more detailed treatment of OE tense, aspect, and voice, see J. M. Wattie, 'Tense', *Essays and Studies* xvi (1931), pp. 121-43, F. Mossé, *Histoire de la Forme Périphrastique être + Participe Présent* (Paris 1938), L. G. Frary, *Studies in the Syntax of the Old English Passive* (*Language* Dissertations, 1929), J. Fröhlich, *Die Indefinite Agens im Altenglischen* (Bern 1951). A very useful historical treatment appears in K. Brunner, *Die Englische Sprache* II (Halle 1951), 267 ff, where further specialised references may be found. On the whole question of aspect in the Gmc languages, see A. Mirowicz, *Die Aspektfrage im Gotischen* (Wilno 1935). Cf also J. Raith, *Untersuchungen zum englischen Aspekt* (Munich 1951).

Mood

132. Indicative

The indicative is the mood of general objective expression and is used in the vast majority of constructions that do not involve grammatical dependence: *hwæt sægst ðū?* 'what do you say?', *Hȳ hergiað and hȳ bernað, rȳpað and rēafiað, and tō scipe lǣdað* 'They ravage and burn, plunder and rob, and carry off shipwards'. It is the mood also of a large number of grammatically dependent expressions. These to a large extent involve 'fact' (as against 'surmise'), 'reality' (as against 'unreality'), but the use of indicative and subjunctive cannot be entirely rationalised in accordance with such dichotomies. In many cases we are simply dealing with linguistic convention, one or other mood being associated (though not invariably used) with a given type of construction.

The indicative is also found with great regularity in:

(a) relative clauses: *þegen þe ǣr wæs his hlāford* 'thane who had formerly been his lord';

(b) noun clauses of various kinds (including, though less frequently, indirect questions) relating to fact or certainty: *þæt is gesȳne . . . þæt ūs Godes yrre . . . on sit* 'it is clear that God's anger rests on us', *ic wāt þæt ic ne eom wyrðe* 'I know that I am not worthy', *ne sceall nān mann āwǣgan þæt hē sylfwylles behǣt* 'no one must revoke what he promises of his own accord', *þæt wearð gefylled . . . þæt his swiðre hand wunað hāl* 'it was fulfilled that his right hand remains whole', *swā hwæt swā him becōm* 'whatever came his way', *sǣde him hwylce gyfe hē onfēng* 'told him what gift he had received';

(c) adverb clauses of place: *tō Scotlande, þǣr se gelēafa wæs þā* 'to Ireland, where the faith was at that time', *swā hwǣr swā hē wæs* 'wherever he was';

(d) adverb clauses of time: *Þā hē þā þās andsware onfēng, ðā ongan hē . . . singan* 'When he received this answer, he began to sing', *þonne hē ādlig bið* 'when he is sick', *sōna swā hē rīces gewēold* 'as soon as he possessed the kingship', *oð þæt þæt hūs . . . on fȳre wearð* 'until the house became on fire', *nū hē on heofonum leofað* 'now that he lives in the heavens';

(e) adverb clauses of cause: *for þām þe hit næfð lēafe þæs Ælmihtigan* 'because it has not the Almighty's permission', *þæs þe hē wann wið heofnes Waldend* 'because he fought against the Ruler of Heaven';

(f) adverb clauses of manner: *swā swā Aidanus him bæd* 'as Aidan had prayed for him';

(g) adverb clauses of result: *flotmen swā strange . . . þæt oft on gefeohte ān fēseð tȳne* 'pirates so strong that often in a fight one will chase ten', *sum fēoll on īse, þæt his earm tōbærst* 'a certain man fell on some ice so that his arm broke';

(*h*) adverb clauses of condition, where the condition is a practical possibility: *gif þū gelȳfan wylt, þū wurþest hāl sōna* 'if you are prepared to believe, you will become well at once', *gif þū ǣnig þincg hæfst* 'if you have anything'.

133. Subjunctive

The subjunctive is the mood of subjective expression, and in general its use is confined to volitional, conjectural, or hypothetical contexts. As indicated in the previous paragraph, however, usage is sometimes determined purely by convention, and it is to some extent variable. The principal uses of the subjunctive are as follows:

(*a*) in non-dependent clauses expressing wishes and commands: *God ūre helpe* 'may God help us', *cild binnan ðrītegum nihta sīe gefulwad* 'let a child be (*or* a child must be) baptised within 30 nights';

(*b*) in noun clauses (including indirect questions) in negative or conjectural contexts or dependent upon verbs of saying, thinking, or suggesting: *Swā mē þæt riht ne þinceð, þæt ic ōleccan āwiht þurfe Gode* 'Thus it does not seem to me right that I should need to flatter God', *is nȳdþearf . . . þæt hē Godes lage gȳme* 'it is necessary that he should heed God's law', *hit nān wundor nys þæt se hālga cynincg untrumnysse gehǣle* 'it is no wonder that the holy king should heal sickness', *se prēost cwæð þæt ān wer wǣre on Īrlande* 'the priest said that there was a man in Ireland', *hēo hine . . . lǣrde, þæt hē weoroldhād forlēte* 'she advised him that he should give up secular life', *cunnian hwā cēne sȳ* 'to find out who is brave';

(*c*) in adverb clauses of concession introduced by *þēah (þe)*: *þēah man swā ne wēne* 'although people do not think so'; the indicative (as in *Beowulf* 2467) is exceptional; the alternative ('willy-nilly') concession has the subjunctive when there is inversion without a conjunction (*bēo hē . . . bēo hē* 'whether he is . . . or whether he is . . . ') and also when a conjunction such as *sam* is used (*sam hit sȳ sumor sam winter* 'whether it is summer or winter');

(*d*) in adverb clauses of condition, the terms of which are extremely hypothetical or quite impossible: *gyf se þegen þæne þræl* ... *āfylle* 'if the thane kills the serf', *būtan God gebeorge* 'unless God saves', *swylce eal Finnsburuh fȳrenu wǣre* 'as though all Finnsburg were on fire', *þǣr mē gifeðe* ... *wurde* 'if it had been granted me'; in 'impossible' conditions, expressed with the pret. subj., both the adverbial clause and the related non-dependent clause have the subjunctive: *him wǣre bettere þæt hē nǣfre geboren wǣre* 'it would have been better for him if he had never been born';

(*e*) in adverb clauses of purpose: *þæt heora geleāfa wurde āwend eft tō Gode* 'in order that their faith might be turned again to God', *þȳ lǣs wē ætgædere ealle forweorðan* 'lest we all perish together', *þȳ lǣs ðe hit ēow ǣðrȳt þince* 'lest it seem tedious to you';

(*f*) in some adverb clauses of result, where the result is anticipated: *Swā sceal geong guma ... gewyrcean ... þæt hine on ylde eft gewunigen wil-gesīþas* 'So ought a young man to bring it about that eager retainers support him in his old age';

(*g*) in temporal and other clauses which relate to future or conjectural events: *Gespræc þā se gōda ... ǣr hē on bed stige* 'The noble one then spoke, before he went (*or* should go) to bed', *oþ þæt ... cunne gearwe* 'until he knows well', *nis nū cwicra nān, þe ic him mōdsefan mīnne durre ... āsecgan* 'there is now no one living to whom I dare speak my heart';

(*h*) in many comparative clauses, with *þonne: sēlre bið ǣghwǣm þæt hē his frēond wrece, þonne hē fela murne* 'it will be better for everyone that he avenge his friend than mourn much';

(*i*) in clauses of various kinds, which are dependent on clauses containing subjunctive verbs: *gecnāwe sē ðe cunne* 'let him know who can (*subj.*)', *þæs ūs scamað swȳðe þæt wē bōte āginnan, swā swā bēc tǣcan* 'we are very much ashamed to (*lit.* that we should) attempt a remedy, as the Scriptures teach (*subj.*)', *Ðēah ... hit æfter þām eft geweorðe þæt wǣpngewrixl weorðe* 'Even though it turns out later on that armed conflict breaks out (*subj.*)'.

134. During the OE period, the subjunctive came to be expressed more and more by means of the 'modal auxiliaries', *willan, sculan, magan, (ic) mōt* (§§ 88, 91, 93, 95). This was

especially so in the preterite, perhaps because it was in the
preterite that the weakening of unstressed vowels to [ə] (see
§ 13) left fewer inflexional mood distinctions. For example:
*Nū ic suna mīnum syllan wolde gūð-gewǣdu, þǣr mē gifeðe swā
ǣnig yrfe-weard æfter wurde* 'Now I would give my son my
war-gear, if I had been granted any heir', *nū wolde ic gebētan,
gif ic ābīdan mōste* 'now I would reform, if I might be spared',
līcette þæt hē sceolde bīon se hēhsta god '(he) pretended that he
was the most exalted god'. In some texts we can see the two
forms of expression alternating in parallel constructions: *þæt
Ādām sceal . . . wesan him on wynne, and wē þis wīte þolien*
'that Adam should live in contentment and we should suffer
this torment'; similarly, *sē þe slēa his fæder . . . sē sceal dēaðe
sweltan* 'he who kills his father is to die', but *sē þe his gewealdes
monnan ofslēa, swelte sē dēaþe* 'he who kills a man of his own
free will is to die'.

135. Imperative

The imperative proper exists only in the second person singular and plural (*Cædmon, sing mē hwæthwegu* 'C., sing me
something', *Lēofan men, gecnāwað þæt sōð is* 'Beloved people,
know what is true'), though there is also a rare first person
plural form in *-an, -on*. Almost the only common example of
the latter is *(w)uton, utan* (which historically is probably an
aorist optative or subjunctive of *wītan* 'go'; see § 214), which
is used in a frequent periphrasis to express the first person
plural imperative of other verbs: *Uton feallan tō ðǣre rōde* 'Let
us fall before the cross', *utan dōn swā ūs nēod is* 'let us do as is
necessary for us'. For the third person (and sometimes also
for the first), exhortations are expressed by means of the subjunctive (see § 133*a*).

136. Infinitive

The infinitive is chiefly used as follows:

(*a*) with a small number of verbs like *cunnan, (ic) dearr,
magan, sculan, þurfan, willan* (and, as we saw in the preceding
paragraph, *uton*) which to a greater or lesser extent act as
auxiliaries, and which almost all survive in Mod.E. as the
'anomalous finites': *hwæt sceal ic singan?* 'what am I to sing?',

ne dear man forhealdan 'one dare not withhold', *ne mōton habban* '(they) cannot have', *Ne þurfe wē ūs spillan* 'We need not destroy each other'. In constructions with such verbs, infinitives relating to *being* or *moving* are often omitted, as being implicit in the context: *wita sceal geþyldig* 'a wise man must *be* patient', *ǣr hē in wille* 'before he is willing *to go* in'. Other infinitives may be omitted if a form of the verb in question occurs in the context: *understande sē ðe cunne* 'let him understand who can (*sc.* understand)';

(*b*) with verbs of causation, intention, and inception. In this group we often find the infinitive used with passive meaning (see above, § 131), and also the 'accusative and infinitive' construction (§ 96). For example: *dō hit ūs tō witanne* 'make us know it', *hēt hine lǣran* 'bade him be taught', *hēt . . . his hēafod ofāslēan* 'ordered his head to be struck off', *ðenceð gegrīpan* 'intends to grasp', *wilnað biscephād tō underfōnne* 'wishes to receive the office of bishop', *ongan fyrene fremman* 'began to do evil';

(*c*) with verbs of motion, rest, and observation, often with durative aspect (see above, § 130), and sometimes with 'accusative and infinitive' (§ 96): *cōm . . . sīðian* 'came travelling', *geseah . . . standan twēgen . . . wēpan* 'saw two standing weeping', *geseah blācne lēoman . . . scīnan* 'saw a bright light shining'.

In the last two classes, the infinitive was sometimes preceded by *tō*; the use of *tō* with the infinitive (almost always inflected, *-anne, -enne*) increased throughout the OE period and was general in the following classes of usage:

(*d*) purpose: *nū gē mōton gangan . . . Hrōðgār gesēon* 'now you may go to see H.', *ūt ēode se sǣdere his sǣd tō sāwenne* 'the sower went out to sow his seed';

(*e*) causal: *ic nū forsceamige tō secganne* 'I am now very much ashamed to say';

(*f*) specificatory (especially with nouns and adjectives) and adverbial: *gierd mid tō prēageanne . . . stæf mid tō wreðianne* 'rod with which to chastise, staff with which to support', *wurþe tō beranne* 'worthy to bear', *geornful tō gehīeranne* 'eager to hear', *hrædest tō secganne* 'to put it briefly';

86

(g) substantival: *dereð ... sumum monnum ... þæt sōð tō gehīerenne* 'to hear the truth hurts some people', *mē ys .. ālȳfad ... þæt yfel tō hatianne* 'I am allowed to hate evil', *nis nān earfoðnyss ... tō helpenne* 'it is no difficulty to help'. There is an important idiom with the copula and dative of the person which usually implies necessity: *nū is tīma ūs of slǣpe tō ārīsenne* 'now it is time for us to arise from sleep', *mǣl is mē tō fēran* 'it is time for me to go', *ūs is suīðe geornlīce tō gehīeranne* 'we must listen very attentively'.

For more advanced and detailed study of mood in OE, students are referred to F. Behre, *The Subjunctive in Old English Poetry* (Gothenburg 1934), H.-O. Wilde, 'Aufforderung, Wunsch und Möglichkeit', *Anglia* lxiii.209-391, lxiv.10-105, M. Callaway, *The Infinitive in Anglo-Saxon* (Washington 1913).

Word-Order

137. It is a truism that the word-order in OE is relatively free as compared with that in Mod.E. But it is easy to exaggerate this freedom and to overlook two important facts: first, that there are in OE considerable areas of conformity to describable patterns; secondly, that these patterns to a great extent coincide with present-day usage. In the paragraphs that follow, we shall be content to draw attention only to the most important and recurrent configurations, leaving to specialist grammars those that are relatively irregular, since these are less significant for the bulk of the OE literature and for the subsequent history of English alike.

Exceptions to the patterns here described are well attested, and we do not follow S. O. Andrew (for example, in *Syntax and Style in Old English*, Cambridge 1940) in holding the statistical norm to be of such overriding importance in OE structure as to empower us to emend these exceptions in order to make them conform to the more frequently recurring patterns.

138. Noun and Pronoun Modifiers

Nouns may be defined by demonstratives or adjectives or both. It is normal for both to precede the noun, the demonstrative coming first: *se* (or *þes*) *mann* 'the (*or* this) man', *gōd mann* '(a) good man', *se* (or *þes*) *gōda mann* 'the (*or* this) good man'. Adjectives used substantivally are preceded by a demonstrative: *sēo æðele* 'the noble (woman)'. Possessives behave like demonstratives: *his brōþur* 'his brother', *mīnne stronglican stōl* 'my sturdy throne'. Pronouns are frequently qualified by *eall* and *self* which they usually immediately precede: *wē ealle* 'we all', *þis eall* 'all this', *mē selfum* 'for me, myself'.

Outstanding exceptions to the rule *demonstrative—adjective —noun* are *eall* and adjectives in *-weard* which usually precede the demonstrative: *eall þēos mǣre gesceaft* 'all this (*or* this whole) glorious creation', *ealle þā hwīle* 'all the time', *on eallum þām gelimpum* 'in all these misfortunes', *on sūðeweardum þǣm lande* 'in the southerly (part of the) land', *of inneweardre his heortan* 'from his inward heart'. *Bēgen* as a noun modifier is placed similarly (*bēgen þā gebrōþru* 'both the brothers'), but numerals follow demonstratives (*þisum twām gebrōðrum* 'to these two brothers'). Thus normally disjoined from the *demonstrative—adjective—noun* sequence, *eall* and adjectives in *-weard* are also frequently found following the noun: *fram þǣm mūþan ūteweardum* 'from the outward (part of the) mouth', *Denum eallum* 'to all the Danes', *bēot eal* 'entire vow'. The adjective *genōg* is normally found in this position: *fēondas genōge* 'foes enough', *þǣr bið medo genōh* 'there is ample mead'.

When a noun is qualified by two adjectives, we may find one before it and one after (*swīðe micle meras fersce* 'very big fresh-water lakes'), or the two adjectives, linked by *and*, may follow the noun (*bill . . . brād and brūnecg* 'broad and bright-edged sword'); both adjectives may also precede the noun, especially when the first concerns quantity: *manege hālige stowa* 'many holy places'.

It is often difficult to decide whether *eal(l)* is adjectival or adverbial; cf *Beowulf* 1567 (and what is said below on the variable position of adverbs, § 142): *bil eal ðurhwōd* 'the whole sword (*or* the sword entirely) penetrated'.

139. It is by no means rare to find modifiers in general (especially adjectives, and especially in poetic usage) following their nouns: *freoðoburh fægere* 'fair stronghold', *wadu weallendu*

'surging waters', *niceras nigene* 'nine water-demons'. Even possessives and emphatic demonstratives can take this position: *ēþel þysne* 'this country', *wine mīn Unferð* 'my friend, U.', *gingran sīnre* 'to her handmaiden'. The simple demonstrative can also follow the noun when it is preceding an adjective: *mīne brōþro þā lēofan* 'my dear brothers (those dear brothers of mine)', *Ēadweard se langa* 'E. the tall'; but it is possible that such adjectives should be interpreted as substantival: 'my brothers, the dear ones', 'E., the tall one'.

Descriptive noun titles such as 'king' and 'abbot' usually follow the names they qualify: *Ælfred cyning* 'King Æ.', *Ælfmǣr abbod* 'Abbot Æ.', *Ēadric ealdormann* 'Governor E.', *Martiānus cāsere* 'M. Cæsar, Emperor M.', *Wǣrferð biscep* 'Bishop W.', *Godwine eorl* 'Earl G.'. With a determining modifier, however, such titles are often found preceding the name: *þone arcebiscop Ælfēah* 'the Archbishop Æ.'.

140. Genitive complements generally precede the words to which they are related: *hira land* 'their land', *þæs landes scēawunge* 'for a surveying of the land', *syxtig mīla brād* '60 miles across', *īglanda fela* 'many islands', *wedera cealdost* 'coldest of weather(s)', *sīþes wērig* 'travel-weary', *þrǣla hwylc* 'any serf' (§ 120*f*). It is normal for the genitive complement to keep this position even when its related noun is in a prepositional phrase: *of hwæles hȳde* 'from whale-skin', *mid Godes fultume* 'with God's help'. But when the noun is already determined by another qualifier, we find the genitive complement following its noun: *on ōðre healfe þæs mōres* 'on the other side of the moor', *sumne dǣl þæs mēoses* 'a part of the moss', *mid þan langan legere þæs dēadan mannes inne* 'with the dead man's lengthy lying-in-state'; yet there are exceptions to this: *se beorna brego* 'the prince of men'. The adjective *full* usually precedes its genitive complement: *full wrǣtta ond wīra* 'full of ornaments and metalwork'. A noun often precedes its complement when the latter is a personal name: *sunu Bēanstānes* 'B.'s son', *cwēn Hrōðgāres* 'H.'s queen'.

For some figures comparing OE and ME in this respect, see C. C. Fries, *Language* xvi.205. See also B. J. Timmer, *English Studies* xxi.49-72.

141. Prepositions

As their name should etymologically imply, prepositions in OE are generally placed in front of the items with which they are grammatically and notionally connected, and in front of any modifiers that may precede such items: *on huntoðe* 'in hunting', *on sumum stōwum* 'in some places', *on his āgnum lande* 'in his own country', *on Godes griðe* 'in God's peace'. But they are postpositive (and should perhaps be called 'postpositions') with the adverbs of place which frequently have pronominal function: *þærtō, þærintō, þæræt, hērinne, hērtōeācan* 'in addition to this'. With pronouns, the prepositions (especially those of more than one syllable) quite frequently follow: *þus cweðende him tō* 'saying thus to him', *him biforan* 'before him', *him betweoh* 'between them'; in verse, stressed postposition is not uncommon even with nouns: *Scedelandum in* 'in Scandinavia'. But postposition is most frequent, both in prose and verse, when it enables the preposition to stand before a verb form: *þā gatu him tō belocen hæfdon* 'they had closed the gates on themselves', *him cēnlīce wið feaht* 'fought stoutly against him', *him māra fultum tō cōm* 'more help came to him'; this is especially common in relative clauses in which the preposition, according to Mod.E. literary style, goes with the relative pronoun: *þe wē gefyrn ymbe spræcon* 'about which we spoke earlier', *þe hēo mid beweaxen wæs* 'with which it (the cross) was overgrown'. Less commonly, we find the preposition following even the verb, either closely or remotely: *Ōswold him cōm tō* 'O. came to him'; *him cōm micel eāca tō* 'a great reinforcement came to them'.

This usage is not to be confused with the adverbial and elliptical use of prepositions: *þā fōron hīe tō* 'then they went to (that place)'. Compound prepositions like *tōweard, betwēonum* sometimes have the governed item(s) between their component parts; thus, *tō scype weard* 'shipwards', *be sæm twēonum* 'between the seas'; compare 'to us-ward', Psalm xl.5 (A.V.).

142. Adverbs

The variety of position taken up by adverbs and adverb phrases in OE as in Mod.E. makes general descriptive statements very difficult. Ælfric writes within a few lines *sōna on slǣpe wearð gehǣled* 'was quickly healed in sleep' and *hī sendon þā sōna* 'they then immediately sent', in one case with his adverbs placed before the verb, in the other with them placed after it. The student will recognise that the free variation available to Ælfric in the position of adverbs is available today likewise, since the translations of these two examples could both be varied considerably. But the variety seems to some extent more chaotic than it actually is because of the unsatisfactory way in which we group under the term 'adverb' words which (for example, *very* and *quickly*) are functionally dissimilar and which occupy mutually exclusive environments. 'Adverbs' may be adjective-modifiers, verb-modifiers, or sentence-modifiers; they may relate to time, place, manner, degree, or simply negation. A full treatment of their positions would have to take these and other factors into account.

143. For the present purpose, however, it may suffice to say that adverbs in general precede the items (words, phrases, clauses) that they modify: *ne mihte* 'could not', *þǣr ārǣrde* 'raised there', *þǣr stōd* 'stood there', *hē wel cūþe Scyttisc* 'he knew Gaelic well', *se biscop þā fērde* 'the bishop then went', *and munuclīce leofode* 'and lived monastically', *swīðe ælmesgeorn* 'very charitable', *tō gelōme* 'too often', *gehwanon cumene* 'come from everywhere', *Ēac wē witan ful georne* 'Besides, we know quite certainly'.

The negative particle *ne* so regularly precedes the items which it modifies that it is frequently agglutinated with them; thus with parts of common verbs (*nis, nǣron, nabban, nolde,* etc.), *nāht* (*ne + ā + wiht*) 'not, by no means', *nǣnig* (*ne + ǣnig*) 'none', *nǣfre* (*ne + ǣfre*) 'never', *nā* (*ne + ā*) 'never, by no means'. In OE usage, multiple negation was perfectly normal, conjunctive *ne* preceding a clause, and *n(e)* preceding verbs, asseverative adverbs, and indefinite pronouns, within the clause: *ne ic ne herige ne ic ne tǣle* 'nor do I praise or blame', *ne þurfan gē nōht besorgian* 'you need not be at all anxious', *nis nǣnig swā snotor* 'there is no one so wise', *hyt nā ne fēoll* 'it by no means fell', *nis nō ðæt ān ... ac ēac ...* 'it is not only this . . . but also . . . ', *ne hit nǣfre ne gewurðe* 'nor may it ever happen'.

As already stated, a good deal of latitude existed in the placing of adverbs; adverbial phrases and adverbs of more than one syllable tended in particular to be placed in a relatively posterior position: *clypode mid geleāfan* 'called out with faith', *wē winnað rihtlīce* 'we struggle righteously', *Ælfred kyning hāteð grētan Wærferð . . . luflīce ond frēondlīce* 'King Æ. sends greetings to W., with love and friendship'.

The dative complement of instrumentality, which is adverbial, also normally precedes the item to which it is related: *mēcum wunde* 'wounded by the sword', *sweordum āswefede* 'slain by the sword'; cf also the dative complement with adjectives (*him eallum lāð* 'hateful to all of them') and to some extent the nominative complement with participles (*Ōswold gehāten* 'called O.').

144. Subject, Object (or Complement), and Verb (S, O/C, V)

All possible permutations of these elements are recorded in both prose and verse, and again it must be stressed that the observations to follow do not constitute an exhaustive description of the facts. There was considerable free variation in OE, and it would not be helpful—even if it were practicable—to tabulate all the factors that led to the selection of pattern in every recorded case.

The prose and to a lesser extent the late verse display a considerable tendency towards the order S V O/C in non-dependent clauses: *þæt Estland is swȳðe mycel* 'Estonia is very large', *and se cyning and þā rīcostan men drincað mȳran meolc* 'and the king and the mightiest men drink mare's milk', *hē lufode forhæfednysse* 'he loved temperance'. Where the verb comprises a finite part plus a participle or infinitive, the two are either close together (*se ādliga . . . wearð gehæled on ðære ylcan nihte* 'the sick man was healed that very night'), or the non-finite part comes at the end (*Hē wolde æfter ūhtsange oftost hine gebiddan* 'After Matins, he would usually pray').

The most frequent occasion for departing from this order is when certain adverbs (especially *ne* and *þā*) come first; the order is then V S O/C: *ne mihte hē gehealdan heardne mēce* 'he could not hold the grim sword', *þā sende se cyning . . . þām*

þearfum þone . . . disc 'then the king sent the dish to the poor';
þær also occurs with this order, especially when used expletively
and not with its full local meaning: *þær bið swȳðe mycel gewinn
betwēonan him* 'There is much strife between them'.

See R. Quirk, 'Expletive or Existential *there*', London *Mediæval
Studies* ii.32. It should be noted that *þā* and other elements, which are
followed by V S O/C when adverbial, do not take this order when conjunctive; in correlative sequences there is thus a sharp distinction
between the order in dependent and non-dependent clauses (see the
examples in § 150).

145. The order V S O/C is regular in questions (*Eart þū se
Bēowulf sē þe . . . ?* 'Are you the Beowulf who . . . ?'), in jussive
and volitional expressions (*Lære mon siððan furður on Læden-
geðīode* 'Let one then instruct further in Latin'), and in conditional clauses without subordinating conjunction (see § 158).
The verb similarly comes first in imperative expressions: *Forgif
nū, Drihten, ūrum mōdum* 'Grant now, oh Lord, to our hearts',
Swiga ðū 'Be silent'. In questions where O/C is an interrogative
pronoun or an interrogative plus noun, however, the order is
O/C V S: *Hwæt sægest þū?* 'What do you say?', *Hwilce fixas
gefēhst ðū?* 'What fishes do you catch?'

146. The common order S V O is also disrupted by *disjunction*, when first place is taken by an element which has special
significance or importance in the context: *Gēa, būtan nettum
huntian ic mæg* 'Certainly I can hunt without nets' (in reply
to the question *Ne canst þū huntian būton mid nettum?* 'Can
you not hunt except with nets?'). Compare also: *sume wīg
fornōm* 'some, war carried off' (in a series where individual
fates are being listed), *him sēo wēn gelēah* 'him expectation
deceived,' *nacode wē wæron ācennede, and nacode wē gewītað*
'naked we were born and naked we die'. Disjunction also
affects final position, especially in the separation of co-ordinate
objects or complements: *hīe wæron . . . gebrocede . . . mid cēapes
cwilde ond monna* 'they were afflicted with the death of cattle,
and of men', *of hwæles hȳde geworht, and of seoles* 'made of
whale's hide and of seal's', *hē hī fēdan sceolde and scrȳdan* 'he
was to feed them, and find them clothes'.

93

One of the minor arrangements that we might note appears in the last example. When O is a pronoun, it frequently precedes V: *þā burgware hīe geflīemdon* 'the townsfolk routed them'. Another recurrent feature is V in initial position, in some cases for special declarative effect (*Wæs hit þā on ælce wīsan hefig tȳma* 'It was then in every way a grievous time', *Gegrētte þā guma ōperne* 'Then the one man saluted the other'), in other cases apparently because individual writers were fond of this style (it is especially common, for instance, in the Ælfredian Bede and in some of the poetry). In the poetry as a whole there is great variety in the disposing of S, O, and V, and it is easier to speak of the word-order in any one poem than in OE poetry as such.

147. In dependent clauses generally, the dominant order is S O/C V. This is fairly regular in relative clauses (*þe æt his mǣges slege . . . fylste* 'who assisted in the killing of his kinsman'), in concessive clauses (*þēah hē him lēof wǣre* 'though he was dear to him'), and is frequent in temporal clauses (*ǣr hē bǣl cure* 'before he chose the funeral-fire', *ðā hē þone cyningc sōhte* 'when he visited the king'), in conditional clauses (*gif wē ðā stilnesse habbað* 'if we have peace'), in causal clauses (*for ðǣm hīe ðǣr sittan ne mehton* 'because they could not stay there'), and in noun clauses (*hē geseah þæt Apollonius swā sārlīce sæt ond ealle þingc behēold ond nān ðingc ne ǣt* 'he saw that A. was sitting sorrowfully thus and looking at everything and eating nothing'). But dependent clauses are also found in large numbers with the order S V O/C, and this seems especially common with causal clauses (*for þǣm hiora cyning wæs gewundod on þǣm gefeohte* 'because their king was wounded in the battle'), result clauses (*þæt hīe gedydon on ānre wēstre ceastre* 'so that they encamped in a deserted fort'), and noun clauses (*hē sǣde ðæt Norðmanna land wǣre swȳþe lang* 'he said that Norway was very long').

This subject can be pursued in more detail in S. O. Andrew, *Syntax and Style in Old English* (Cambridge 1940) and *Postscript on Beowulf* (Cambridge 1948), John Ries, *Die Wortstellung im Beowulf* (Halle 1907), H. Kuhn, 'Zur Wortstellung und -betonung im Altgermanischen',

P.B.B. lvii (1933), 1-109, and C. R. Barrett, *Studies in the Word-Order of Ælfric's Catholic Homilies and Lives of the Saints* (Cambridge 1953). See also C. C. Fries, 'On the Development of the Structural Use of Word-Order in Modern English', *Language* xvi.199-208.

148. Order of Clauses

Although the criteria distinguishing dependent from non-dependent clauses in OE have not yet been completely worked out, enough is known for us to be able to state that as a rule dependent clauses follow the dependent or non-dependent clauses to which they are related: *For þȳ ne sceall nān mann āwǣgan þæt he sylfwylles behǣt þām ælmihtigan Gode þonne hē ādlig bið, þē lǣs þe hē sylf losige, gif hē ālīhð Gode þæt* 'Thus no one must nullify what he promises Almighty God of his own free will when he is sick, lest he should perish, if he denies God this'. This is true of prose and verse alike: *gehwylc hiora his ferhþe trēowde, þæt hē hæfde mōd micel, þēah þe hē his māgum nǣre ār-fæst æt ecga gelācum* 'each of them trusted his heart, that he had great courage, even though he had not been merciful to his kinsfolk in sword-play'.

Certain types of dependent clause are found more readily in initial position than others, notably conditional clauses (*gyf þār man ān bān findeð unforbærned, hī hit sceolan miclum gebētan* 'if a single bone is found there incompletely burnt, they have to pay dearly for it') and indefinite relative clauses of various kinds (*swā hwider swā hē cōm, hē cȳdde þās wundra* 'wherever he came, he proclaimed these miracles'). But on the whole, initial position has to be supported by correlation (see § 150): *swā hwæt swā him becōm ... þæt hē hraðe dǣlde* 'whatever came his way, this he promptly shared'. Thus correlated, many types of clause appear initially: *Nū ic sceal geendian earmlicum dēaþe ... nū wolde ic gebētan* 'Now that I must perish in a wretched death, I would like to make amends', *þā hē þā þās andsware onfēng, ðā ongan hē sōna singan* 'When he got this answer, he at once began to sing'.

Clauses of most kinds are found also medially: *Hē hæfde þāgȳt, ðā hē þone cyningc sōhte, tamra dēora unbebohtra syx hund* 'He had still, when he visited the king, 600 tame deer unsold'.

Relationship

149. Co-ordination and Parataxis

In Mod.E. and other languages, notional relationships such as cause and condition can be given linguistic expression in a sequence of non-dependent constructions related by a simple conjunction ('co-ordination') or, without a conjunction, by a feature like intonation or some kind of juncture which is not usually symbolised in a written record ('parataxis'). So too, throughout OE, such expressions were very common: *hē þē æt sunde oferflāt, hæfde māre mægen* 'he beat you at swimming —(he) had greater strength' (cause), *hē his feorh generede and hē wæs oft gewundod* 'he saved his life but he was wounded many times' (concession). Sometimes the relationship is made more explicit by the presence of a relational adverb, as in another version of the latter example: *and þēah hē wæs oft gewundad* 'and yet . . .'.

150. Correlation and Hypotaxis

Subordinate or grammatically dependent ('hypotactic') constructions constitute a more complex means of expressing relationship, and in OE these frequently involved correlation, that is, the linking of members in a relationship by the presence in each member of corresponding demonstrative elements: 'God *so* loved the world, *that* he gave his only begotten Son'. There are many sets of correlative elements in OE; among the commonest are *þā* (. . . *þā*) . . . *þā, þonne* . . . *þonne, nū* . . . *nū, þæt* . . . *þæt, þȳ* . . . *þȳ, þæs* . . . *þæt, swā* . . . *swā*. For example, *þā hē þā þās andsware onfēng, ðā ongan hē sōna singan* 'when he received this answer, he (then) at once began to sing', *þonne hē geseah . . . þonne ārās hē* 'when he saw . . . he (then) arose', *nū ic sceall geendian . . . nū wolde ic gebētan* 'now that I have to die, I would like to make amends', *þā þæt Offan mæg . . . onfunde, þæt se eorl nolde yrhðo geþolian* 'when Offa's kinsman saw (this), that the earl would not tolerate cowardice', *ðæt hēr þȳ māra wīsdōm . . . wære ðȳ wē mā geðīoda cūðon* 'that there should be the more wisdom here the more languages we knew', *bǣdon þæs on mergen þæt hī mōston þone sanct ... underfōn* 'begged in the morning (for this,) that they might receive the saint', *hēo ne dorste ... him swā lēanian swā hē hire tō geearnud hæfde* 'she dared not reward him in such a way as he had deserved of her'. The correlatives are often juxtaposed, the one at the end of one member, the other at the beginning of the next; this is particularly common with relative clauses: *tō wyrcanne þæt þæt þū worhtest* 'to make that which you made'. Examples of some of the less common correlatives will appear in the paragraphs that follow.

In dealing with the phenomenon of correlation, we see the link between 'parataxis' and 'hypotaxis'; indeed, some of the correlative elements (for example, *oððe ... oððe, gē ... gē*) are to be regarded as co-ordinating conjunctions: *þā scipu ... oððe tōbrǣcon oþþe forbǣrndon oþþe tō Lundenbyrig brōhton* 'the ships they (either) broke up or burnt or brought to London', *gē wið fēond gē wið frēond* 'both against foe and against friend'. On the relation between parataxis and hypotaxis in OE, see further, G. Rübens, *Parataxe und Hypotaxe* (*Studien zur englischen Philologie*, vol. lvi, 1915), and A. H. Smith, *The Parker Chronicle (832-900)*, London 1935, p. 15.

151. Hypotactic expression is found extensively also without correlation, notably with the causal, conditional, and concessive relations, and especially where the dependent clause follows the related non-dependent clause: *hē hī him eft āgeaf, for þǣm þe hiora wæs ōþer his godsunu* 'he gave them back to him, because one of them was his godson', *wēne ic þæt hē mid gōde gyldan wille uncran eaferan, gif hē þæt eal gemon* 'I expect that he will requite our sons with good, if he remembers all this', *hī wǣron þæs Hǣlendes gewitan, ðēah ðe hī hine ðāgȳt ne cūðon* 'they were the Saviour's witnesses, though they did not yet know Him'.

152. Dependence without Finite Verb

Notional relationships were often expressed in OE by means of prepositional, participial, or other phrases; thus in the following example, *hē cōm ðā þurh Godes sande* ('he came then by reason of God's summons'), we have a phrase expressing a causal relation equivalent to 'he came then because God had

AN OLD ENGLISH GRAMMAR

summoned him'. Similarly, with present and past participles:
þæt man his hlāford ... of lande lifigendne drīfe 'that anyone
should drive his lord, living (i.e. while he lived), from the land',
gedrēfed on his mōde, hē gebæd hine '(as he was) troubled in his
mind, he prayed'. Often, in imitation of the Latin ablative
absolute, such expressions appear in the dative (§ 111): *ðā ...
fērde hē tō heofonum, him on lōcigendum* 'then he proceeded to
the heavens, while they looked on', *him andweardum* 'with them
present (i.e. in their presence)', *āstrehtum handum* 'with hands
outstretched'. Absolute expressions are most frequently temporal in function, but they often relate to manner; they are
also used causally, conditionally, and concessively.

153. Expression of Relationship

A given relationship thus found linguistic expression in
several different ways.

The descriptive function usually associated with the **relative**
clause could, for example, be expressed (*a*) by means of a participial expression: *fram Brytta cyninge, Ceadwalla gecīged* 'from
the king of the Britons, (who was) called C.'; (*b*) with an infinitive
expression: *stæf mid tō wreðianne* 'a staff with which to support'
(§ 136*f*); (*c*) with various relative pronoun constructions (often
involving correlation), the most important of which are illustrated in the following examples (see also § 120*a* and *b*): *for
Ōswoldes geearnungum þe hine æfre wurðode* 'for O.'s merits,
who constantly worshipped Him', *tō Westseaxena kyninge ...
sē wæs ðāgīt hæðen* 'to the king of the West Saxons who was
still heathen', *Eart þū se Bēowulf, sē þe wið Brecan wunne?* 'Are
you the Beowulf who competed with Breca?', *understande sē
ðe wille* '(let him) understand who will', *þæt lȳtle þæt hē erede*
'the little that he ploughed', *on þǣm æhtum þe heora spēda on
bēoð* 'in those possessions in which their wealth lies', *of ðǣm
mere, ðe Trūsō standeð in stæðe* 'from the lake on whose shore
T. stands', *nis nū cwicra nān, þe ic him mōdsefan mīnne durre
... āsecgan* 'there is now no one living to whom I dare speak
my heart', *ān mægð þæt hī magon* 'a tribe who can'; (*d*) with
no relative pronoun: *mid heora cyningum, Rædgota ond Eallerīca
wæron hātne* 'with their kings who were called R. and E.'.

98

154. Various **temporal** relations are expressed by means of dependent clauses introduced by common conjunctions (frequently correlated) such as *siððan* (*siððan Ēbrēas ... gegān hæfdon* 'after the Hebrews had gone'), *þā* or *þā* (. . .) *þā* (*ðā þā scipu gearwe wǣron* 'when the ships were ready'), *þonne* (*ðonne ðæt flǣsc bið geswenced* 'when the flesh is afflicted'), *þenden* (*þenden hē on ðysse worulde wunode* 'while he dwelt in this world'), *nū* (*nū wē hit habban ne mōton* 'now that we cannot possess it'), *ǣr þǣm þe* (*ǣr ðǣm ðe hit eall forhergod wǣre* 'before it was all completely ravaged'), *oð þæt* (*oþ þæt Crīst sylf cōme* 'until Christ Himself should come'); those relating to the future require subjunctive verbs for the most part (§ 133*g*), but in general the mood in temporal clauses is indicative. Frequently, time relations are indicated by means of temporal adverbs in non-dependent constructions: *þā, þonne, ǣr, nū, sōna, gȳt,* and many others; for example, *wæs Hæsten þā þǣr cumen* 'H. had then arrived there', *gȳt mē twēonað* 'I still doubt'. Time is also expressed by means of participial and absolute expressions (see above, § 152).

155. **Purpose** is generally expressed by a dependent clause containing a subjunctive verb; the clause is usually introduced by *þæt(te)* (*ūs gedafenað ðæt wē ... ondswarigen* 'it is fitting for us that we (should) answer'), less frequently by *tō þǣm* (. . .) *þæt* (*ic cōm ... tō þǣm þæt hē wǣre geswutelod* 'I came in order that he should be made manifest'); negative purpose clauses are introduced by *þȳ lǣs* (*þe*): *þē lǣs þe hē sylf losige* 'lest he himself perish'. Purpose can also be expressed with a co-ordinate construction familiar in Mod.E.: *uton faran ... and gesēon* 'let's go and see', *ic sende minne engel beforan ðē and drīfe ūt ... (mittam ... ut ēiciam)* 'I shall send my angel before thee to drive out ... '. The inflected infinitive is also common in this function: *hē ... cōm eorðan tō dēmenne* 'he came to judge the earth'. Finally, we should mention several 'purpose-equivalent' constructions, that is, constructions in which purpose is expressed simultaneously with other relationships, notably cause: *ēode ... aweg ... for ðan ðe hē ne mihte gesēon* 'he went away so that he might not see (*or* because he could not bear to see)'.

99

156. **Result** clauses are again usually introduced by *þæt(te)*, but the verb in these is indicative: *ðæt him tōbærst sēo heorte* 'so that his heart burst'; frequently, they are introduced by *swā* (...) *þæt(te)*, as in *swā þæt hē hrēas ... on eorðan* 'so that he fell to the ground'; the subjunctive is of course used when it is required in a particular context (see § 133*h*): *ic wille þæt hī hit hælden swā kynelīce ... þæt þǣr ne bē numen of nā geld* 'I want (this,) that they may possess it so royally that there be no payment taken from it'. Result-equivalent expressions include clauses of time and degree: *þā sǣton hīe ūt on ðām īglande ... oþ þone first þe hīe wurdon swīðe metelēase* 'then they stayed out on the island until (*or* so that) they became very short of food', *swā him mon māre selð swā hine mā lyst* 'the more he is given the more he wants'. The **modal** relation (manner, attendant circumstances, comparison) is best regarded as embracing the result relationship. In OE it is most often expressed by means of clauses introduced by *swā* (*swā*): *swā swā hī from þē hider cōmon, swā hī ēac tō þē hionan fundiað* 'just as they have come here from Thee, so they likewise hasten hence to Thee'; but we also find participial and absolute expressions: *hē ealle woruldcara āwearp fram his heortan, nānes þinges wilnigende* 'he cast away all thoughts of the world from his heart, desiring nothing', *ūpāhafenum handum langlīce bæd* 'with upraised hands (he) prayed long'.

157. **Causal** clauses contain indicative verbs and the common conjunction is *forðon* (*þe*), with its variants such as *forðǣm* (*þe/þæt*), *forðȳ* (*þe/þæt*): *for þām ðe nān mihtigra þē nis* 'because there is none mightier than Thou'; *forðon* (*-ðȳ*) is also a common connective or relational adverb in co-ordinate causal expressions: *ond hīe forðȳ ūt oðrēowon* 'and they therefore rowed away'. Various forms of correlation are found: *hē for þǣm nolde, þȳ hē mid his folce getruwade* 'for this reason he would not, (namely) that along with his force he was confident', *ic for þon ... ūt ēode ... for þon ic nōht cūðe* '(for this reason) I came out because I could in no way (*sc.* sing)'. Cause is frequently expressed paratactically or with simple co-ordination, particularly where the second member of the relationship contains a

verb of intending, saying, or thinking: *þā fērde hē tō Rōme, wolde his hǣle biddan* 'he then journeyed to Rome (because he) wanted to pray for his salvation', *se cyng mid his here fērde tōweard Hrōfeceastre, and wēndon þæt se biscop wǣre þǣrinne* 'the king with his force travelled towards Rochester because they thought that the bishop would be there'. Causal members may be phrases: prepositional phrases with *for* or *þurh* (*hē cōm ðā þurh Godes sande* 'he then came because of God's summons'), appositional phrases (*gedrēfed on his mōde, he gebæd hine* 'being troubled in his mind, he prayed'), and absolute phrases (*ðā gelamp onbryrdendum þām fēonde . . . þæt se cyning . . . wearð ofslægen* 'then, at the instigation of the devil, it came about that the king was slain'). In addition, we often find cause-equivalence in relative, temporal, modal, and conditional clauses: *þæt hē ēode in tō ānum his gefērena, sē wæs mid þā grimmestan untrumnesse hefegad* 'that he should go in to one of his companions who (*or* because he) was afflicted with a most serious illness', *hit is swutol þæt hēo wæs ungewemmed mǣden, þonne hire līchama ne mihte formolsnian* 'it is clear that she was an undefiled maiden, when (*or* since) her body could not decay', *þā wearð hē on slǣpe swā swā God wolde* 'then he fell asleep just as (i.e. because) God wished', *gif hē ðurhwunað on yfelnysse . . . þonne sceal hē . . . ðrōwian* 'if he persists in wickedness, then he must (*sc.* therefore) suffer'.

158. The usual **conditional** conjunctions are *gif, þǣr,* (and for negative conditions) *būtan, nefne* (*nemne*) and *nymðe*; on the mood in conditional clauses, see above, §§ 132*h*, 133*d*. For example: *gif īow swǣ ðyncð* 'if it seems so to you', *þǣr ic āhte mīnra handa geweald* 'if I had command of my hands', *būton hī him māran andlyfne sealdon* 'unless they gave him more food', *nymðe mec God scylde* 'unless God protects me'. In conditions with *gif*, there is often a correlative *þonne*: *gif ic eft gefare . . . þonne mæg ic . . .* 'if I later achieve . . . then I can . . .'. The inversion construction occurs but is not common: *āhte ic mīnra handa geweald* 'if I had command of my hands'; phrases, such as absolute expressions, are also rare conditionally. On the other hand, conditional-equivalent expressions are common;

the following relative clause translates a Latin formal condi-tion: *sē ðe biscephāde gewilnað, gōd weorc hē gewilnað* 'he who (*or* if anyone) desires the office of bishop, he desires good works'; similarly, in OE temporal constructions, we find *nū* sometimes corresponding to *sī* in a Latin original, and Ælfric has on one occasion *þonne ǣr* alternating with *gif* in parallel clauses. Modal clauses may be conditional (*swā swā hēo lēohtlīce gebylged wǣre* 'as (if) she were slightly angered'), and likewise noun clauses: *nȳttre . . . þæt ān cweornstān sȳ gecnytt ābūtan his swīran* 'better that a millstone be fastened about his neck' (corresponding to the Vulgate, *ūtilius . . . sī lapis molāris impōnātur circa collum eius*).

On *þǣr*, see H. Meroney, 'Old English *ðǣr* "if" ', *J. Engl. and Germ. Phil.* xli (1942), pp. 201-9.

159. Dependent **concessive** clauses (which have subjunc-tive verbs) are introduced by *þēah* (*þe*): *þēah ðe hit his rīce wǣre* 'although it was his kingdom'. In the related non-dependent clause we sometimes find such correlative items as (*swā*) *þēah, hwæðere, þēahhwæðere*, and we very often find these words indicating the concessive relation in co-ordinate expres-sions: *hē wæs Crīste swā þēah lēof* 'he was nevertheless dear to Christ', *hwæþre mē gyfeþe wearð* 'yet it was granted me'. While *hwæðere* as the sole concessive relational item is largely con-fined to poetic usage, co-ordinating *ac* in this function is largely confined to the prose, where it is extremely frequent: *hē wolde ofstingan Ēadwine cininge, ac hē ofstang Lillan his ðegn* 'he wanted to stab King Edwin, but he stabbed Lilla his thane'. Co-ordination with *and* may also express concession (*mūð habbað, and ne meldiað wiht* 'they have a mouth, yet do not speak at all'), and paratactic expression is also well attested: *hē fela findeð, fēa bēoð gecorene* 'he finds many but few are chosen', *ic eorþan eom ǣghwǣr brǣdre . . . folm mec mæg bifōn* 'I am everywhere broader than the earth, yet a hand can encompass me', where the Latin original has *et tamen*. There are many forms of indefinite concession, but perhaps the most character-istic is the 'challenge' form, with imperative or with jussive subjunctive (§ 133*a*): *hycge swā hē wille* 'let him think as he

will'; the alternative concession is often on the pattern V S V S, with the subjunctive (*wylle wē nelle wē* 'whether we will or no', *swelte ic lybbe ic* 'whether I live or die'), but it may take the form of contrastive pairs separated by *ne* or *oððe* (*feor oððe neāh* 'whether far or near'). Concessive prepositional phrases are not uncommon (*for eallum þissum* 'for all this'), but appositive and absolute participles are fairly rare in this function. Concessive-equivalent relative clauses are very frequent; the prose Boethius, for example, has *þe ðū . . . geōt . . . hafst* where the poetic version has *ðeāh ðū . . . gēta . . . hæbbe* 'which *or* though you yet have'. Concession is also commonly expressed in modal, temporal, causal, degree, and other clauses: *swā hit riht ne wæs* 'although it was not right', *ne swylteð hē . . . þonne syllan sceal innað* '(the bellows) does not die when (*or* even when *or* although) he has to surrender his entrails', *mōd sceal þē māre, þē ūre mægen lȳtlað* 'courage must be the greater as our strength lessens'.

For further reading on the OE expression of notional relationships, see G. W. Small, 'On the Study of Old English Syntax', PMLA li.1-7; M. Callaway, *The Absolute Participle in Anglo-Saxon*, Baltimore 1889, and 'The Appositive Participle in Anglo-Saxon', PMLA xvi.141-360; L. L. Schücking, *Die Grundzüge der Satzverknüpfung im Beowulf, Studien zur englischen Philologie* xv; A. Adams, *The Syntax of the Temporal Clause in Old English Prose*, New York 1907; H. G. Shearin, *The Expression of Purpose in Old English Prose*, New York 1903, and 'The Expression of Purpose in Old English Poetry', *Anglia* xxxii.235-52; A. R. Benham, 'The Clause of Result in Old English Prose', *Anglia* xxxi.197-255; F. J. Mather, *The Conditional Sentence in Anglo-Saxon*, Munich 1893; J. M. Burnham, *Concessive Constructions in Old English Prose*, New York 1911; R. Quirk, *The Concessive Relation in Old English Poetry*, New Haven 1954. For data on the causal relation, we are indebted to Miss Elizabeth Liggins, University of New England, who is writing a study of the subject. On possible nominative and accusative absolute participial constructions, see the recent monograph by Else von Schaubert, *Vorkommen, gebietsmässige Verbreitung und Herkunft altenglischer absoluter Partizipialkonstruktionen in Nominativ und Akkusativ* (Paderborn 1954).

IV

WORD-FORMATION

160. Just as our knowledge of syntax enables us to express ourselves by grouping words of our own selection into conventional arrangements without our needing to know that the particular words we choose have ever been in these particular arrangements before, so our knowledge of word-formation habits enables us to express ourselves by using words or word-elements in conventional arrangements without our needing to know whether such a compound has existed before or whether a word has been given such a function before. *Gas-turbine* is possible not only because we already had *gas-stove* and *steam-turbine*, but because we had the pattern in *motor-car*. Words like *evacuee*, *macadamize*, and *psychopathology* are possible through our knowledge of the function of the various affixes involved. We can use *coffee* and *contact* with both noun and verb inflexions because for centuries we have had words like *copy* and *count* used similarly as both nouns and verbs. This does not mean, on the other hand, that the total word-stock in use today consists of parts which we can still use in making new formations; we can recognise that *bishopric*, *knowledge*, and *wedlock* have suffixes without being able to use these suffixes in other environments.

In OE, where we can observe a set of word-formation patterns of a complexity similar to that obtaining in Mod.E., it is often impossible for us to distinguish processes that were active and flourishing during the OE period from those that had ceased to be formative before the Anglo-Saxons left the continent of Europe but whose products were still very much in use. Nor, for the purposes of learning OE, would there be much object in distinguishing them.

161. Formative Conversion

The nearest approach in OE to the functional change of

Mod.E. *we coffeed,* **a good buy** is to be seen in the regular correspondence between many nouns and verbs; for example:

(*a*)	bite 'bite'	:	bītan '(to) bite'
	gripe 'grip'	:	grīpan 'grip'
	hrine 'sense of touch'	:	hrīnan 'touch'
	slite 'tear'	:	slītan 'tear'
	cyme 'arrival'	:	cuman 'come'
	cyre 'choice'	:	cēosan 'choose'
	flyge 'flight'	:	flēogan 'fly'
	gyte 'flood'	:	gēotan 'pour'
	hryre 'fall'	:	hrēosan 'fall'
	lyre 'loss'	:	lēosan 'lose'
	scyte 'blow'	:	scēotan 'shoot'
(*b*)	dōm 'judgment'	:	dēman 'judge'
	bōt 'remedy'	:	bētan 'improve'
	blōd 'blood'	:	blēdan 'let blood'
	frōfor 'comfort'	:	frēfran 'comfort'
	gold 'gold'	:	gyldan 'gild'
	weorc 'deed'	:	wyrcan 'work'
	camb 'comb'	:	cemban 'comb'
	lār 'learning'	:	lǣran 'teach'
	lāst 'track'	:	lǣstan 'follow'
	scrūd 'clothing'	:	scrȳdan 'clothe'
(*c*)	cuma 'guest'	:	cuman 'come'
	flȳma 'fugitive'	:	flȳman 'rout'
	gefēra 'companion'	:	-fēran 'travel'
	gesaca 'opponent'	:	-sacan 'contend'
	wita 'wise man'	:	witan 'know'
(*d*)	andswaru 'answer'	:	andswarian 'answer'
	eard 'dwelling place'	:	eardian 'dwell'
	ende 'end'	:	endian 'end'
	lēan 'reward'	:	lēanian 'reward'
	lufu 'love'	:	lufian 'love'
	sorg 'sorrow'	:	sorgian 'sorrow'
	þing 'matter'	:	þingian 'beg, agree'
	wuldor 'glory'	:	wuldrian 'glorify'
	wundor 'wonder'	:	wundrian 'wonder at'

162. There are similar correspondences between many adjectives and verbs; for example:

(a)
beald 'bold'	:	byldan 'embolden'
ēaðmōd 'humble'	:	ēaðmēdan 'humble'
full 'full'	:	fyllan 'fill'
fūs 'eager'	:	fȳsan 'impel'
georn 'eager'	:	gyrnan 'yearn for'
hāl 'whole'	:	hǣlan 'heal'
scearp 'sharp'	:	scyrpan 'sharpen'
wōd 'mad'	:	wēdan 'rage'

(b)
beorht 'bright'	:	beorhtian 'shine'
fūl 'corrupt'	:	fūlian 'decay'
gōd 'good'	:	gōdian 'improve'
lȳtel 'little'	:	lȳtlian 'diminish'
open 'open'	:	openian 'open'
sweotol 'clear'	:	sweotolian 'reveal'
trum 'firm'	:	trumian 'grow strong'
yfel 'evil'	:	yflian 'inflict evil'

163. The type *cyre : cēosan* (§ 161*a*) is one of several in which noun and verb are related through *gradation* (see §§182f), in this case also with *i*-mutation (see §§ 208ff). The types *dōm : dēman* (§ 161*b*), *full : fyllan* (§ 162*a*), also with *i*-mutation, go back to a pre-OE process involving the use of a suffix *-ja-*. This suffix also produced a number of important causative verbs in which the stem is related to the pret. sg. form of vocalic verbs, with *i*-mutation; thus *rīsan* 'rise', pret. sg. *rās*, corresponds to *rǣran* 'cause to rise, raise' (for the *s : r* correspondence, see § 180); similarly, *licgan* 'lie' beside *lecgan* 'lay', *sittan* 'sit' beside *settan* 'set'. The types *ende : endian* (§ 161*d*), *fūl : fūlian* (§ 162*b*) are similarly the OE reflexes of a much earlier process of suffixing, in this case with *-ōja-*, but it seems likely that this correspondence continued to be productive in the OE period, since for many of the verbs in these sets (*lufian, andswarian, beorhtian,* for example) there are no cognates in other Gmc languages.

On this question, as well as on the wider issue of the relation between cognate parts of speech in OE, see the first chapter of D. W. Lee,

Functional Change in Early English (Menasha, Wis., 1948). Minor suffixes in OE verb-formation are *-sian* (as in *mǣrsian* 'proclaim'), *-ettan* (as in *lāðettan* 'loathe'), and *-lǣcan* (as in *geānlǣcan* 'unite'); see the alphabetical list in § 172.

164. In lists (*a*) and (*c*) of § 161 we see two patterns on which nouns were at one time formed from verbs. One of the most prolific ways of doing this was by the use of the suffix *-ung* (also found as *-ing*), yielding feminine abstract nouns, especially from consonantal verbs of Class II; thus *weorðung* 'honour', *þrōwung* 'suffering'. Agent-nouns were often formed from verbs by means of the suffix *-end* (as in *dēmend* 'one who judges', *hǣlend* 'one who heals, saviour') and *-ere* (as in *cwellere* 'killer', *leornere* 'learner').

Nouns were also formed from adjectives in several ways; the frequency of the suffix *-nes(s)* (*-nis*, *-nys*) is particularly noteworthy; for example, *beorhtnes* 'splendour', *hǣðennes* 'heathendom', *unrihtwīsnes* 'injustice'.

165. New adjectives were formed chiefly from existing nouns. The commonest suffixes were *-ig* (*blōdig* 'bloody', *cræftig* 'strong', *fāmig* 'foamy'), *-ful* (*geleāfful* 'pious', *sorgful* 'sad', *þoncful* 'thankful'), the corresponding negative suffix *-lēas* (*ārlēas* 'impious', *feohlēas* 'moneyless', *frēondlēas* 'friendless'), and *-lic* (*dēofollic* 'diabolical', *lēohtlic* 'bright', *þrýðlic* 'mighty').

166. Adverbs were formed chiefly from adjectives, with the endings *-e*, *-līce*, *-inga* (*-unga*); for example, *dēope* 'deeply', *fæste* 'firmly', *rihte* 'rightly', *wīde* 'widely'; *blindlīce* 'blindly', *sōðlīce* 'truly', *openlīce* 'openly', *frēondlīce* 'amicably'; *eallunga* 'entirely', *nīwinga* 'recently', *yrringa* 'angrily'.

It is not easy to distinguish the formations in *-e* and *-līce* because many adjectives had two forms, with and without *-lic*, and it is impossible to tell from which form the adverb in *-līce* comes; thus, for example:

sār, *adj.* 'grievous'	sārlic, *adj.* 'grievous'	sārlīce, *adv.* 'grievously'
wrāð 'furious'	wrāðlic 'furious'	wrāðlīce 'furiously'
gesǣlig 'happy'	gesǣliglic 'happy'	gesǣliglīce 'happily'
mōdig 'proud'	mōdiglic 'proud'	mōdiglīce 'proudly'

Other adverbial terminations are *-es* and *-a* (extensions of the use of the genitive mentioned in § 102), as in *ealles* 'entirely', *elles* 'otherwise', *hāmweardes* 'homewards', *ungemetes* 'exceedingly', *geāra* 'formerly', *sōna* 'at once', *tela* 'well', *þriwa* 'thrice'; *-um* (which, like *-e*, is an extension of the use of the dative and instrumental mentioned in § 112), as in *furðum* 'even', *hwilum* 'at times', *unwearnum* 'irresistibly'; *-an* (usually signifying 'from the place or direction indicated in the stem'), as in *ēastan* 'from the east', *feorran* 'from afar', *gystran* 'yesterday', *heonan* 'hence', *siððan* 'afterwards'. One might also mention the relatively infrequent adverbial use of adjectives in n.a.sg.neut., notably *eal* 'entirely', *ful* 'very'.

167. Modification

Just as in Mod.E. we can modify the noun *turbine* and create a new word by using the existing word *gas* as a prefix, so in OE new words, especially nouns and adjectives, were freely formed by modifying existing ones which might, where they existed as separate words, be various parts of speech.

(*a*) *Nouns.* With noun prefixes: *bōccræft* 'literature', *dēaðdæg* 'day of death', *folclagu* 'law of the people', *mannslyht* 'man-slaughter', *tūngerēfa* 'district officer'; in some cases, the prefixed noun is inflected: *Englalond* 'England', *hellewīte* 'torment of hell', *Sunnandæg* 'Sunday'.

With adjective prefixes: *eallwealda* 'the Almighty', *godspel* (*gōd*) 'gospel', *hēahburg* 'capital', *wīdsǣ* 'ocean'.

With adverb prefixes: *eftsīð* 'return', *inngang* 'entrance'.

(*b*) *Adjectives.* With noun prefixes: *beadurōf* 'bold in battle' *dōmgeorn* 'eager for glory', *fyrdhwæt* 'bold in arms'.

With adjective prefixes: *glēawhȳdig* 'wise-minded', *efeneald* 'of equal age', *scīrmǣled* 'brightly adorned'.

With adverb prefixes: *felamōdig* 'very brave', *ǣrwacol* 'early awake', *welwillende* 'benevolent'.

In addition, there are many compound adjectives on the pattern commonly known by the Sanskrit term *bahuvrīhi*, in which the second element is a noun; among the best known of these are *brūnecg* 'bright-edged', *glædmōd* 'glad-hearted', *mild-heort* 'gentle', *stercedferhð* 'stout-hearted', *yrremōd* 'angry'.

168. A considerably more widespread method of modification was the use of a large number of recurrent prefixes, many of which did not occur in the language as separate words (compare *un-* in Mod.E.). Prefixed to verbs, the commonest

single effect of these elements was to cause a shift in *aspect*, particularly from durative to perfective (see § 129), just as in Mod.E. many verbs undergo a similar shift in becoming phrasal verbs (for example, *eat up*, beside *eat*). Thus scores of common verbs are made perfective by the prefix *ā-* (for example, *āheawan* 'cut off', *āfȳsan* 'drive away', *āsendan* 'dispatch') and hundreds more by *ge-*: for example, *fēran* 'go' but *gefēran* 'reach', *frignan* 'ask' but *gefrignan* 'learn', *hlēāpan* 'leap' but *gehlēāpan* 'mount', *winnan* 'fight' but *gewinnan* 'win'. It will be seen also that *ge-* often makes intransitive verbs transitive. An example of a common noun-modifier is *and-*, which has the force of 'opposite' or 'corresponding to' (compare Go. *and*, Greek *anti*); for example, *andefn* 'proportion', *andlēan* 'reward', *andsaca* 'adversary', *andswaru* 'answer'. With adjectives and adverbs, an extremely common prefix is *un-*, by which the antithesis of the stem-meaning is indicated: for example, *unforht* 'unafraid', *unlȳtel* 'much', *unrihte* 'wrongly'; see further, § 170, *un-*.

169. Recurrent Affixes

The processes of conversion and modification already discussed may be studied in more detail in the following lists of suffixes and prefixes that recur in the most frequently read texts. For the convenience of the learner, the lists are graded; those containing the affixes of highest frequency (§§ 170, 171) should be learnt in turn and studied carefully, the other used at first rather for reference purposes.

170. *Very high frequency*:

ā-: used to modify verbs; in many cases it changes the aspect from durative to perfective, in many it is a mere intensifier, and in many others it appears to have no semantic function. Examples: *āfȳsan* 'drive away', *āheāwan* 'cut off', *āhebban* 'lift up', *ālecgan* 'lay down', *āsendan* 'dispatch', *ābysgian* 'occupy', *ārǣran* 'exalt'; *ābīdan* 'wait', *āriman* 'count'. The prefix appears also with nouns and adjectives derived from verbs; for example: *ācennednes* 'birth', *ārǣd* 'resolved'.

an-: see on-.

be-, bī- : used primarily (as *be-*) to modify verbs, often adding the sense 'round, over', often with only intensifying or perfective effect; examples: *bebūgan* 'surround', *beclȳsan* 'confine', *begēotan* 'pour over'; *belūcan* 'lock up', *bescūfan* 'hurl', *bestrȳpan* 'despoil'. With many verbs, *be-* has the effect of making the intransitive transitive: *bestȳman* 'make wet', *bewēpan* 'bewail'; with others again, it has privative force: *bedǣlan* 'deprive', *beniman* 'take away'. With many nouns we have the special stressed form *bī-* (*big-*), with others the same form as with verbs: *bigleofa* 'sustenance', *bismer* 'insult', *bīword* 'proverb', *bebod* 'command', *behāt* 'promise', *begang* 'region'. The prefix *be-* appears also with some common adverbs and prepositions: *beforan* 'before', *beheonan* 'on this side of', *behindan* 'behind', *beneoðan* 'beneath', *betwēonum* 'between'.

for- : used chiefly with verbs, the action of which it usually intensifies (especially in a destructive sense), often with a shift to perfective aspect: *forbærnan* 'burn up', *fordōn* 'destroy', *forhogian* 'despise', *forlǣdan* 'lead to destruction', *forniman* 'carry off, destroy', *forscyppan* 'transform', *forweorðan* 'perish'. It appears also with some nouns derived from verbs: *forhergung* 'devastation', *forlorennes* 'perdition', *forsewennes* 'contempt'. With adjectives and adverbs it is equivalent to the modification 'very': *forheard* 'very hard', *formanig* 'very many', *foroft* 'very often'.

ge- : commonest with verbs, but used also with many nouns and to a lesser extent with other parts of speech. With verbs, it is used chiefly to denote perfective aspect (see § 168) and this association with 'result' is seen above all in its use as a past participle inflexion; further examples: *geāscian* 'discover', *gesceran* 'cut through', *gesittan* 'inhabit'; as was pointed out in § 168, some of these examples show a shift also from intransitive to transitive, and this is further illustrated in *gerīdan* which is used in the sense 'ride round (somewhere)' or 'ride up to (some point)' as well as 'occupy'. With some verbs, *ge-* gives a special sense (as with *gestandan* 'endure, last'), but with others it is not possible to detect the special significance of the prefix: for example, *gehātan* 'call, promise', *gehealdan* 'hold, keep' *gesecgan* 'say, tell'. The nouns involved are mainly derived from verbs, and the *ge-* indicates either completeness of the verbal action or collectiveness; for example, *gesceaft* 'that which has been created, creation', *gelimp* 'that which has happened, event, calamity', *gestrēon* 'wealth, property', *gepring* 'crowd'. With many nouns and adjectives, and with several adverbs and pronouns, *ge-* introduces the idea of assembly or association: *gebrōðorscipe* 'fraternity', *gefēra* 'comrade', *genēat* 'colleague'; *gelīc* 'similar', *gemǣne* 'common', *gesib* 'akin'; *gehwanon* 'from all quarters', *gehwǣr* 'everywhere'; *gehwā* 'each', *gehwilc* 'each' (compare the grouping function in *ge . . . ge* 'both . . . and'). With other nouns, adjectives, and adverbs, no special function can be discerned, and it is likely that in many cases the *ge-* has been carried over from related verbs; for example, *gereord* 'voice', *gepyldig* 'patient', *gepungenlīce* 'virtuously'.

-ig : used in the formation of adjectives, mainly from nouns; examples: *ādlig* 'sick', *blōdig* 'bloody', *crǣftig* 'strong', *cystig* 'excellent', *dyrstig* 'daring', *grǣdig* 'greedy', *scyldig* 'guilty', *spēdig* 'rich', *wlitig* 'beautiful'; *-ig* goes back to two earlier suffixes, *-īg-* and *-ag-*, the one causing *i*-mutation (§§ 208ff), the other not.

-lic : used in the formation of adjectives, usually from nouns or existing adjectives; examples: *cynelic* 'royal', *dēofollic* 'diabolical', *earmlic* 'wretched', *geōmorlic* 'sad', *hyhtlic* 'pleasant', *munuclic* 'monastic', *sellic* 'rare', *torhtlic* 'glorious', *prȳðlic* 'strong', *ungelȳfedlic* 'incredible', *woruldlic* 'worldly'.

-nes(s), -nis, -nys : used in the formation, especially from adjectives, of feminine abstract nouns; examples: *ǣfæstnes* 'piety', *ānrǣdnes* 'firmness', *beorhtnes* 'brightness', *dȳgolnes* 'secrecy', *ēcnes* 'eternity', *gehȳrnes* 'hearing', *gewemmednes* 'defilement', *onbryrdnes* 'inspiration', *sārnes* 'pain', *prīnes* 'trinity', *unrihtwīsnes* 'injustice'.

on- (with nouns, also **an-**): used with several parts of speech. With verbs, it often indicates the inception of an action; for example, *onbærnan* 'incite', *onbryrdan* 'inspire', *ongytan* 'perceive', *onhǣtan* 'inflame', *onlȳhtan* 'enlighten', *onspringan* 'spring forth', *onwæcnan* 'awake'; with other verbs (where *on-* is the unstressed form of *un-*), it indicates the antithesis of the action of the stem: *onbindan* 'unbind', *ongyrwan* 'undress', *onlūcan* 'open', *onsǣlan* 'untie', *onwrēon* 'reveal'. In nouns (usually derived from verbs), where *on-* or *an-* is an unstressed form of *and-*, the prefix often clearly indicates 'against, in reply to': *onlīcnes* 'appearance', *onrǣs* 'attack', *onscuning* 'detestation', *onscyte* 'calumny'; so also with other parts of speech: *onemn* 'alongside', *ongean* 'against, opposite', *onsǣge* 'impending, attacking'.

un- : used mainly with adjectives and adverbs, but also with nouns and a few verbs. For the most part it is used to indicate the antithesis of the stem-meaning: *unforht* 'dauntless', *ungearu* 'unprepared', *ungelīc* 'dissimilar', *unlȳtel* 'large', *unēaðe* 'with difficulty', *unrihte* 'unjustly', *untela* 'amiss', *unfrið* 'hostility', *unsnotornes* 'folly'; it is rare with verbs (see *on-*, above): *unscrȳdan* 'undress', *untrumian* 'weaken'. In some cases the form with *un-* is not simply the antithesis of the unprefixed form; compare *unorne* 'simple, humble' with *or(e)ne* 'excessive'. With a fair number of nouns, *un-* is pejorative in force; for example, *uncræft* 'malpractice', *unlagu* 'injustice', *unþēaw* 'evil habit', *unweder* 'bad weather'; in a few cases, it merely intensifies; thus, *uncoðu* 'disease', and possibly also *unforht* 'very afraid' (*Dream of the Rood* 117) and *unhār* 'very grey' (*Beowulf* 357, MS).

-ung, often -ing : used to form feminine abstract nouns, especially from consonantal verbs of Cl. II; examples: *bodung* 'preaching', *earnung* 'merit', *hēofung* 'lamentation', *þrōwung* 'suffering', *weorðung* 'honour', *wilnung* 'desire'; *hrǣding* 'hurry', *onscuning* 'detestation', *rǣding* 'lesson', *-ing* being especially associated with formations from consonantal verbs of Cl. I.

171. *High frequency:*

and- (ond-) : used with nouns, with verbs which are usually derived from nouns, and in a few cases with other parts of speech; the prefix often retains its original sense of 'against, opposite, towards', and corresponds to *on-* in many verbs

(§ 170). Examples: *andefn* 'proportion', *andgyt* 'sense', *and-lēan* 'reward', *andsaca* 'adversary', *andswaru* 'answer', *ond-slyht* 'onslaught', *andettan* 'confess', *andswarian* 'answer', *ondhweorfan* 'turn against'; *andweard* 'present', *andgytfullīce* 'intelligibly', *andlang* 'along'.

-dōm: forms abstract nouns from other nouns and from adjectives; examples: *crīstendōm* 'Christianity', *ealddōm* 'age', *hlāforddōm* 'lordship', *lǣcedōm* 'medicine', *martyrdōm* 'martyrdom', *swicdōm* 'treachery', *þēowdōm* 'slavery', *wīsdōm* 'wisdom'.

-end: forms masculine agent nouns (compare present participles in *-ende*) from verbs; examples: *dēmend* 'judge', *eardiend* 'dweller', *hǣlend* 'saviour', *healdend* 'chief', *nergend* 'saviour', *rǣdend* 'ruler', *scyppend* 'creator', *wrecend* 'avenger'. A few such forms in *-end* (notably *āgend* 'owner', *berend* 'bearer', *būend* 'dweller', *hæbbend* 'owner', *wīgend* 'fighter') appear over and over again as the second elements in poetic compounds; for example, *folc-*, *foldāgend* 'ruler of people, of land', *gār-*, *helmberend* 'spear-, helmbearer (=warrior)', *eorð-*, *fold-*, *woruldbūend* 'earth-, land-, world-dweller'.

-ful(l): used to form adjectives, especially from abstract nouns; for example, *andgytfull* 'sensible', *bealofull* 'evil', *egesfull* 'terrible', *hyhtfull* 'joyful', *synnfull* 'sinful', *weorðfull* 'illustrious', *wuldorfull* 'glorious'; in some cases, the suffix is added to existing adjectives: *geornfull* 'eager', *gesundfull* 'unimpaired'.

in-: used with various parts of speech but in two usually distinct ways. It can have the directional force of 'in', and in this function appears also as *inn-*; for example, *ingān* 'enter', *ingenga* 'invader', *ingesteald* 'household goods', *ingeponc* 'cogitation', *innweard* 'inward'. It also acts as an intensifier (*indryhten* 'distinguished', *infrōd* 'very wise'), and sometimes, like *on-* (§ 170), indicates the inception of an action (*indrencan* 'intoxicate', *inlȳhtan* 'enlighten'), in which function it may be an Angl. characteristic.

-lēas: forms adjectives from nouns, with the sense of 'bereft of'; examples: *ārlēas* 'impious', *cwidelēas* 'speechless', *dōmlēas* 'inglorious', *drēamlēas* 'joyless', *feohlēas* 'destitute', *gȳmelēas* 'careless', *griðlēas* 'unprotected', *reccelēas* 'careless', *sāwollēas* 'lifeless', *winelēas* 'friendless', *wynnlēas* 'joyless'.

of- : used primarily with verbs, to which it usually gives perfective aspect; examples: *offaran* 'overtake', *offerian* 'carry off', *ofgyfan* 'give up', *oflǣtan* 'give up', *ofsendan* 'send for', *ofscēotan* 'shoot down', *ofsēon* 'see, understand', *oftorfian* 'stone to death'.

ofer- : commonest with verbs, where it often has straightforward adverbial sense; with nouns it indicates superiority in degree or quality; examples: *ofercuman* 'overcome', *oferhelmian* 'overhang', *oferhycgan* 'despise', *oferswīðan* 'overpower', *oferwrēon* 'cover'; *oferēaca* 'surplus', *oferfæreld* 'passage', *ofermægen* 'superior force'.

-scipe : forms masculine abstract nouns from other nouns and to a considerable extent also from adjectives; examples: *dryhtscipe* 'valour', *eorlscipe* 'courage', *gālscipe* 'pride', *gebēorscipe* 'convivial gathering', *gefērscipe* 'fellowship', *hǣðenscipe* 'heathenism', *þegenscipe* 'service', *unwærscipe* 'carelessness'.

tō- : with several parts of speech, it implies motion towards, addition to, or presence at; examples: *tōnēalǣcan* 'approach', *tōcyme* 'arrival', *tōweard* 'towards', *tōēacan* 'in addition to', *tōemnes* 'besides', *tōmiddes* 'in the midst of', *tōdæg* 'today'. With many verbs, especially verbs of force, it gives perfective aspect: *tōbrecan* 'break up', *tōdǣlan* 'scatter', *tōhlīdan* 'split open', *tōlūcan* 'wrench apart', *tōstregdan* 'scatter', *tōweorpan* 'destroy'.

172. *Other common affixes:*

ā-, ō- : gives generalised meaning to pronouns and adverbs (see also *ǣg-*): *āhwæðer* 'either (of two)', *āhwǣr* (*ōhwǣr*) 'anywhere', *āhwanon* 'from everywhere'.

ǣ- : gives sense of 'without': *ǣgilde* 'without payment', *ǣmynde* 'forgetfulness'.

æf- : used with nouns and corresponds to *of-* (§ 171): *æfþonca* 'grudge', *æfwyrdla* 'damage'.

æfter- : as in *æfterfylgan* 'pursue', *æftergenga* 'successor'.

ǣg- : like *ā-*, gives generalised meaning to pronouns and adverbs: *ǣghwā* 'everyone', *ǣghwǣr* 'everywhere', *ǣghwider* 'in all directions'.

-að : see *-oð*.

-bǣre : forms adjectives signifying 'productive of' the stem-meaning: *lustbǣre* 'agreeable', *wæstmbǣre* 'fertile'.

-bora : forms masculine agent nouns from other nouns: *mundbora* 'protector', *rǣdbora* 'councillor'.

-cund : forms adjectives signifying 'of the nature of' the stem-meaning: *dēofolcund* 'diabolical', *godcund* 'sacred, divine'.

ed- : modifies various parts of speech, adding the sense 'again, back'; examples: *edhwyrft* 'return, change', *edlēan* 'requital', *edwenden* 'reversal', *edwīt* 'reproach'; *edstaðelian* 're-establish'; *ednīwe* 'renewed'.

-ed : forms adjectives (compare *-ed* as past pple inflexion of consonantal verbs), usually from nouns; examples: *fǣted* 'plated', *hilted* 'hilted', *hringed* 'made of rings', *micelhēafded* 'big-headed'. In a number of words, *-ed* appears to signify 'deprived of', as in *copped* 'with the top off'.

el- : signifies 'foreign, from elsewhere' (cf. Lat. *alius*, OE *elra* 'other', *elles* 'otherwise'); examples: *elland* 'foreign country', *elþēodig* 'foreign'.

-el, -ol (-ul) : these noun-forming suffixes appear with some common heterogeneous nouns, mostly masc., some fem.; examples: *bydel* 'messenger', *gyrdel* 'belt', *þyrel* 'hole', *stapol* 'pillar', *staðol* 'foundation', *swaðul* 'flame'.

-els : forms masculine concrete nouns: *byrgels* 'tomb', *fǣtels* 'vessel', *rēcels* 'incense'.

-en : (1) adjective suffix (as distinct from the *-en* of vocalic past pples used adjectivally, as *geþungen* 'excellent'): *ǣttren* 'poisonous', *gylden* 'golden', *þællen* 'purple', *silfren* '(made) of silver', *stǣnen* 'of stone';

(2) various noun suffixes which by the OE period had fallen together as *-en(n)*; it is difficult to distinguish the functions of the suffix, and all genders of noun occur with it. Examples: *dryhten* 'lord', *pēoden* 'prince'; *menen* 'handmaid', *nȳten* 'animal', *scypen* 'cow-shed', *byrgen* 'burial-place', *land-*

hæfen 'tenure of land', *ræden* 'condition', *þinen* 'woman-servant'.

-ere: forms masculine agent nouns, especially from other nouns (compare *sangere* 'singer' from *sang* 'song', where in Mod.E. the agent noun is formed from the verb); examples: *bōcere* 'scholar', *cwellere* 'killer', *fuglere* 'fowler', *godspellere* 'evangelist', *rӯpere* 'plunderer', *wyrdwrītere* 'historian'.

-erne: adjectival, used with the points of the compass; for example, *sūðerne* 'southern'.

-estre: used in forming agent nouns, originally feminine and then also masculine; for example, *miltestre* 'harlot'.

-et(t): forming neuter abstract, and later concrete, nouns: *bærnett* 'burning', *rӯmet* 'space'.

-ettan: used to form intensive or frequentative verbs: *lāðettan* 'loathe', *ōnettan* 'hasten'.

-fæst: used in forming adjectives from nouns and from other adjectives; examples: *ǣrendfæst* 'bound on an errand', *blǣdfæst* 'glorious', *sōðfæst* 'righteous', *wynnfæst* 'pleasant'; *wīsfæst* 'wise'.

-feald: used to form adjectives, especially from numerals: *ānfeald* 'single, simple', *þrifeald* 'threefold'; *manigfeald* 'various'.

fore-: used to modify various parts of speech with the sense of 'precedence' or 'pre-eminence'; examples: *foregān* 'precede', *foresecgan* 'mention before'; *foregenga* 'attendant', *foresprǣc* 'preamble', *foreþanc* 'forethought'; *foremǣre* 'very famous', *foresnotor* 'very wise'.

forð-: modifies various parts of speech, but especially verbs and forms derived from verbs, with the sense of 'motion towards': *forðbringan* 'bring forth', *forðfaran* 'pass onwards, die', *forðgeorn* 'eager to advance'.

ful-: modifies various parts of speech with the sense of 'completeness': *fulgān* 'accomplish', *fullǣstan* 'help', *fulwyrcan* 'complete'; *fultum* 'help', *fulwīte* 'full penalty'; *fulfremed* 'perfect'; *fulneāh* 'almost'.

-hād: forms masculine abstract nouns: *geogoðhād* 'time of youth', *mægðhād* 'virginity', *woruldhād* 'secular life'.

-iht: used in a few cases to form adjectives from nouns; thus, *finiht* 'having fins', *þorniht* 'thorny', *-hōcyht- (Beowulf* 1438) 'hooked'.

-ing : (1) forming masculine concrete nouns from adjectives and from other nouns, often with the sense of 'proceeding or derived from (the stem)' or 'associated with (the stem)'; biblical forms like *Lēving* 'son of Levi', *Nathaning* 'son of Nathan' show that the formation was still productive in the OE period. Examples: *æðeling* 'prince', *brenting* 'ship', *cyning* 'king', *earming* 'wretch', *hōring* 'adulterer', *pen(n)ing* 'penny', *wīcing* 'pirate'. See also *-ling*;

(2) forming feminine nouns: see *-ung*, § 170.

-isc : forming adjectives from nouns, including the names of persons and peoples; some of the forms in *-isc* are also used substantivally. Examples: *folcisc* 'secular', *mennisc* 'human' (or 'humanity'), *Ebrēisc* 'Hebrew', *Englisc* 'English' (as noun, means 'the English language').

-lāc : used to form neuter abstract nouns: *rēaflāc* 'robbery', *wrōhtlāc* 'calumny'.

-lǣcan : used to form verbs, usually from adjectives and nouns: *geānlǣcan* 'unite', *nēalǣcan* 'approach'.

-ling: used to form masculine concrete nouns, usually diminutives: *dēorling* 'favourite', *sibbling* 'relative', *yrðling* 'farmer'. See also *-ing*.

mis- : modifies various parts of speech with the sense of 'amiss, wrongly': *misdǣd* 'misdeed'; *miswende* 'erring'; *misbēodan* 'ill-treat', *misfōn* 'fail to get', *mislimpan* 'go wrong'.

ō- : see *ā-*.

-ol : (1) see *-el*;

(2) used to form adjectives, especially from verbs; examples: *hetol* 'hostile', *swicol* 'deceitful', *þancol* 'thoughtful'.

or- : makes nouns adjectival with sense of 'lacking, without (the stem)'; intensifies existing adjectives. Examples: *orleahtre* 'blameless', *ormōd* 'despairing', *orsāwle* 'lifeless', *orsorg* 'free from care'; *oreald* 'very old', *ormǣte* 'intense'.

oð- : modifies verbs, some with the sense of 'at, close to' (thus *oðstandan* 'stand still'), more often with the sense of 'away': *oðberan* 'carry off', *oðfeallan* 'decline', *oðrōwan* 'row away', *oðwindan* 'escape'.

-oð, -að : forms masculine nouns, many of them abstract: *drohtoð* 'way of life', *faroð* 'sea', *fiscað* 'fishing', *hergað* 'plundering', *langað* 'longing', *waroð* 'shore'.

-ræden : forming feminine abstract nouns: *mannræden* 'allegiance'.

sām- : modifies adjectives with the sense of 'half'; for example, *sāmworht* 'half-built'.

-sian : used to form verbs, usually from adjectives and nouns; for example, *mǣrsian* 'proclaim', *yrsian* 'be angry'.

sin- : modifies various parts of speech with the sense of 'extensive, lasting': *syndolh* 'serious wound', *sinfrēā* 'permanent lord', *sinniht* 'perpetual night', *singāl* 'continual'.

-sum : forms adjectives, especially from nouns: *langsum* 'enduring', *wynnsum* 'delightful'.

-ð(o), -ð(u) : forms feminine abstract nouns, especially from adjectives; examples: *fǣhð(o)* 'hostility', *getrēowð* 'fidelity', *hȳhðu* 'height', *mǣrðu* 'glory', *myrgð* 'mirth', *yrgðu* 'cowardice', *yrmð(u)* 'misery'.

þurh- : modifies various parts of speech, especially verbs, with the sense of 'through, completely': *þurhbrecan* 'break through', *þurhdrīfan* 'pierce', *þurhetan* 'consume', *þurhtēon* 'accomplish', *þurhwunian* 'persist'; *þurhwacol* 'sleepless'.

under- : modifies various forms, especially verbs, with the actual or figurative sense of 'underlying': *underfōn* 'receive', *undergytan* 'understand', *understandan* 'perceive', *underþēodan* 'subjugate'.

up- : modifies various forms with the sense of 'up, away': *uplang* 'upright'; *upgang* 'landing', *upāstīgnes* 'ascension'; *upāspringan* 'spring up'.

ūt- : modifies various forms with the sense of 'out, away': *ūtfūs* 'eager to set out', *ūtlag* 'outlaw' (adopted from ON), *ūtgān* 'go out'.

wan-, won- : privative or negative prefix, used especially with nouns and adjectives: *wonhȳd* 'recklessness', *wansceaft* 'misery', *wanhāl* 'sick', *wanspēdig* 'poor'.

-weard : forms adjectives with the sense of 'in the direction indicated (by the stem)': *ēasteweard* 'eastward', *hāmweard* 'homeward', *ufeweard* 'further up, upper'.

-wende : used to form adjectives from existing adjectives and from nouns: *hālwende* 'healthy', *hwīlwende* 'transitory', *lēofwende* 'amiable'.

wið- : used to modify various parts of speech with the sense of 'away, against': *wiðbregdan* 'snatch away', *wiðfōn* 'lay hold on', *wiðhabban* 'resist', *wiðsacan* 'oppose, deny'; *wiðinnan* 'within', *wiðsūðan* 'to the south of'; *wiðlǣdnes* 'abduction'.

wiðer- : modifies various parts of speech with the sense of 'opposing, counter'; examples: *wiðerlēan* 'requital', *wiðersaca* 'adversary', *wiðertrod* 'retreat'; *wiðerrǣhtes* 'opposite'.

ymb(e)- : modifies various forms with the sense of 'around': *ymbgang* 'circuit', *ymbesprǣc* 'comment'; *ymbbeorgan* 'shield, protect', *ymbhycgan* 'consider', *ymbsittan* 'besiege'; *ymbūtan* 'around'.

For further and more detailed study, see H. Paul, 'Wortbildungslehre' in *Deutsche Grammatik* (Halle 1920); F. Kluge, *Nominale Stammbildungslehre der Altgermanischen Dialekte* (3rd ed.: Halle 1926); F. Holthausen, *Altenglisches Etymologisches Wörterbuch* (Heidelberg 1934); M. L. Samuels, 'The ge-Prefix in the OE Gloss to the Lindisfarne Gospels', *Trans. Phil. Soc.* 1949; on -ing and other noun suffixes, see above all A. H. Smith, *English Place-Name Elements* (Cambridge 1956).

V

PHONOLOGY

Preliminary Notes

173. The attempt to describe the sounds or 'phones' of a language and to classify and arrange them in their more common patterns is termed *phonology*. But whereas the phonology of a living language can be determined with exactness and verified, the phonology of a language such as OE, which is inferred from written remains and the later history of the language, can be treated only approximately and no verification is possible through the ear or with the help of scientific equipment.

174. There are many different sounds in a language, but it is convenient to distinguish two ways in which sounds differ from each other. In the first place, speakers may recognise sounds as differing and use the contrast to distinguish different words; for example, the Mod.E. [t] and [k] in *till* and *kill*, or the [p] and [b] in *cap* and *cab*, or the [ɔ] and [ʌ] in *hot* and *hut*. Sounds so differing we call *significantly* differing sounds; they are said to be in *contrastive distribution* and are called *phonemes*. But there are other differences between the sounds of a language which are not usually noticed by the speakers of that language; careful observation will show a speaker of Mod.E. that he has, for instance, four distinct *k*-sounds in *keep*, *cool*, *look*, and *looked*, two distinct vowel sounds in *pit* and *bid*, two distinct *t*-sounds in *lot* and *eighth*. Differences like these, which occur in Mod.E. accidentally, as it were, through the influence of neighbouring sounds, are not used to distinguish one word from another; the different sounds are said to be in *complementary distribution* and are called *allophones* of the contrastive sounds or phonemes to which they are related. It must be emphasised that a given classification of sounds into phonemes and allophones belongs only to the language for which it is made; what are allophones in one language may be phonemes

ın another, and *vice versa*. Thus the *l*-sounds in Mod.E. *plead* (where the *l* is often entirely unvoiced) and *lead* (where it is voiced) are allophones, but in Welsh this difference between *l*-sounds is contrastive, that is, *phonematic* (or *phonemic*); on the other hand, some languages make no distinction between voiced and voiceless plosives such as we make in Mod.E., and in Tamil for instance [k] and [g] are allophones.

The concept of the *phoneme* has played an important part in the development of linguistic science and the term has been used in many and often conflicting senses; it is used here in its most convenient practical significance. For its early history and theory, see W. F. Twaddell, *On Defining the Phoneme, Language* Monographs, 1935, and for a recent clear exposition, Daniel Jones, *The Phoneme, its Nature and Use* (Cambridge, Heffer, 1950). On its importance for historical phonology, see H. Hoenigswald, *Language* vol. xxii, pp. 138-43 and H. Penzl, *ibid.* vol. xxiii, pp. 34-42.

175. In the sections on pronunciation (§§ 14ff, see also 11ff) the sounds of OE have been described apart from their phonetic contexts: but in order that the student may understand the more or less regular series of sound-changes which seem to upset the normal inflexional patterns, it is necessary to describe at least the more common ways in which the sounds changed of themselves (*isolatively*) or were affected by neighbouring sounds (*combinatively*). Apparent anomalies will then be seen to conform in fact to the basic patterns of OE; moreover, once the sound-changes have been grasped, the student will be able to recognise new (and seemingly irregular) forms of words and to anticipate what forms words already known are likely to have in particular linguistic circumstances.

176. In what follows it will sometimes be necessary to discuss or explain sounds not clearly represented in the OE writing or the exact relationship between spelling and sound. For this purpose it is necessary to use a *phonetic alphabet*, that is, one in which the value of each symbol is known and constant, on the principle of 'one sound, one symbol'. The most convenient way to do this will be to use symbols from the alphabet of the *International Phonetic Association* as they are needed for transcribing the OE sounds. Phonetic symbols will, as is customary, be placed in square brackets, a colon placed after any

symbol indicating that the sound is *long*. A phonetic transcription which seeks to indicate every phonetic feature, whether phonematic or not, is called a *narrow transcription*, as distinct from a *broad transcription* which seeks to indicate sounds only in so far as they are contrastive and which is the more convenient for practical purposes.

Vowels. It is the vocalic elements in speech sounds that form, as it were, 'syllable-centres'. Vowels may be classified as *back*, *central*, and *front*, and *low*, *mid*, and *high*, according to the part of the tongue used and its relative proximity to the palate, and *low* vowels may be said to be more *open* or less *close* than *high* vowels. They may also be described as with or without (*lip-*)*rounding*, and they may be classified as *slack* or *tense* according to the relaxed or tense condition of the muscles. In the following list of phonetic symbols there are indications of the values intended by means of descriptive notes and words from current languages:

Phonetic Symbols	OE Symbols	Modern Examples	Phonetic Transcriptions	Description
[ɑ]	a	Fr. pâté	[pɑte]	low, back
[ɑː]	ā	Fr. lâche	[lɑːʃ]	low, back, long
[æ]	æ	h*a*t (RP)	[hæt]	medium-low, front
[æː]	ǣ	h*a*nd (drawled)	[hæːnd]	[æ] lengthened and tenser
[ɛ]	e	l*e*t	[lɛt]	medium, front
[eː]	ē	Germ. w*e*g	[veːg]	high-medium, front, long
[ə]	a, e, o (unstressed)	chin*a*	[tʃainə]	medium, central
[œ]	oe	Germ. Göttingen	[gœtiŋən]	medium, front, slack, rounded
[ɸː]	oē	Germ. sch*ö*n	[ʃɸːn]	high-medium, front, tense, rounded, long
[ɪ]	i	b*i*t	[bɪt]	medium-high, front
[iː]	ī	f*ee*t	[fiːt]	high, front, long
[ɔ]	o	sp*o*t	[spɔt]	medium-low, back, rounded

Phonetic Symbols	OE Symbols	Modern Examples	Phonetic Transcriptions	Description
[o:]	ō	Germ. wo*h*l	[vo:l]	medium, back, rounded, long
[u]	u	p*u*ll	[pul]	medium-high, back, rounded
[u:]	ū	fool	[fu:l]	high, back, rounded, long
[y]	y	Germ. f*ü*llen	[fylən]	medium-high, front, rounded
[y:]	ȳ	,, fü*h*len	[fy:lən]	high, front, rounded, long

It will be seen that we can describe the OE *æ, e, i, y* as *front* vowels, and *a, o, u* as *back* vowels.

Semivowels. The sounds [j] and [w] may be called semivowels, because one may think of them as very short [i] and [u] respectively, or as consonants with a vowel-like quality. They are respectively palatal and labio-velar and are sounded like the initial sounds in *your* and *wagon*. OE [w] is printed with *w* for the MS (runic) symbol ᚹ, and [j] is commonly represented in OE spelling by *g, ge, gi, i,* or *ig*.

Consonants function as the *boundaries* of syllables. They may be treated summarily, since the phonetic symbols for them correspond in general to the uses made of the consonant symbols in ordinary Mod.E. writing. But some indication of the more important phonetic descriptions will be needed in discussing some of the OE sound-changes, and a few symbols must be explained. The consonants [b], [d], [g] are *voiced plosives* or *stops*, and [p], [t], [k] are the corresponding *voiceless* plosives; [b], [p], [m] are *bilabials*, and [f], [v] *labio-dentals*; [d], [t], [n], [r], [s], [z] are called *(post-)dentals* or *alveolars*. [m], [n], [ŋ] (as in *thing*) are *nasals*, and the first two, with [l] and [r] (the 'liquids'), have a vowel-like quality by which they may constitute syllables (compare the *l*-sound in *middle*); in phonetic transcription, the *syllabic* property may be indicated by a small mark, thus: [ḷ, ṃ, ṇ, ṛ]. [ŋ], [g], [k], [x] (which sounds like the consonant in Germ. *ach*) are *velars* (formerly called *gutturals*). The *fricatives* (or *spirants*) are the voiced [ð] (heard initially in *then*), [v], [z], [ʒ] (the second consonant in *measure*), [ɹ] (the usual initial sound in *road*), and [ɣ] ([x] voiced; see § 20); a velarised form of [ɹ] is heard postvocalically in Somerset and elsewhere, formed with the tip of the tongue curled up, and is called *retroflex r*. The voiceless fricatives are [θ] (heard initially in *thin*), [f], [s], [ʃ] (heard initially in *shed*), [ç] (heard finally in Germ. *ich* and sometimes initially in Mod.E. *huge*), [x] (see above). *Affricate* consonants consist of a plosive followed by a fricative, as [tʃ] and [dʒ], heard initially and finally in *church* and *judge* respectively.

Sounds are termed *palatal* when they are produced (like the [k] of *keep*) in conjunction with the hard palate, and *velar* when they are produced (like the [k] of *lock*) in conjunction with the soft palate (*velum*). In OE there were important consequences of the difference between palatal and velar consonants; see, for example, § 204.

For an introduction to phonetics so far as English is concerned, see D. Jones, *Outline of English Phonetics* (Cambridge, Heffer, 1956), Ida C. Ward, *The Phonetics of English* (Cambridge, Heffer, 1945); more general in scope are K. L. Pike, *Phonetics* (Ann Arbor 1943) and E. Dieth, *Vademecum der Phonetik* (Berne 1950). Throughout this Grammar, [r] is used in 'broad' transcription for any *r*-sound; [ɹ] is here used only occasionally, in 'narrow' transcription, when special attention is being drawn to the fricative or 'burred' *r*.

177. In the following sections are described what may be called 'significant' sound-changes, that is, such changes whose understanding and memorising are necessary for the mastery of the patterns and practice of OE grammar. The changes in OE sounds and the influence upon them of neighbouring sounds are part of the history of English as a whole; we shall therefore try, in describing them, to give some idea of the phonetic processes involved, and the student will find that some understanding of these processes will be an aid to their intelligent memorising and practical employment.

In addition to works cited elsewhere in this Grammar, K. Luick, *Historische Grammatik der englischen Sprache* (Leipzig 1914-29) should be consulted for a particularly full account of everything pertaining to OE sounds.

178. For illustrating specifically Gmc features, Latin forms will be cited in contrast, since Latin is *cognate* with English—that is to say, of the same ultimate IE origin—and has preserved features which the Gmc languages have changed. By *Gmc* is meant a mass of common features which must have been shared by the ancestors of the Gmc languages; properly, these features are best described as *Common Germanic* rather than *Primitive Germanic*, since though the Gmc languages all, as it were, look back to them, it is by no means certain that all such phenomena existed at the same time or in the same place so as to form a single language. Gmc forms, being older than any written representations, are *reconstructions* (and are marked with an asterisk) from cognate written forms. Gothic however often provides forms, attested in writing, which are useful to illustrate Gmc developments, since they are very close to the assumed Gmc. By *Gothic* is meant the partial translation of the Bible into one of the Gothic dialects made by Bishop Wulfila at the close of the fourth century and preserved in the Codex Argenteus MS from the early sixth century with astonishing consistency of spelling. It comprises the oldest written remains of a Gmc language. By *Pr(imitive) OE* is meant the reconstructed forms from a period before the seventh century, when the earliest written remains begin. This Pr.OE will naturally be most used in indicating the nature of the OE sound-changes, while Latin, Gothic, and Gmc will be brought in more for comparative and historical purposes.

Some Gmc Sound-Changes Affecting OE

179. The First Gmc Consonant Shift

A most outstanding differential characteristic of Gmc is a complex series of regular consonant changes which occurred in prehistoric times. Though these changes were in part known earlier, Jakob Grimm (in 1822) was the first to formulate their basic principles, and for this reason they have been known collectively as *Grimm's Law* or the *First Sound Shift*. For the purposes of OE, the two most important of these shifts are (*a*) that the series of IE voiced plosives [b], [d], [g], [gw] became respectively the corresponding voiceless plosives [p], [t], [k], [kw], and (*b*) that the series of originally voiceless plosives of IE became respectively the voiceless fricatives [f], [θ], [x], [xw]. Compare the following pairs of Latin and OE words, the relevant symbols being italicised:

(*a*) la*b*or 'I fall' : slē*p*an 'sleep'   *d*entem : tō*þ* 'tooth'
    *g*enu : *c*nēō(w) 'knee'   *v*ēnī (< **guē*nī) : *c(w)*ōm 'came'

(*b*) *p*edem : *f*ōt 'foot'   *t*ertius : *þ*ridda 'third'
    *c*ollem : *h*yll 'hill'   *qu*od : *hw*æt 'what'

While a knowledge of Grimm's Law is useful rather to the Gmc philologist than to the student of OE, it may form a valuable background for his studies and at times afford clarification in difficulties. Thus, for instance, the relationship between such pairs as *bycgan* 'buy' and its pret. *bohte*, *scyppan* 'create' and *gesceaft* 'creation', *hycgan* 'think' and *hyht* 'hope', *magan* 'be able' and the 2 sg. pres. indic. *meaht* or *miht*, etc. become clearer if we know that already in IE any labial or velar when followed by *t* (IE had a formative *t*-suffix) had produced respectively *pt* (from labials) and *kt* (from velars). Thus, where the *p* in *scyppan* had regularly developed in the unvoicing of Grimm's Law, the *ft* of *gesceaft* comes from the *pt* of IE by the second part of Grimm's Law. We need the Go. *bugjan* to clarify the *bycgan*—*bohte* pair, since the *g* had been fronted and lengthened in OE (see § 184). It should further be noted that the *g* in *bugjan* (as also in *hugjan*, OE *hycgan*) came about by a third series of changes under Grimm's Law not yet mentioned, by which IE aspirated voiced plosives (which may be symbolised [bh], [dh], [gh]) had lost their aspiration and took the place of the voiced plosives shifted under (*a*) above. The *g* of Go. *bugjan*, then, goes back to IE [gh], while the *ht* of the pret. goes back to the IE group *kt* formed as outlined above.

J. Grimm, in the second edition of his *Deutsche Grammatik* (Vol. I,

1822) first used the term 'the first sound shift' (*die erste Lautverschiebung*). For the best recent monograph on the phonetic processes of the shift, see J. Fourquet, *Les Mutations consonantiques du germanique* (Paris 1948); cf also R. A. Williams in *Trans. Phil. Soc.* 1934, pp. 71 ff.

180. The Second Gmc Consonant Shift

In IE and early Gmc the place of the stress in a word varied with grammatical function, but some time after the operation of Grimm's Law the stress became fixed, usually upon the root syllable. Before this happened, however, an important change in consonant pronunciation took place, the conditions of which were first clearly seen in 1877 by the Dane, Karl Verner, and which has therefore often been known as *Verner's Law*. The change was that the voiceless fricatives [f], [θ], [x], [xw] (from IE [p], [t], [k], [kw], by Grimm's Law), and [s] were voiced to [v], [ð], [ɣ], [ɣw], [z] when the main stress did not fall on the immediately preceding syllable, provided the change was not prevented by the proximity of other voiceless consonants. By subsequent sound-changes in West Gmc (reflected in OE), the resulting series was further modified by [ð] becoming [d], [z] becoming [r], [ɣ] remaining [ɣ] or becoming [j] according to whether the neighbouring vowels were back or front, and [ɣw] becoming [w] or [ɣ] or [j]. Since *f* represents both [f] and [v] in OE, Verner's Law appears in writing as interchanges between *þ/ð* and *d*; *h* (unless lost between vowels) and *g*; *h(w)* (again, unless lost) and *w* or *g*; and also *s* and *r*. Examples may most easily be seen in the vocalic verbs, for the original stress in the pret. pl. and past pple came *after* the consonant in question; thus, unless otherwise affected by analogy, the 2 sg. and 1-3 pl. pret. indic., the pret. subj., and the past pple of vocalic verbs in OE show the consonants resulting from Verner's Law when the stems of such verbs end in one of the consonants affected; compare:

weorðan 'become' beside *wurdon* &c, with [θ > ð > d];

tēon 'draw' (< **tēohan*), pret. sg. *tēah*, beside *tugon* &c, with [x > ɣ], past pple *togen*;

cēosan 'choose' beside *curon* &c, with [s > z > r];

к 127

sēon 'see' (cf Go. *saíhwan*, Lat. *sequor*) beside *sāwon, sǣgon*
&c, with [xw > ɣw > ɣ *or* w], past pple *sewen, segen*, with
[w] and [j] respectively.

Similarly are related the medial consonants in various other
corresponding forms, such as *hrēosan* 'fall' beside the related
noun *hryre, rīsan* 'rise' beside the related causative verb *rǣran*
'raise'.

The name 'second consonant shift' here given to the phenomena of
Verner's Law is commonly reserved for the series of consonant changes
which distinguish Old High German and which were called *die zweite
Lautverschiebung* by Grimm; but as this OHG shift does not concern OE
at all, the term has long been used in English studies for the Verner
series. This sound-shift was in fact the second chronologically, the OHG
shift being the third.

Grimm, noting a fairly regular interchange in Gmc languages between
pairs of words contrasted as in the Verner series, used the term 'grammatical change' (*grammatischer Wechsel*) to describe the relationship.
Thus it is sometimes said that there is 'grammatical change' as between
the pret. sg. *cēās* and the pl. *curon*. Karl Verner set forth his views
tentatively in Vol. xxiii of the German periodical *Kuhn's Zeitschrift*
(pp. 97 ff) in 1877, as a result of his studies in Slavonic languages, which
have preserved something of the freer IE stress. The voicing of fricatives when stress does not immediately precede them can be seen in the
second word of such pairs as Mod.E. *éxecute* and *exécutor, ábsolute* and
absólve, éxercise and *exért*.

The *d* in OE *fæder* 'father' as against the fricative in *brōðor* is to be
accounted for by Verner's Law; study of Sanskrit cognates showed
Verner that *pitár* and *bhrátar* reflected a difference also in the IE
accentuation of the two words. Hence the [t] of IE **pǝt-*, after becoming [θ] by Grimm's Law, was voiced to [ð] by Verner's Law, becoming
[d] in OE; on the other hand, the [t] of *bhrát-* remained voiceless by
reason of the preceding stress after the operation of Grimm's Law and
until after the West Gmc change of [ð > d].

The process by which Gmc [z] resulting from IE [s] by Verner's Law
became [r] in West and North Gmc is often termed *rhotacism* (Germ.
Rhotacismus). The [z] evidently had a kind of buzzing quality and thus
easily shifted to become what was probably a trilled *r*. Something like
this phonetic process, but in reverse, occurred with the West Slavonic
sounds written *rz* in Polish and *ř* in Czech, as in Polish *dobrzy* 'good'
and the name of the Czech composer *Dvořak*; compare also Go. *dags*
and ON *dagr* for a similar phenomenon. Further on Verner and this
consonant shift, see O. Jespersen, *Linguistica* (Copenhagen and London
1933) in which more than one essay is devoted to the subject (ʃf especially pp. 12 ff and 229 f). Cf. also Lat. *ero* < *es-o, *ez-o.

181. Such apparently irregular verbs as *hōn* 'hang' and *fōn* 'seize' become clearer if we remember the lost *h* that alternated with *g* in the present and pret. pl. forms: **hōhan*, **fōhan* beside *hēngon, -fangen* etc. The Gmc forms of the infinitives were approximately **haŋhanan* and **faŋhanan* respectively, and with the rounding of the stem vowel to *o* and loss of nasal in this position, followed by lengthening, we get **hōhan* and **fōhan* which, with the usual loss of medial [x] give the OE forms *hōn* and *fōn* (see §§ 185, 189f). But by Verner's Law the [x] in forms like the pret. pl. became [ɣ] and subsequently [g] before the loss of nasals preceding voiceless fricatives, thus determining the markedly different *-ng-* cluster in these forms.

In OE *hw* remained only initially, as in *hwā* 'who'; medially it had become *h* early, and this *h* was then lost between vowels, with consequent contraction, along with original *h*. Hence *sēon* (Go. *saíhwan*, Gmc **sehwan*, Pr.OE **sehan*) can be seen to be a vocalic verb of Class V, with the effects of Verner's Law giving pret. pl. *sāwon, sǣgon, sēgon*, past pple *-segen, -sewen* as noted in § 180. The 1 and 3 pret. sg. show the *h* (from **hw*), with diphthongisation before velarised consonants: *seah*.

The alternation between *g* and *w* arose through Gmc [xw] becoming [ɣw] by Verner's Law, and subsequently [w] or [ɣ] in W.Gmc according to whether the proximate vowels were front or back. Angl. tended to generalise forms with *g* (*sēgon*, etc.), WS and Kt forms with *w* (*sāwon*, etc.).

182. Vowel-Gradation ('Ablaut')

Vowel-gradation, which Grimm termed Ablaut, may be defined as the patterned variation of vowel-sounds, in relation to meaning, in forms of the same root. Taking the consonants of a word as its minimal root, one may vary the vowel between the consonants, as in *drīfan* 'drive', *drāf, drifon, -drifen*. This is called *root-gradation* and may still be seen in Mod.E. *drive—drove—driven*. One may similarly vary the vowel of the suffix in inflecting words, and this is termed *suffix-gradation*. This varying of vowel existed in IE, and was probably closely connected with variations of stress, pitch, and intonation; one may compare Mod.E. varieties such as [wɔz] and [wəz] for *was*.

In particular, root-gradation was used in IE as one of the means of conjugating verbs, and it is as a development of this practice that the Gmc (and therefore the OE) vocalic verbs are differentiated in their tenses to a large extent by variation of their root-vowel in accordance with regular series (see §§ 74ff).

Gradation may be *qualitative*, when the vowel is varied in quality (as in *drīfan*, *drāf*), or *quantitative*, when the variation is a matter of length (as between the pret. sg. and pl. of *metan* 'measure': *mæt*, *mǣton*). Besides the conjugation of the vocalic verbs, many other groups of words sharing the same root are said to be in *gradation-relationship* (while, in some cases, shewing also the results of later sound-changes); thus, *beran* 'bear', *gebǣre* 'behaviour', *byre* 'son'; *bēodan* 'command', *gebod* 'an order', *bydel* 'a messenger'.

183. In IE there was the basic gradation series, *e*, *o*, lengthened, and reduced grades. That is to say, the basic vowels *e* and *o* might also be lengthened or reduced to either vanishing-point (zero-grade) or to the slight indeterminate sound [ə] called *schwa*, this reduction being caused by lack of stress and related factors. Thus for instance the IE base of the OE verb *cuman* 'come' was *gwem, *gwom, and *gwm̥ (with zero-grade and syllabic m̥). These forms in Gmc would become *kwem, *kwam, *kwum, short *o* being regularly *a* in Gmc and the zero-grade in conjunction with the syllabic consonants (m̥, n̥, l̥, r̥] giving rise in Gmc to -um, -un, -ul, and -ur. Hence the Gmc principal parts corresponding to those of OE *cuman* were something like *kweman-, *kwam, *kwǣmun, *kwuman-; the actual parts in Go. (with *e* raised to *i* in the infin.) are as follows: *qiman, qam, qēmun, qumans*. Zero-grade was a characteristic feature of the *aorist* form of the IE verb, and for this reason Gmc verbs of the vocalic type which have formed their present stem from the zero-grade (*u* plus syllabic consonant in Gmc) are termed *aorist-presents*; OE *cuman* is an example of this phenomenon, though, as we have just seen, the Go. form is not. The *w* is lost in OE before *u*. In the pret. pl. the OE verb shows the usual rounding of *ā* before the nasal *m*, giving *cwōmon*; this lengthened *ō* is then analogically extended to the

sg., giving *cwōm*; before the *ō*, the *w* later falls, and hence we have forms both with and without it in OE: *cwōm*(-), *cōm*(-). Similarly, though not in being an aorist-present, *niman* 'take' has pret. pl. *nōmon* as well as *nāmon*, and the *ō* is often extended to the sg., giving *nōm* beside the historically expected form *nam* (see § 186*e*). Other aorist-presents are *murnan* 'lament' and *spurnan* 'kick'. A few further verbs, otherwise of the regular vocalic classes, because they have lengthened *u* in the pres. stem, are termed aorist-presents perhaps inaccurately, since the origin of the -*ū*- is not clear; it may however be a lengthening, by some sort of analogy, of the short *u* of the aorist-grade type. Of this sort are *brūcan* 'enjoy', *būgan* 'bend', *lūcan* 'shut', *scūfan* 'push', and a few others.

There were, then, in the root-gradation series full grade (IE *e* and *o*), lengthened grade, and reduced grade (schwa or zero). From these forms, together with new combinations involving the diphthongal elements *i* and *u*, were formed the series of gradation which are behind most of the classes of vocalic verbs in OE:

		'*e*'	'*o*'(*Gmc a*)	leng-thened	reduced
I	Gmc	**ī** (IE ei)	**ai**		**i** (zero + *i*)
	OE	**bīdan**	**bād**		**bidon, biden**
II	Gmc	**eu**	**au**		**u, o** (zero + *u*/*o*)
	OE	**bēōdan**	**bēād**		**budon, boden**
III	Gmc	**e, i**	**a**		**u, (o)**
	OE	**helpan**	**healp**		**hulpon, holpen**
IV	Gmc	**e**	**a**	**ǣ**	**o**
	OE	**beran**	**bær**	**bǣron**	**boren**
V	Gmc	**e**	**a**	**ǣ**	**e**
	OE	**metan**	**mæt**	**mǣton**	**meten**

In Cl. V, the vowel of the past pple has perhaps been influenced or replaced by that of the present stem. See further on the Gmc sound-changes A. Meillet, *Caractères généraux des langues germaniques* (Paris, 3rd ed., 1926); see also W. Streitberg, *Urgermanische Grammatik* (Heidelberg 1896), H. Hirt, *Handbuch des Urgermanischen* (Heidelberg 1932-34), and F. Kluge, *Urgermanisch* (Strassburg 1913); for a good summary of the whole question of IE accent, see A. Campbell, *Trans.*

Phil. Soc. 1936, pp. 1 ff; cf also Sigmund Feist, *Indogermanen und Germanen* (Halle 1924).

The Class I series of gradation can be seen in the Lat. cognates *fidus* (<*feidus*), *foedus* (<*foidus*), and *fīdes*. The *o* in the reduced grade of Classes II, III, and IV arises because *u* was lowered to *o* in past pples except before nasals. It is not easy to explain the lengthened grade vowel *ǣ*; we may compare the Lat. perfect *ēdi* of *edere* with the OE pret. *ǣt* of *etan* 'eat', and reckon upon some kind of reduplication process. The series in Cl. VI is different from the others; Greek *ago* 'drive' and *ogmos* 'furrow' point to an IE *a/o* series, and with a lengthened grade *ō*, the two short vowels falling together in Gmc, there would result the *a/ō* alternation that we find in OE *faran* 'go' and its pret. *fōr*.

184. Lengthening of Consonants

In West Gmc all consonants except *r* were lengthened after short syllables by the influence of an immediately following [j]. This is the cause of most of the doubled consonants in OE, though there were earlier Gmc changes which had produced for instance the *-ll* and *-nn* in such words as *eall* and *mann*, as well as later purely orthographic doublings (see § 199) to indicate vowel-shortening as in *hlæddre* 'ladder' for earlier *hlǣdre*, *næddre* 'adder' for earlier *nǣdre*, *moddrie* 'maternal aunt' for earlier *mōdrie*. The long consonants of earlier OE were indicated graphically by doubling, and for this reason the term *gemination* (Lat. *gemini* 'twins') has been commonly used, especially in the expression 'West Gmc Gemination'; but phonetically the process is consonant *lengthening* and not consonant doubling, while the use of double letters to indicate it is merely a graphic device. Examples of W.Gmc consonant-lengthening after short vowels by means of a following *-j-* are: *fremman* 'perform' (Gmc *framjan*), *trymman* 'strengthen' (cf the adj. *trum*), *biddan* 'pray' (Go. *bidjan*), *sittan* 'sit' (cf ON *sitja*), *scyppan* 'create' (Go. *-skapjan*), etc. It will be seen that the *j* which caused lengthening also mutated the vowel (see §§ 208f) or caused raising from *e* to *i* (§ 207) in the preceding syllable; *fremman* for instance is a consonantal verb of Class I, formed from *fram* 'forward' plus the suffix *-ja-* (see §§ 161-3), the *j* having mutated the vowel as well as lengthening the consonant *m*.

The semi-vowel *j*, being a palatal sound, must have palatalised the immediately preceding consonant and then become absorbed in this palatalised form, thus lengthening it. Thus *cynn* 'race' (Go. dat. sg. *kunja*), *bed(d)* 'bed' (Go. *badi*), etc. But *r* did not undergo this lengthening, nor did it absorb the following *j*; thus we have such verbs as *nerian* beside Go. *nasjan* 'save', and the noun *here* 'raiding party' (Go. acc. sg. *hari*) with its gen. and dat. sg. *heri(g)es*, *heri(g)e* (Go. *harjis*, *harja*). That the *g* of such forms as *licgan* 'lie' and *bycgan* 'buy' was palatalised by the following *j* (cf ON *ligja*, Go. *bugjan*) is shown by the OE spelling *-cg-* and later forms. Compare also *hycgan* 'think' (Go. *hugjan*).

The consonant-lengthening did not take place when the *j* was immediately followed by *i*; in such cases the *j* coalesced with the *i*. This is the explanation of the contrast between the lengthened consonants in 1 sg. pres. indic. of Class I consonantal verbs such as *fremman* (*ic fremme*) and the short consonant of 2 and 3 sg. (*þū frem(e)st*, *hē frem(e)ð*), while the pl. again has the long form (*fremmað*). The original Gmc endings of 2 and 3 sg. pres. indic. were *-jis*, *-jiþ*, whereas the 1 sg. and all the pl. had the *j* but not followed by *i*. Thus for example the Go. forms of *bidjan* (OE *biddan*) are *bidja*, *bidjis*, *bidjiþ* for the sg. pres. indic., corresponding to OE *bidde*, *bid(e)st*, *bid(e)þ* (WS *bit(t)* by syncope and assimilation). In all Class I consonantal verbs with short stem-vowel we have the same phenomena of doubled consonant for 1 sg. and 1-3 pl. pres. indic. but single consonant for 2 and 3 sg.

This lengthening is important also because there are several vocalic verbs with present forms constructed originally with *-j-* (like consonantal verbs) but otherwise regular. Thus in Cl. V, *biddan*, *licgan*, and *sittan* are of the same gradation series as *metan* 'measure', but their lengthened consonant and their *i* raised from *e* disguise the connexion. Similarly in Cl. VI, beside *faran* 'go', we have *scyppan* 'create' and *sceððan* 'harm' where *j* has caused lengthening and mutation (compare Go. *skapjan*, *skaþjan*). In the same class, *hebban* 'raise' has the same '*j*-present', with lengthening and mutation, but here the alternation in the pres. indic. is between *-bb-* and *-f-* (*ic hebbe*, *þū hef(e)st*, etc.). This is because the second consonant shift

133

operates in most verbs with *j*-present since the stress was originally after the root; hence the Gmc *f* (a voiceless bilabial fricative
[ɸ]) would be voiced to a bilabial fricative [β]. This voiced
fricative [β] would become a plosive when lengthened in W.Gmc
and this form appears in OE as -*bb*-; compare *swebban* 'put to
sleep' and *habban* 'have'. More irregular is the vocalic verb
swerian 'swear', originally Class VI; it shews the usual absence
of lengthening of *r* and the preservation of the *j* as *i* (Gmc
*swarjan), and is thus parallel to the consonantal verb *nerian*
'save'; but *swerian* went over to Cl. IV in its past pple *gesworen*.
Other *j*-presents in Cl. VI are *hlihhan* 'laugh' (Go. *hlahjan*) and
steppan 'go' (Gmc **stapjan*).

185. Loss of nasal consonants

There was a tendency for nasal consonants to disappear in
pronunciation in later Gmc before the voiceless fricative [x],
and in the West Gmc group which included OE, nasals in
general were lost before all voiceless fricatives, with compensatory lengthening of the preceding vowels and rounding of
a to *o*. Hence Go. *fimf* (compare Welsh *pump*) beside OE *fīf*,
OHG *gans* beside OE *gōs*, etc. The Gmc combination -*aŋh*-
produced OE *ō* and thus Gmc **faŋhanan* gave Pr.OE **fōhan*,
OE *fōn* 'seize', as already explained in § 181. Similarly, OE
þencan, Go. *þagkjan* 'think' and *þyncan*, Go. *þugkjan* 'seem'
(Go. -*gk*- = [ŋk]) shew retention of the nasal consonant, while
the corresponding pret. forms *þōhte*, Gmc **þaŋxta*, and *þūhte*,
Gmc **þuŋxta*, shew loss of the nasal before the voiceless
fricative together with lengthening.

OE Minor Sound-Changes

186. Influence of nasals

(*a*) In OE the nasals tended to nasalise a preceding *a* and
sometimes rounded it; it is these factors which probably under-
lie the variations in spelling in different dialects and at varying
periods between *a* and *o* in such words as *mann* (*monn*) 'man',
cann (*conn*) 'can' (see also (*e*) below).

(b) The nasals *m* and *n* raised *e* to *i* when this vowel immediately preceded; thus we have *niman* 'take', beside ON *nema*, and *bindan*, in vocalic verb classes IV and III respectively, whose pres. stem normally has *e*; compare also Lat. *gemma* with the OE adopted form *gim(m)* 'gem'.

(c) When an original *u* was followed in Gmc by a low or mid back vowel, as in the past pple of vocalic verbs, the OE form has the lowered vowel *o*; but this phenomenon was generally prevented by a following *m* or *n*; thus we have *geholpen*, *-boren* as the past pples of *helpan* and *beran*, with the regular lowering of *u* to *o*, while those of *bindan* and *niman* are *-bunden* and *-numen*, with the original *u* preserved by the nasals. See also § 207.

(d) The normal fronting of Gmc *ǎ* to *ǽ*, which characterises OE, is prevented by a following nasal; compare the pret. forms *brægd* and *band* of *bregdan* 'pull' and *bindan* 'bind' respectively, members of the same class of vocalic verbs; note also *mann* or *monn* beside *bæð* 'bath', both words having Gmc *a*, and the pret. pl. forms of the same class *nāmon* (from *niman* 'take') and *bǽron* (from *beran* 'bear').

(e) Finally, the proximity of a nasal tends to round *ā* to *ō*, so that we have pret. pl. *nōmon* beside *nāmon*, and *c(w)ōmon* for the historically expected *c(w)āmon* (with *ā* instead of the normal *ǽ* of Cl. IV as explained in (d) above).

187. Influence of *w*

The semi-vowel *w* has the following effects on contiguous vowels:

(a) it changes a following *eo* to *u* in late WS; thus *weorðan* 'become' > *wurðan*;

(b) it may round a following *ǐ* to *ў̆*, as in *swȳðe*, earlier *swīðe* 'very much'; compare also *nyllan* (*ne* + *willan*) 'be unwilling'; a later instance of the rounding influence of [w] is the Mod.E. pronunciation of *quality* [kwɔliti], as compared with the French cognate where the *w* has been lost;

(c) retracts a contiguous *ǽ* to *ā*, as in the pret. pl. *sāwon* (beside *sǽgon*) of *sēon* 'see', Cl. V (see § 180), *hlā(w)* 'mound' beside *hlǽw*, and *hrā(w)* 'corpse' beside *hrǽ(w)*.

Being a consonantal form of *u*, *w* becomes *u* finally after short syllables ending in a consonant; thus *bearu* 'grove', but gen. sg. *bearwes*; *gearu* 'ready', but *gearwes*; *beadu* 'battle', but *beadwe*. But after long stems this *w* or *u* disappears in pronunciation like any other *u* (see § 188); hence gen. sg. *mǣdwe*, but *mǣd* 'meadow'. See further §§ 38, 51, 52.

Before *u*, *w* tends to be lost; hence the past pple *cumen* from **cwumen* 'come', and the noun *sund* 'swimming' beside the verb *swimman*; *w* is sometimes lost also before *ō*, as in the pret. *cōm* 'came' beside older *cwōm*.

188. Vowel alternations

We have seen in the immediately preceding paragraphs some examples of the interchange of vowels under the influence of their phonetic environment. Thus, in vocalic verbs of Cl. III we find *helpan* beside *bindan*, and their past pples *-holpen* beside *-bunden*. Again, short and long *u* alternate in parts of *cunnan* 'be able' because of the loss of the nasal in the pret. and past pple, *cūðe* (Go. *kunþa*) and *cūð* (Go. *kunþs*). Here the lengthened vowel is the result of 'compensation' for the loss of the nasal. Then we have *man(n)* beside *mon(n)*, *ongan(n)* beside *ongon(n)* (pret. sg. of *onginnan* 'begin'), and similar pairs. It will be seen, therefore, that besides the major variations in vowels brought about by gradation (§§ 182f) and *i*-mutation (§§ 208ff), there are several fairly regular interchanging pairs of vowels. Those described so far are the results of the influence of nasals and of *w*. Other vowel alternations, similarly caused by neighbouring consonants, include the unrounding of *y̆* in proximity to *c*, *g*, and *h*, as in *drihten* beside *dryhten* 'lord', late WS *brīcð* beside *brȳcð* (3 sg. pres. indic. of *brūcan* 'enjoy'), and the replacement of *e* by *y* between *s* and *l* in frequent late WS spellings of *self* 'self', *sellic* 'marvellous', *sellan* 'give', resulting in the forms *sylf*, *syllic*, *syllan*.

There is a kind of alternation between final *-u* and zero as between short and long stems of nouns and adjectives, with *u* lost after long syllables. Thus we get the pairs *scipu* 'ships' beside *land* 'lands' (both neut. pl.; see § 31), *sunu* 'son' beside *hand* (Go. *handus*) 'hand', nouns of the same declension (§ 43), *mǣd* 'meadow' beside *beadu* 'battle' (both fem.; see § 38), the adjective forms *gōd* beside *trumu* (n.sg. fem. and n.a.pl. neut.; see §§ 50-52). For the alternation between *æ* and *a* as in *dæg* 'day' beside *dagas*, *glæd* 'happy' beside *glades*, see § 192.

189. Loss of *h*

The voiceless velar fricative [x] represented by *h* was lost very early when it came between vowels and between the liquids *l* or *r* and a vowel. Thus verbs whose roots originally ended in *-h* have lost it in most of the OE paradigms; compare *tēon* 'draw', *(ic) tēo*, *(wē) tēoð* with the reconstructed early forms **tēohan*, **tēohu*, **tēohaþ*; so too with the rest of the present forms, except the 2 and 3 sg. pres. indic., on which see § 191. The original *h* remained of course finally, as in the sg. imperat. *tēoh* and 1, 3 sg. pret. *tēah*. Original Gmc *hw*, appearing in OE as *h* except initially (*hwā* 'who'), was treated in the same way; thus Gmc **sehwan* 'see', Pr.OE **sehan* and by diphthongisation before velarised consonants (§ 201) **seohan*, appears as *sēon*, beside pret. sg. *seah*; in the same way, Gmc **līhwan* 'lend' (Go. *leihwan*) > **līhan* > **līohan* > *līon* > *lēon*. Nouns and adjectives ending in *h* generally lose it in inflexions; thus *hēah* 'high' but gen. sg. masc. *hēas* (§ 52), *feorh* 'life' but gen. sg. *feores*, *wealh* 'foreigner' but *weales* (§§ 33, 27).

In all the instances of the loss of intervocalic *h*, there was contraction of the first vowel or diphthong with the second vowel (§ 190), giving a long vowel or diphthong whatever the length of the first vowel originally; thus *feōs* (< **feohes*), gen. sg. of *feoh* 'property', *sc(e)ōs*, gen. sg. of *sc(e)ōh* 'shoe'. On the other hand, when *h* was lost between a liquid and a vowel, the vowel or diphthong in the preceding syllable remained unchanged in length; thus *weales* (gen. sg. of *wealh*), *feores* (gen. sg. of *feorh*).

Grammarians have generally concluded without much discussion that there was the same compensatory lengthening of the vowel or diphthong when *h* was lost after liquids as when it was lost between vowels. The only evidence usually cited for this is drawn from OE metre, but this is inconclusive; indeed, some half-lines in *Beowulf* seem to require a short diphthong in the oblique cases of *feorh*: thus *Beowulf* 1843a *on swā geongum feore*, where the B type requires the 'resolution' of *feore* as two short syllables with the weight of one long one; a parallel example is *Beowulf* 933b. The modern pronunciation of place-names such as *Wales* and *Hale* (from Angl. *walh*, *halh*, and thus without diphthongisation) suggests only unlengthened OE forms, nor do records reveal ME forms like *woles or *hole which would be expected if there were an OE starting point *-ā-*. See A. H. Smith, *English Place-Name Elements* (Cambridge 1956), s.v. *walh*, and J. Vachek, *Zeitschrift für Anglistik und Amerikanistik.* vol. v (1957), especially pp. 25f. But cf also K. Brunner (ref. as in § 24) § 218.1 and R. Girvan, *Beowulf and the Seventh Century* (Methuen) p. 16.

190. **Contraction.** Vowels and diphthongs, upon loss of intervocalic *h* (§ 189), absorb the following vowel; thus *tēoan, resulting from *tēohan, appears as *tēon* 'draw', and *hēaes, from *hēahes, as *hēas*, masc. gen. sg. of *hēah* 'high'; short vowels or diphthongs under these conditions were lengthened: *seohan >*sēon* 'see'. Contraction similarly takes place where stem-vowels and inflexional vowels are contiguous, without there having been a medial *h*; thus from *dōan, *dōað we get in OE *dōn* 'do', *dōð*, etc.; cf also *gān* 'go', *gāð*. In many cases, however, the uncontracted forms remain in early texts and in Angl., and sometimes also inflexional syllables were restored by analogy with other words not subject to contraction.

Analogical re-formations among contracted forms are discussed by R. Quirk, 'On the Problem of Morphological Suture in Old English', *Mod. Lang. Rev.* vol. xlv, pp. 1-5.

191. **Syncope and assimilation in verbs**

The unstressed vowel of the final syllable in the 2 and 3 sg. pres. indic. is commonly reduced to zero or 'cut from between' in what is termed *syncope* in the OE verbs of Kt and WS, while Angl. tends to retain the 'unsyncopated' forms. Pr.OE endings *-is* and *-iþ*, after mutating the preceding vowel where this was possible (§§ 207, 209), became in historical times *-es(t)* and *-eð*, and it was the vowel in these forms that was syncopated. Hence the 2 and 3 sg. pres. indic. *dēmst* and *dēmð* of *dēman* 'judge', *hilpst* and *hilpð* of *helpan* 'help', *fylst* and *fylð* of *feallan* 'fall', etc. It will be seen that this syncope brought together the consonant(s) of the stem with those of the inflexions, and where this produced unfamiliar consonant clusters, assimilation

PHONOLOGY

took place (see § 69). Thus from earlier *bindes(t)*, *bindeþ* (from *bindan* 'bind') would arise *bindst* and *bindþ*, usually resulting, by assimilation, in *bintst* and *bint*; similarly *cwið(ð)* from *cwið(e)þ* (*cweðan* 'say'), *cȳst* from both *cȳs(e)st* and *cȳs(e)þ* (*cēosan* 'choose'), and the 3 sg. forms *stent* (*standan* 'stand'), *sent* (*sendan* 'send'), *bit(t)* (*biddan* 'ask'), *birst* (*berstan* 'burst'), *it(t)* (*etan* 'eat'). The Angl. unsyncopated forms, however, usually have unmutated vowels; see § 76, note.

It is important to remember that the loss of *h* between vowels (§ 189) took place at a period later than the completion of syncope; thus verbs whose roots originally ended in *h* (such as *sēon* 'see', *lēon* 'lend') retain the *h* in the 2 and 3 sg. pres. indic., there being no inflexional vowel left in these forms when the time came at which *h* was lost. Thus, for example, *sēon* 'see' has 2 and 3 sg. pres. indic. *sihst* and *sihð*, while Angl., which had no syncope, lost the *h* giving the contracted and lengthened (§§ 189, 190) forms *sīs(t)* and *sīð*. Similarly from *fōn* 'seize', WS has *fēhst* and *fēhð*, from *slēan* 'strike', *slihst* and *slihð*, from *gefēon* 'rejoice', *-fihst* and *-fihð*, etc.

For a recent full treatment of syncope, see J. Hedberg, *The Syncope of the Old English Present Endings* (Lund 1945), and also M. T. Löfvenberg, *On the Syncope of the Old English Present Endings* (Uppsala 1949).

192. **Alternation of æ and a**

West Gmc *ă* were fronted to *ǽ* in the earliest OE period, but the anticipatory or attractional influence of a following back vowel (*a*, *o*, or *u*) either prevented this normal fronting in the case of the short vowel (and at times also of the long) or caused the fronted sound to be retracted again. Thus, *dæg* 'day' but pl. *dagas* and *mæg* 'kinsman' but pl. *māgas* (though *mǣgas* also occurs); so too *bæð* 'bath' with pl. *baðu*, *fæt* 'vessel' with pl. *fatu*, *glæd* 'happy' with n.sg. fem. and n.a.pl. neut. *gladu*, etc. (see §§ 27, 32, 51); *licgan* 'lie' has a pret. pl. *lāgon* beside *lǣgon*. In this alternation, we have a kind of vowel-harmony; in pronouncing the front vowel *æ*, the fact that a back vowel was to follow immediately after a single consonant induced a more retracted variety of vowel.

139

193. **'Unstable *i*'**

The diphthongs *ĭe̯*, which were a special feature of early WS (on their origin, see below §§ 204, 210), had come by King Alfred's time to be pronounced as simple vowels; this is shown by such reverse spellings as *hiene* for *hine* 'him', *hieder* for *hider* 'hither' in the contemporary Hatton MS of King Alfred's version of the *Cura Pastoralis* of St Gregory, and by *hīran* for *hīeran* 'hear', *gelīfan* for *gelīefan* 'believe' in the Cotton MS (as copied by Junius in the seventeenth century) of the same text. The *ĭ* thus monophthongised from the earlier diphthongs *ĭe̯* must have been for some time different phonemes from the original *ĭ*, because they regularly became *ȳ* in classical OE, which the original *ĭ* did not. The new *ĭ* are termed *'unstable ĭ'* because they often alternate in spelling with *ie* and *y*, and are generally spelt *y* in classical texts of the time of the Benedictine revival, being thus distinct from original *ĭ*; compare *gelȳfan* 'believe' with *bīdan* 'wait', and note that *gelȳfan* has earlier variant spellings *geliefan* and *gelifan* while *bīdan* remains constant in general. The exact pronunciation of this Alfredian unstable *i* pair of sounds is not known, but it must have been of a nature to develop into high front rounded [y] and [y:]. When it is said, therefore, that in late WS the diphthongs *ĭe̯* were monophthongised to *ȳ*, this is a loose and misleading way of indicating that unstable *ĭ* were rounded to *ȳ*. The new *ȳ* sounds proceeded to share the development of the other *ȳ* which resulted from the *i*-mutation (§ 208) of *ŭ* (as in *trymman* 'strengthen' beside the adjective *trum* 'firm'). It will be remembered, however, that all OE *ȳ* were frequently unrounded to *ĭ* in proximity to *c*, *g*, or *h* (see § 188), and hence such common forms as *gifan* 'give', from early WS *giefan*, instead of *gyfan*, *ongitan* 'perceive' (early WS *ongietan*) instead of *ongytan*.

Similarly, *iernan* 'run' and *biernan* 'burn' (in which the *ie*, *y* seem to have arisen through the influence of the *r* or *rn*) are early WS forms of *yrnan* (*irnan*) and *byrnan* (*birnan*). But these verbs have undergone an early metathesis of the initial consonant and vowel, for they are vocalic verbs of Class III, developing respectively from *rinnan* and **brinnan* (compare *winnan* 'struggle', in the same class); Go. has in fact *brinnan* as well as *rinnan*. Because of this metathesis, they have diphthongisation before velarised consonants (§ 201) in the I and 3 sg. pret. (*earn, bearn*), but they retain *u* in the past pple by reason of the nasal which still immediately followed it at the period when *u* was otherwise lowered to *o* in past pples (§ 186c).

194. Miscellaneous notes on minor sound-changes

Some considerable variation arises in the forms of OE through the working of *analogy*, the tendency for less 'ordinary' forms to imitate those that are more familiar. Many nouns passed from less frequent declensional forms which they once had, and were 'levelled' with commoner types; others again seem to have fluctuated between two originally distinct ways of being declined. Thus *mete* 'food', which developed regularly from Pr.OE **mæti* (Gmc **matiz*, Go. *mats*), also had a form *met(t)* as if from a Gmc **matja* which would produce consonant-lengthening; indeed, in the pl. the double-consonant type, *mettas*, is the preferred form; similarly, *hyse* 'man', though going back to a Gmc form **husiz*, shows forms with lengthened consonant as if from Gmc **husja*. There was originally a separate declension with stems ending in the vowel *i* (compare **matiz* above), and also a subdivision of the common masc. and neut. declension with stems in *-ja*: and while these two types have mostly been absorbed in the commoner ones, forms like *mete, mettas, hyse, hyssas* remind us of these facts. Traces of the '*i*-declension' survive in the gen. pl. *wini(ge)a* (beside *wina*) of *wine* 'friend', and *Deni(ge)a* (beside *Dena*) of *Dene* 'Danes'. Of the *ja*-stem declension, traces survive in the nom. pl. *rīc(i)u*, gen. pl. *rīc(e)a*, and dat. pl. *rīc(i)um* of *rīce* 'kingship'.

OE had a number of noun declensions which are descended from well-known IE types, but relatively few examples of most of them are current, so that these 'minor declensions' may simply be treated as 'irregularities' by the non-philological student. We are able to recognise and reconstruct these declensions because, in addition to the Gothic remains, Runic inscriptions from as early as the 4th century survive to indicate something very near to the common Gmc types, and comparison with cognate languages confirms these findings. Thus we know that there was a common masc. and neut. declension with stem in -*a*, as shown in Runic *stainaz* 'stone', of which the final -*z* is merely the mark of the nom. sg., the stem being *staina*-. Similarly we know of the *i*-declension (compare Lat. *hostis*) from Runic *gastiz* 'stranger', which lies behind OE *gi*(*e*)*st*. Again, a *u*-stem declension is to be inferred from Go. *sunus* (OE *sunu*) 'son' and *handus* (OE *hand*) 'hand'. Go. dat. sg. *harja* enables us to recognise the *ja*-stem type which survives in OE *here*; and so on. For a selection of early Runic inscriptions, see A. Jóhannesson, *Urnordische Runenschriften* (Heidelberg 1923) and H. Arntz, *Handbuch der Runenkunde* (Halle 1944).

195. The liquid and nasal consonants *l, r, m, n* tend to make possible the syncope of a preceding unstressed vowel in medial syllables, and this feature is common throughout the OE inflexions; thus *dryhten* 'lord' beside gen. sg. *dryhtnes, engel* 'angel' beside nom. acc. pl. *englas, frōfor* 'comfort' beside sg. oblique cases *frōfre*.

On the other hand, a slight vowel-sound sometimes develops between these same consonants and another consonant, such vowels being front or back according to the phonetic environment. Thus *burg* 'fortress' has dat. sg. and nom. acc. pl. *byr*(*i*)*g*, while the nom. sg. sometimes appears as *buruh*; so too *þuruh* beside *þurh* 'through'.

A convenient term for these 'intrusive' or 'parasitic' vowels, as they are sometimes called, is the ancient Indian grammarians' term *svarabhakti* (Sanskrit), literally *svara* 'sound' and *bhakti* 'part'. In pronouncing the name of the Hindu deity *Indra*, the old grammarians tell us, there was a sound somewhere between between a half and a quarter of a full vowel between the *d* and the *r* : *ind*(*ə*)*ra*; such a sound, a 'partial vowel' is a svarabhakti. This is a more exact term than any of the others.

196. The long ('doubled') consonants of early OE (§ 184) were later often written as single letters, the reason for this being that the phonematic distinction between long and short consonants had ceased to exist in final position for the most part. Thus the distinction between *mann* 'man' and *man*, the pron. 'one', was indicated by early scribes in the final consonant, but later both words were often written *man* or *mon*. Similarly, such nouns as *cynn* 'race', *wedd* 'pledge', *wēstenn* 'desert' are often written with single final consonant, though the lengthened consonant continues to leave its mark in the inflected forms (*cynnes, wēstennes,* etc.), and medially in general (*sittan* 'sit').

197. There was often assimilation of consonants in the course of inflexion, quite apart from that occasioned by syncope (§ 191). Thus *h* tended to be lost between a vowel and a following *n*, as in the acc. sg. masc. of *hēah* 'high', *hēanne* or *hēane* from earlier *hēahne*. Again, *g* tends to disappear before a following *d* or *n* with compensatory lengthening of a preceding short vowel; thus *sǣde* beside *sægde*, pret. of *secgan* 'say', *lēde* beside *legde*, pret. of *lecgan* 'lay', *brǣd* beside *brægd*, pret. of *bregdan* 'pull', *þēn* beside *þegn* 'retainer', *frīnan* beside *frignan* 'ask', etc. Before *t*, *c* often becomes *h*, as in *tǣhte*, pret. of *tǣcan* 'show', *worhte*, pret. of *wyrcan* 'work', *īhte*, pret. of *īcan* 'increase', etc.

OE palatal *g* tended to be vocalised and become absorbed in a preceding front vowel, and it would probably be more accurate to describe the phenomena of *sǣde*, *þēn*, etc. as examples of the absorption of such a vocalised *g* in the preceding *æ*, *e*, etc. Similarly, the 3 sg. pres. indic. of *licgan* 'lie' is often *liþ* in WS, from *ligþ* (Angl. *ligeþ*).

198. Before an unstressed vowel, *w* often ceases to be pronounced, and this phenomenon is frequently seen in the pret. and past pple of consonantal verbs formed from nouns and adjectives with stems ending in *w*; for example, *gyrwan* 'prepare' (compare the adj. *gearu*) has pret. *gyrede* beside *gyrwede*, and similarly *syrwan* 'deceive' (compare the noun *searu* 'trick') has pret. *syrede* beside *syrwede*.

Final unstressed *u* is often lowered to *o*, or even to *a*. Hence *gearo* beside *gearu* 'ready', *sido* beside *sidu* 'custom'; there are neut. pl. noun-forms in -*a* in Ælfric MSS, such as *dēofla* (for *dēoflu*) 'devils'.

199. **Changes in vowel-length.** During the OE period, though mainly in the latter part, there was lengthening of short vowels before -*ld*, -*mb*, -*nd*, sometimes also before -*rl*, -*rn*, -*rs*, -*rþ*, and possibly before -*rd* and -*ng*. Thus *cild* > *cīld*, *gold* > *gōld*, *findan* > *fīndan*, and similarly we have *bīndan*, *clīmban*, *hūnd* 'dog', and *mūrnan* 'care'. This lengthening was brought about by the vowel-like properties of liquids and nasals (and in this way may have some affinity with diphthongisation before velarised consonants). A vocalic element from the *l*, *r*,

m, *n* may be thought to have coalesced with the preceding vowel and so given it length. The lengthening did not take place if a third consonant immediately followed the lengthening cluster; compare *cīld* with the pl. *cildru* (§ 44) which was never lengthened (compare Mod.E. *child* and *children*). Nor did the lengthening occur in less stressed words and positions; thus *and* 'and', *sc(e)olde* 'should', and *wolde* 'would' remained with short vowels. The *ē* and *ō* resulting from this lengthening were always the close vowels; thus *fēld* was [feːld] and *gōld* [goːld].

Just as the above lengthening failed to occur before groups of three consonants, as in *wŭndrian* 'wonder' beside *wūndian* 'wound', so too any pair of consonants, other than the lengthening clusters, might cause shortening of preceding long vowels in the later OE period. Thus *blǣdre* 'bladder' became *blǎddre*, *fōdres*, *fōdre*, etc. became *fŏddres*, *fŏddre*, and so by analogy the nom. *fōdor* 'nourishment' also became *fŏddor*; similarly, *ātor* 'poison' became *ǎttor* by reason of oblique forms with shortening before *-tr-* (*ǎttres*, for example). Other instances are *hlǣddre* from *hlǣdre* 'ladder', *nǎddre* from *nǣdre* 'adder'. Doubled consonants, earlier a method of indicating contrastive consonant length (see § 184), came to be used to indicate the shortness of preceding vowels, when consonant length was no longer such a prominent phonematic feature.

Some Major OE Sound-Changes

200. Here are grouped some sound-changes which are especially important to the student, either because they play a major part in the varied forms of inflexion or because their phonetic nature is of particular interest or difficulty. They are treated in the probable order of their occurrence and in relation to other changes already described. They are severally the cause of the development of new front-round vowels and of new diphthongs beside the *ēa*, *ēo*, *īo* which had come down from Gmc and (in WS only) of the diphthongs *ie* which later became 'unstable *i*' and then *ȳ*, as explained in § 193.

201.   **Diphthongisation before velarised consonants** ('Breaking'). The front vowels *ǣ*, *ĕ*, *ĭ* were diphthongised to *ēa*, *ĕŏ*, *ĭŏ* (later *ĕŏ*) when immediately followed by velar or velarised consonants or consonant groups. The consonants which had this effect were *ll* or *l* plus another consonant, *rr* or *r* plus a consonant, and *h* or *h* plus a consonant, though only *ǣ* was diphthongised before all these. Thus Gmc **harduz* (cf Go. *hardus*) > Pr.OE **hærd* > *heard* 'hard'; Gmc **armaz* (cf Go. *arms*) > Pr.OE **ærm* > *earm* 'poor'; **herte* > *heorte* 'heart' (cf Go. *haírto* = **herto*); **werpan* > *weorpan* 'throw' (cf ON *verpa*); **fehu* > *feoh* 'cattle' (cognate with Lat. *pecu*; see § 179), etc.

No diphthongisation took place before the combination *rj* as in *nerian* 'save' or before the *ll* produced by West Gmc consonant-lengthening (§ 184) as in *sellan* 'give' and *tellan* 'count' (Go. *saljan, taljan*). In WS no diphthongisation of *e* took place before *ll* or any *l*-group except *l* plus *h* (hence the regular form *helpan* 'help') but in the pret. sg. of verbs like *helpan* and *sellan* it will be noted that diphthongisation took place: *healp*, *sealde*; here we have dipthongisation of *æ* before *l* plus consonant, the doubled *ll* of *sellan* belonging only to the present.

It is important to remember that this diphthongisation is the addition of a vowel glide to the front vowel through the influence of certain velar qualities in following consonants; thus it is Pr.OE *æ*, not the earlier form *a*, that is diphthongised, and it is inaccurate to speak of 'undiphthongised *a*' in cases where the usual diphthongisation has not occurred, or of the 'diphthongisation of *a* to *ea*'.

The term 'breaking' was first used in 1822 by Jakob Grimm in his *Deutsche Grammatik* to cover the formation of *all* the OE diphthongs developed from front vowels; it therefore included the analogous changes produced by diphthongisation before back vowels (§ 214) as well as the diphthongisation after palatal consonants (§ 204). What we here call 'diphthongisation before velarised consonants' was termed *fracture* by Mayhew in his *Synopsis of OE Phonology* (Oxford 1891), and Sievers was the first to apply to it the term *brechung* in his fundamental *Angelsächsische Grammatik*. The term *breaking* is merely the English translation of the German word by J. Wright and others, and is regrettable, since the vowels involved were in no sense 'broken' into a diphthong but rather had something added to them.

202. We may infer that the phonetic processes underlying this diphthongisation were as follows. Since the sounds of speech are continuous and not discrete, 'glides' arise between different sounds as our speech-organs, while still producing one sound, form themselves into the position for producing the next. If the difference in the position of the organs is great, the glide is considerable; compare in London English today the back-vowel glide heard between the [ɪ] and [lk] of *milk*: [mɪɔlk]. In OE the vowels diphthongised were front, and in words like **feh-* the speech organs, in forming themselves into the position to make the voiceless velar fricative [x] would give *u*-quality to the off-glide from *e*: [fex > feux > feox > feəx], spelt *feoh*. With the consonant groups beginning with *l* and *r* on the other hand (as in *healp*, *heard*), there would also be the consonantal on-glides to contribute to the diphthongisation, since *l* and *r* have vocalic properties. The *l* in these groups must have had 'dark' or velarised quality, like that in the Londoner's *milk* already mentioned, and *r* was probably a 'burred' retroflex (produced with the tongue-tip curled up) rather like that heard today in Somerset, and also with *u*-timbre. Thus *heard* may be supposed to have gone through the following stages in early OE, [hæɹd > hæuɹd > hæəɹd], the second element of the diphthong being made up not only (as in *feoh*) of the off-glide from the front vowel as the speech-organs moved towards the position to form the velarised consonant, but also of the on-glide to the consonant itself. It appears then, that at particular periods in particular dialects the difference in the positions required of the speech-organs for these contiguous sounds became so extreme as to produce glides between the sounds clearly enough heard for the scribes to notice and record them in their orthography. The glides then formed diphthongs with the original vowels, and these diphthongs often remained after the special conditions that produced them had ceased to obtain.

For recent discussion of this diphthongisation, see the references given in § 18. In her article there referred to, Miss Daunt sought to deny the diphthongal nature of the phenomenon, attributing the second element in the digraphs to the influence of Irish scribal practice in which it is generally believed that back vowels written before certain consonants merely show the 'dark' quality of such consonants. Thus, for instance, OIr. *fer* 'man' has gen. sg. *fir*, dat. sg. *fiur*, the function of the *u* in the latter being to show the 'colour' of the 'dark' *r*. OE scribes, Miss Daunt thinks, might have developed the habit of showing by the second elements in the digraphs *ea, eo, io* simply the type of resonance or timbre of the following *l* or *r*. The Irish parallel however would imply a phonematic distinction in OE between the various types of consonant so indicated, and this is most unlikely. Moreover, since the same digraphs *ea, eo, io* were also being used for the known diphthongs from Gmc *au, eu, iu* respectively, it is not likely that the specifically OE use of the digraphs would be for simple vowels. The chief authorities still accept the theory of a glide-vowel origin of the digraphs, and in the article by S. M. Kuhn and R. Quirk cited in § 18 evidence is presented in favour of the view that such diphthongs, while originating as positional variants (allophones) of the original vowels, achieved phonemic status within the OE period. See, however, further exchanges of views in *Language* vol. xxxi (1955), pp. 372-401.

203. Diphthongisation before velarised consonants is important in OE grammar, especially in understanding the conjugation of vocalic verbs. *Bregdan, helpan, bindan* are all members of the same (Cl. III) gradation-series, but just as the influence of the nasal has given us *bindan* instead of **bendan* and *band* instead of **bænd*, so diphthongisation has produced the pret. *healp* beside *brægd*; to this same class belongs also *weorðan*, with a diphthong, instead of **werðan*. Again, the diphthongisation before a subsequently lost *h* produces forms where the gradation relationships are obscured; thus *sēon* and *metan* both belong to Cl. V, where Gmc **sehwan* passed through the stage **sehan*, was then diphthongised as **seohan*, and so with loss of *h* and contraction became *sēon* (§§ 189, 190). The Cl. I verbs include *lēon* 'lend' beside *drīfan*; in this case we have Gmc **līhwan > *līhan > *līohan > līon > lēon*; so too, *wrēon* 'cover'. The verb *þēon* 'prosper' (§ 75) was originally of Cl. III (later Cl. I) and its history is reflected in the past pple form used adjectivally, *geþungen* 'excellent'; the stages here are **þiŋhan > *þīhan* (§ 185) *> *þīohan > þīon* and *þēon*. In Cl. VI, *slēan* 'strike' has come through the stages **slahan > *slæhan > *sleahan*; so too, *lēan* 'blame', *þwēan* 'wash'. The diphthongisation did not take place in the infin. or pret. of verbs like *berstan* 'burst' and *þerscan* 'thresh' (pret. sg. *bærst*,

þærsc), because the post-vocalic position of *r* in these forms is the result of metathesis which occurred after the period of diphthongisation when they had the forms *brestan, *þrescan, etc.

The diphthongisation was far less frequent in Angl. dialects because their consonants developed differently and either did not occasion diphthongisation or soon removed its results. The Angl. *l* and *r* seem to have been pronounced in a way that prevented the general fronting of Gmc *a* to *æ* or that caused it to be retracted again; thus *all* beside WS *eall* 'all', *þarf* beside *þearf* 'need'. It should be noted that the *ll* in *eall* and *feallan* 'fall' does not result from West Gmc lengthening (§ 184) but from a far older formation, and this *ll* was of the sort that occasioned diphthongisation (compare § 201). The so-called Angl. 'smoothing', by which diphthongs were reduced to simple vowels before *c*, *g*, and *h*, also removed the results of diphthongisation before velarised consonants; thus, Angl. *werc* beside WS *weorc* 'work', *fehtan* beside *feohtan* 'fight'.

204. Diphthongisation after palatal consonants

When a palatal *c*, *g*, or *sc* immediately preceded $\bar{\breve{æ}}$ or *ĕ*, these vowels developed into the diphthongs *ĕa* and *iĕ* respectively. This was a characteristically WS development, and it is well illustrated in the principal parts of *gifan* (early WS *giefan*) 'give', a verb of Cl. V whose expected forms would be like those of *metan* 'measure' (§ 81): *gefan*, *gæf*, *gǣfon*, *-gefen*; these forms in fact occur in non-WS. Early WS, on the other hand, has *giefan*, *geaf*, *gēafon*, *-giefen*. Similarly *geldan* 'pay' of Cl. III has the early WS infin. form *gieldan* (*ld* did not cause diphthongisation of *e*); likewise *giellan* 'scream', *gielpan* 'boast'. In Cl. IV *sceran* 'cut' has the early WS infin. *scieran*, with sg. and pl. pret. *scear*, *scēaron*. Other examples include *geat* 'gate' (non-WS *gæt*), pl. *gatu* (like *fatu*, pl. of *fæt* 'vessel', by reason of the following back vowel: § 192), *gist* (early WS *giest*, non-WS *gæst*) 'stranger', *gīet* 'yet', and *gīen* 'yet'. By King Alfred's time, *iĕ* had become 'unstable *ĭ*' (§ 193), so that classical OE forms have *i* or *y* (*gifan*, *gyfan*, *gildan*, *gyldan*, etc.).

It would seem that a front vowel-glide (*i* or *e*) developed between the strongly palatal consonant and the following vowel in these cases, giving the rising diphthongs *iė*, *iǣ*, etc. which later became falling diphthongs. For further remarks on their pronunciation, see § 17. In *ceorl* 'man', *gearu* 'ready', and some others, the diphthongs arose through the influence of velarised consonants (§ 201).

205. Notes on diphthongs

As stated in § 18, classical OE had four diphthongs, *ea*, *ēa*, *eo*, and *ēo*. The *ēa* developed regularly from Gmc *au* and had its OE form by the eighth century; thus *dēað* 'death' beside Go. *dauþus*. Most of the examples of IE *eu* were raised to *iu* in Gmc, and *eu* and *iu* gave OE *ēo* and *īo* respectively, but these diphthongs fell together as *ēo* in late WS or classical OE, while in other dialects and in earlier periods they were sometimes kept apart and sometimes levelled as *īo*. Thus, Alfredian WS and Kt frequently show the levelling of both *ēo* and *īo* as *īo* (for example, *bīodan* 'offer', in the Hatton MS of the Alfredian version of *Cura Pastoralis*). Kt in all periods tended to level the two under *īo*, while Nb tended to mix *ēa* with *ēo*, as in *dēoth* in Bede's *Death Song* for *dēað* 'death', *ēore* in the *Lindisfarne Gospels* for *ēare* 'ear'. The short diphthongs *ea* and *eo*, as in *geaf* 'gave', *heard* 'hard', *leomu* 'limbs', *feorh* 'life', were produced in OE itself by the various diphthongisations. Here again early WS tends to use *io* for *eo* (as in *liornian* 'learn'), and Kt normally raises *eo* to *io* as with the long diphthong.

Both short and long diphthongs are subject to the Angl. smoothing or monophthongisation before *c*, *g*, *h*, singly or preceded by *r* or *l*; thus Angl. *hǣh*, *hēh* for *hēah* 'high', *ēc* for *ēac* 'also', *eh* for *eoh* 'horse'. In most late OE MSS *ĕa* are replaced occasionally by *æ* in spelling (though careful scribes retain *ea*-forms); such forms as *hærm* for *hearm* 'harm' in Classical OE texts are 'occasional spellings' indicative of the monophthongisation of all the OE diphthongs which was complete in most areas by the time of the earliest ME texts.

In addition to that arising from the influence of preceding palatal consonants, long and short *ie*-forms arose in early WS by the *i*-mutation (§§ 206, 210) of *ĕa*, *ĕo*, *ĭo*; thus corresponding to *gelēafa* 'faith', we have the consonantal verb *gelīefan* 'believe' and beside *searu* 'device' the verb *sierwan* 'plot'. Such *ie*-spellings were partly replaced by *i*-forms by the end of the ninth century (thus *hīran*, early WS *hīeran* 'hear', in the Cotton MS of

Cura Pastoralis), and these in turn by forms indicative of rounded vowels by the tenth century (as *hȳran*, *syrwan*). See further § 193. Outside the area of classical OE, the *i*-mutation of *eā* is represented generally by *e*; thus non-WS *hēran* for late WS *hȳran* 'hear', *heldan* for late WS *hildan* or *hyldan* 'bend'. Sometimes Mercian texts have *æ* for the *i*-mutation of Angl. *ă*, WS *eă*, as *hældan* 'bend', *hlæhhan* (early WS *hliehhan*) 'laugh'. For *i*-mutation of *eŏ*, *ĭo*, non-WS texts generally have *io*-spellings, as *iorre* (WS *ierre*, later *yrre*) 'angry', *hiorde* (WS *hierde*, later *hyrde*) 'shepherd', but Mercian (as represented in the *Vespasian Psalter Gloss*) usually has *eo*, and for the foregoing words has *eorre*, *heorde*.

In later OE, especially in the combination *ht*, *h* often became palatal [ç] and monophthongised and frequently raised the diphthongs *eŏ* and *eā* to *ĭ*; thus early WS *feohtan* 'fight', *cneoht* 'boy', *lēŏht* 'light', *meaht* (from *magan*) 'might' become *fihtan*, *cniht*, *liht*, *miht*. This tendency was checked, however, by a back vowel in the syllable immediately following, so that the pl. of Alfredian and late OE *cniht* is often *cneohtas* and of *Piht* 'Pict' *Peohtas*.

On the OE diphthongs, there is a useful recent study in the light of findings in acoustic phonetics by L. F. Brosnahan, *Some Old English Sound-Changes* (Cambridge, Heffer, 1953).

206. Mutations

Mutation, for which Grimm first used the term *Umlaut* which is still widely current, is the change from one vowel to another through the influence (by attraction, assimilation, or anticipation) of a vowel in an immediately following syllable. We have two important mutations to consider: first, the early Common Gmc mutations, and secondly, Pr.OE *i*-mutation.

207. Common Gmc mutations

There are two which significantly affect OE; first, the raising of *e* to *i* through the influence of an *i* or *j* in the immediately following syllable, or through its being in an unaccented position, or through the influence of a following nasal (see § 186*b*); secondly, the lowering of *u* to *o* through the influence of a back vowel in the next syllable (see § 186*c*). For example, *bir(e)ð*, 3 sg. pres. indic. of *beran* 'bear' (Pr.Gmc **beriþi*), *niman* 'take', from *neman-, god 'god', from Gmc *guþan (compare Go. guþ), and OE gold 'gold', from Gmc *gulþan (compare Go. gulþ). It is important to remember that the lowering of u to o was prevented by a following nasal (hence gebunden beside geholpen, past pples of the same class), and by an i or j in the next syllable; such an i or j caused i-mutation of the 'unlowered' u. So it is that the OE adj. corresponding to gold is gylden, because the Gmc form of the latter was *gulþin-, with subsequent i-mutation of the u, whereas in the noun the original u was lowered to o by the following a (Gmc *gulþan). A similar relationship exists between OE god 'god' and gyden 'goddess', fox 'fox' and *fyxen 'vixen'. OE had no short o other than this one by the lowering of Gmc u, though a subsequent source of OE o lay in Lat. adoptions; ele 'oil', from (late) Lat. olium, had such an o, as one can tell from the mutated form e (see § 208). Analogy, however, occasionally transferred the o lowered from u to another inflected part of a word which originally ended in i and which should therefore have retained the u, having it later i-mutated to y. This is the explanation of the dat. sg. of OE dohtor 'daughter' (§ 47), which is dehter apparently from a Gmc *dohtri; in this case, Gmc u has been analogically lowered to o before the period of i-mutation, whereas a dat. from *duhtri (the regular form) would be the rare OE dyhter. Similarly OE oxa 'ox' has a pl. (from an i-declensional type) exen, where one would have expected *yxen (compare the fox—*fyxen example above).

208. i-mutation

i-mutation, shared in varying degrees by all Gmc languages except Gothic, had been completed in OE by the time of the earliest written records. It is closely related to the raising of e to i (§ 207) inasmuch as it is the direct result of the influence of i or j on the vowel in an immediately preceding syllable. By i-mutation, Pr.OE ă (before nasals), ǽ, ā, ŏ, ŭ are fronted or raised to mid or high front vowels:

OE a before nasals (Gmc a) > e, as in menn, n.a.pl. of mann (monn) 'man';

OE *æ* (Gmc *a*) >*e*, as in *bed(d)* 'bed', Gmc **badja* (cf Go. *badi*);

OE *ā* (Gmc *ai*) >*ǣ*, as in *hǣlan* 'heal', Gmc **hailjan* (cf Go. *háiljan* and the OE adj. *hāl* 'whole', Go. *háils*);

OE *o* (sometimes Gmc *u* analogically lowered; cf § 207) >*œ* [œ] >*e*, as in *ele*, Lat. *olium*, and *exen*;

OE *ō* >*ǣ* [ø:] >*ē*, as in *gēs* 'geese', sg. *gōs* (Pr.OE **gōsi* < Gmc **gansiz*, with loss of nasal and rounding: §§ 181, 185);

OE *u* >*y*, as in the verb *trymman* (<**trumjan*) 'strengthen', beside the adj. *trum* 'strong';

OE *ū* >*ȳ*, as in *rȳman* 'make space', beside the adj. *rūm* 'spacious'.

Angl. retained the mid-front-round forms spelt *oe*, as *oexen* 'oxen', *fōet* 'feet'; the sounds are found unrounded to *ě*, however, in classical OE: *exen*, *fēt*, etc. The alternation of *o* and *y* in such pairs as *fox* and **fyxen* is, as has been shown in § 207, really a case of the *i*-mutation of *u* beside other forms of the same root in which the *u* had been lowered to *o* before the OE period.

209. Other examples of *i*-mutation are very commonly to be found, and this sound-change is of special importance and frequency in the structure of OE. In learning the conjugation of vocalic verbs, the student needs to know the 'mutation pairs' of vowels because in the 2 and 3 sg. pres. indic. there is normally *i*-mutation of the stem-vowel or raising of *e* to *i* (§ 207). Secondly, consonantal verbs are often formed from nouns and adjectives and from other verbs with the suffix **-ja-* (§ 163), with consequent mutation; compare *dōm* 'judgment' with the verb *dēman* 'judge' (Go. *dōmjan*). Thirdly, a number of common adjectives and adverbs formed their comparative and superlative with the Gmc suffixes **-izo*, **-isto* (West Gmc **-iro*, **-isto*), and therefore have mutation in OE; thus *eald* 'old', comp. *yldra*, early WS *ieldra*, where there has been *i*-mutation of the diphthong: *ea* >*ie* >*y* (for the *i*-mutation of diphthongs, see § 210). Again, there are nouns related to the past pples of vocalic verbs (see § 161*a*), with *i*-mutation of the reduced-grade vowel; thus *byre* 'son' beside *-boren*

(earlier *-buren*), past pple of *beran* 'bear', where we have an
i-declensional type of noun (§ 194, note), **buri*, with subsequent mutation of the *u* to *y*, while in the past pple the *u* was
lowered to *o* (*-boren*: § 186c). Compare also *hryre* 'fall' with
the verb *hrēōsan* 'fall', *cyre* 'choice' and *cēōsan* 'choose', *cyme*
'coming' and *cuman* 'come', *fyll* 'death' and *feallan* 'fall',
wyrd 'fate, what happens' and *weorðan* 'become', etc. The
inflexion of a group of nouns, too, shews these mutation
pairs; for example, *fōt* 'foot' and *fēt*, *dohtor* 'daughter' and
dohter, *āc* 'oak' and *ǣc*, *burg* 'fortress' and *byr(i)g*, *frēōnd* 'friend'
and *frīend* or *frȳnd*, etc. (see §§ 47-49).

210. The diphthongs *ĕa*, *eŏ*, *iŏ* were all subject to *i*-mutation
(see § 205). In WS they were all mutated to *iĕ* and these,
iĕ are a special mark of early WS; later, in classical OE,
such forms appear as *i* or *y* (§ 193). Examples are *eald*
'old' but comp. and superl. *yldra*, *yldest* (earlier *-ie-*), *heald*
'sloping' but *hyldan* (also *-i-*, earlier *-ie-*) 'bend', *heord*
'herd' but *hyrde* (early WS *hierde*) 'shepherd', *lēas* 'deprived of'
but *lȳsan* (earlier *-īe-*) 'release', *bēag* 'ring' but *bīgan* (earlier
-īe-) 'cause to bend', *gelēafa* 'faith' but *gelȳfan* 'believe', etc.
For the corresponding forms in other dialects, see § 205.

211. Varying forms of consonantal verbs within the conjugation, such as *wyrcan* 'work' beside pret. *worhte*, *bycgan* 'buy'
beside pret. *bohte*, *hycgan* 'think' beside pret. *hogde* (on the
consonant alternations, see §§ 179, 184, 197), are to be explained by the alternation between the *u* of the present stem
(which underwent *i*-mutation because these verbs had the
suffix **-ja-*) and the *u* of the pret. and past pple which was
regularly lowered to *o* as explained in §§ 186c, 207 and which
had no *j* in the suffix to cause mutation. On *þyncan* and *þūhte*,
þencan and *þōhte*, see § 185.

212. The generally accepted phonetic explanation of *i*-muta-
tion is that the high front *i* or *j* palatalised the preceding
consonant and that this in turn pulled the vowel of the stem
towards its own position, raising or fronting it. The *i* or *j*
which had thus fronted a preceding back vowel (or raised a
front one) by strong attraction in articulation through and by

means of the intervening consonant, was then absorbed into the palatalised consonant. This theory may be called 'mechanistic', because it is based entirely on the assumed workings of the speech-organs. An alternative explanation is that in pronouncing the back vowel in the root-syllable the speaker unconsciously allows his mind and his tongue to 'anticipate' the *i* or *j* that is to come in the immediately succeeding syllable, and that the sounds first resulting from *i*-mutation were the original vowel plus an anticipatory high front vowel which then coalesced with the original stem-vowel to constitute the new form. Thus, for instance, in pronouncing **dōmjan* 'judge', the *j* is supposed to have been mentally anticipated by the speaker, so that he would say something like *dō-i-mjan*, and that later this *ō* and *i* would unite to form the compromise front-round vowel [œ:] written *oe*, **dōimjan* becoming *dōēman*, a form preserved in Angl. but with unrounding to *dēman* in WS. This is a 'mentalistic' or psychological theory of *i*-mutation. The orthodox view of articulatory influence through the consonant is a theory of attraction and assimilation, while the mentalistic view is one of anticipation.

The accepted theory is supported in some measure by the OE and later spellings of the medial consonant in such words as *secgan* 'say' as compared with the related noun *sagu*. Pr.OE **sægjan* has had its *g* palatalised by the following *j* as well as lengthened, and the palatalising and lengthening are both symbolised in the spelling *cg*; it is through this palatalised *g* that the vowel has been mutated. Compare also the verbs *lecgan* 'lay', *bycgan* 'buy', *hycgan* 'think' or nouns like *brycg* 'bridge', *hrycg* 'back'. On the other hand, there are eighth-century spellings which seem to preserve just such *oi* forms as the 'mentalistic' theory would assume to be the first stage of *i*-mutation; the proper name *Cēnwulf*, for instance, appears in Bede as *Coinuulf*, the first element being *cēn(e)* 'bold', from Gmc **kōniz*. It may be suggested that *i*-mutation was brought about by the joint working of both the 'attractional' and the 'anticipatory' influences, that the *i* or *j* pulled the immediately preceding consonant towards a palatal articulation and that this in turn mutated the stem-vowel, while at the same time this vowel was being affected by the anticipation of the *i* or *j*. Note, however, *drȳ* 'wizard', earlier *drūi, where there was no intervening consonant.

Bede's *Historia Ecclesiastica* in its earliest MSS (Moore and Leningrad) contains a number of English names in the Latin text, and Bede seems to have been careful to preserve traditional forms of earlier centuries in writing them. Names with *-oi-* for later *-oe-* and *-e-* occur, and these forms are confirmed by some words in eighth-century glossaries; they include *Coinualch* for *Cēnwealh* and a number ending in *-thruid* or *-thruith* (for *-þrȳð* in such names as *Æðelþrȳð*). The latter element is OE *þrȳð* 'strength', from *þrūþi, and it may be supposed that this *þrūþi became *þrūiþi, with later coalescence of the *ū* and *i* to give *ȳ*. That *ū* > *ȳ* passed through a stage *ŭi* is further suggested by the Runic *fuþorc* or alphabet in which the rune for *u*, called *ūr*, was modified to form the rune called *ȳr* used in *i*-mutation positions; the new rune is merely the old *ūr* (⌐) with the single stroke for *i*, the rune called *is*, inserted at the bottom (⊓).

With regard to the diphthongs subject to *i*-mutation, it seems that in *ēa* both elements were raised in early WS, giving *ĭē*, whereas in Angl. there was a raising (or fronting and raising) only of the second element, giving *ĕ* (thus Angl. *gelēfan* 'believe' beside early WS *-līefan*, where both dialects have the related noun in the form *-lēafa*). The Angl. *ĭō* or *ĕŏ* by mutation show no modification of the second element. The diphthong forms by mutation, therefore, are inconclusive from the point of view of explaining the phonetic processes. In Kt and S.E. dialects, the *ȳ* resulting from *i*-mutation were generally unrounded and lowered to *ĕ*; thus Kt *sen(n)* beside WS *syn(n)* 'sin'.

213. The working of *i*-mutation, like other sound-changes, is sometimes disturbed or altered by the influence of analogy or levelling. For instance, the *i*-declensional (§ 194) pl. noun *Seaxe* 'Saxons' has had the *ea* restored by analogy, where a mutated vowel or diphthong would have been expected; compare *Dene* 'Danes', where mutation (earlier *dani) has occurred. In the 2 and 3 sg. pres. indic. of vocalic verbs, too, analogy seems sometimes to have replaced the expected mutated vowel by the more frequently recurring unmutated one; thus *weorðeð* from *weorðan* 'become', and not the usual early WS *wierð* (later *wyrð*), occurs in the Hatton MS of *Cura Pastoralis*, and in the same text we find *hāteþ* from *hātan* 'call' for the expected *hǣtt* (with mutation, syncope, and assimilation). Similarly *bereð*, from *beran* 'bear', is found beside *bir(e)ð*. Such

forms, without syncope or mutation, are fairly common in lOE.

214. **Diphthongisation before back vowels** ('Back Mutation'). Like diphthongisation before velarised consonants (§ 201), this diphthongisation changes the Pr.OE vowels *æ*, *e*, *i* into the diphthongs *ea*, *eo*, *io* respectively. As with the other diphthongisation, too, the change affects only front vowels (that is, *æ* and not the earlier Gmc *a*). The rule in general is that in the early OE period, while the earliest written records were being made, the front vowels *æ*, *e*, *i*, when followed after a single consonant by a back vowel, became respectively the diphthongs *ea*, *eo*, *io*. Thus *lim* 'limb' has, beside *limu*, pl. forms *liomu* and *leomu* (with the usual lowering in WS and Mercian of *io* to *eo*); *hlið* 'slope' has pl. *hliðu*, and also, by this diphthongisation, *hlioðu*, *hleoðu*; *sidu* 'custom' has the alternative Alfredian form *siodu*; *witan* 'know' appears also as *wiotan* and *weotan*; *wita* 'counsellor' appears also as *wiota*, *weota*, and (through the influence of the *w*, § 187a) *wuta*; similarly we have *heofon* 'heaven', *ealu* 'ale', etc. For the most part, this sound-change belongs to the non-WS dialects, but in classical OE it is found to some extent, particularly before liquid, labial and dental consonants. It is the last of the major vowel-changes in OE, and was still apparently in progress in the earlier eighth century, on the evidence of the glossaries of that period.

The cause of the diphthongisation seems to be the rise of a glide as the speech-organs anticipated the articulation of the back vowel in the following syllable; the process is therefore very similar to that presumed in the diphthongisation before velarised consonants (§ 202). It should be noted however that while the latter affected also long vowels to some extent, the present phenomenon concerns only short vowels.

There is also something of a parallel between this diphthongisation and *i*-mutation (see § 212). In Kentish, the diphthongisation is very widespread and seems to have occurred even through two consonants (compare Kt *siondon* with WS *sindon* 'are', and *sioððan* with WS *siððan* 'afterwards'). In Angl. too it is common, but before *c*, *g*, *h* its effects are removed by Angl. smoothing. Mercian of the *Vespasian Psalter*

Gloss, however, often has the diphthongisation even before *c* and *g* (thus *spreocan* 'speak', *weogum*, d.pl. of *weg* 'way'). Forms like *beoran* 'bear', *eotan* 'eat' are common to non-WS dialects.

Diphthongisation before back vowels is often referred to as 'back mutation' or by the various vowels that caused it: thus '*o/a*-mutation' (the common type) and '*u*-mutation' (the less common type); '*u*-mutation' of *æ* is for the most part found only in Mercian: it is not normal in WS, and *ealu* (§ 46) 'ale' seems to be an Angl. loan-form in WS, remaining as the regular form in classical OE; two other words, *beadu* 'battle' and *bealu* 'evil', perhaps originally poetical and Angl., occur commonly with this diphthongisation of *æ* in classical OE. Kt has *alop* and (on the evidence of proper names containing the elements) *badu* and *balu*. The diphthongisation of *i* after *w* produced *io*, and this through the influence of the *w* (§ 187a) sometimes became *u* in some areas; hence *wutan* 'counsellors' in the Cotton MS of *Cura Pastoralis* beside *wiotan* in the Hatton MS version. This development has left one common mark on Classical OE in the form *wuton*, later *uton* (with loss of *w* before *u*: § 187), which is used for periphrastic 1st pers. imperative or hortatory expressions (§ 135) as in (*w*)*uton dōn* 'let us do'. The origin of (*w*)*uton* is not known, but it seems to be a part of the verb *witan* 'go'.

215. **Conclusion.** There are many problems in OE sound-changes and many unsolved puzzles connected with individual words which have not been touched upon in the foregoing paragraphs. The phonology presented has been for the most part confined to those matters which the student needs to understand in order to learn the grammar of OE efficiently, and those aspects have been especially emphasised which are of the greatest structural importance. The student of the history of the language will consult specialist works devoted to the subject, and it is hoped that the references supplied in the notes throughout will enable the philologist to pursue further studies effectively.

INDEX

This comprises a subject-index to the whole, together with a word-register to Parts II and V. References are to the numbered paragraphs.

INDEX